Collaborative Action Research for
English Language Teachers

CAMBRIDGE LANGUAGE TEACHING LIBRARY

A series covering central issues in language teaching and learning, by authors who have expert knowledge in their field

In this series:

Collaborative Action Research for English Language Teachers

Anne Burns

CAMBRIDGE
UNIVERSITY PRESS

PUBLISHED BY THE PRESS SYNDICATE OF THE UNIVERSITY OF CAMBRIDGE
The Pitt Building, Trumpington Street, Cambridge CB2 1RP, United Kingdom

CAMBRIDGE UNIVERSITY PRESS
The Edinburgh Building, Cambridge CB2 2RU, United Kingdom
40 West 20th Street, New York, NY 10011–4211, USA
10 Stamford Road, Oakleigh, Melbourne 3166, Australia

First published 1999

Printed in the United Kingdom at the University Press, Cambridge

Typeset in Sabon 10.5pt/12pt

A catalogue record for this book is available from the British Library

Library of Congress cataloguing in publication data applied for.

ISBN 0 521 63084 3 Hardback
ISBN 0 521 63895 X Paperback

For Ross, Douglas and Catherine

Contents

Acknowledgements   x
Preface   1

1   **Why should teachers do action research?**   7

1.1   Action research: a case study   7
1.2   A collaborative perspective on action research   12
1.3   Teachers' responses to action research   14
1.4   Summary   17
     Group discussion tasks   18

2   **Definitions and processes**   20

2.1   Introduction   20
2.2   Quantitative approaches to research   21
2.3   Qualitative approaches to research   22
2.4   Action research   24
2.5   What are the origins of action research?   26
2.6   What does action research involve?   29
2.7   What are the processes of doing action research?   35
2.8   Summary   43
     Group discussion tasks   44

3   **Getting started**   45

3.1   Introduction   45
3.2   Constraints and impediments   45
3.3   Finding a focus   53
3.4   The role of theory in question formulation   68
3.5   Ethical considerations   70
3.6   Summary   75
     Group discussion tasks   76

Contents

4   Observational techniques for collecting action
    research data   78

4.1   Introduction   78
4.2   Observation   80
4.3   Notes and diaries   85
4.4   Audio and video recording   94
4.5   Photographs   101
4.6   Charting the social organisation of the classroom   105
4.7   Summary   115
      Group discussion tasks   116

5   Non-observational techniques for data collection   117

5.1   Introduction   117
5.2   Interviews   118
5.3   Surveys and questionnaires   129
5.4   Life and career histories   136
5.5   Documents   140
5.6   Metaphor development   147
5.7   Summary   150
      Group discussion tasks   151

6   Analysing action research data   152

6.1   Introduction   152
6.2   What is data analysis?   153
6.3   When should data be analysed?   154
6.4   Processes of analysis   156
6.5   Validity and action research   160
6.6   Enhancing trustworthiness in action research   162
6.7   Techniques for analysing data   166
6.8   Summary   179
      Group discussion tasks   180

7   Disseminating the research and sustaining the action 181

7.1   Introduction   181
7.2   Disseminating the research   181
7.3   Sustaining the action   201
7.4   Summary   212
      Group discussion tasks   212

8   Collaborative action research in practice   214

8.1   Introduction   214

8.2   Action research as professional development   215
      Jane Hamilton
8.3   Using English outside the classroom   221
      Janette Kohn
8.4   The Teams/Competencies Project   225
      The staff of Wilkins Intensive English Centre
8.5   Strategies for 'non-language' outcomes   229
      Lenn de Leon
8.6   Concluding remarks   233

      Further reading   236
      References   243
      Index   255

Acknowledgements

Numerous people have supported and encouraged me in the writing of this book. My appreciation and thanks are first due to the many teachers who have collaborated with me as practitioner researchers. Their names are too numerous to list individually, but their contributions as well as their enthusiasm for teacher research are hopefully well reflected throughout the book.

Chris Candlin, Geoff Brindley and Catherine du Peloux Menagé, my colleagues at the National Centre for English Language Teaching and Research at Macquarie University, must also be thanked for their ongoing support and encouragement of my work. I am grateful also to the staff of the Resource Centre at NCELTR for their endless patience in chasing up books, articles and references whenever I needed them. Jenny Hammond and Helen Joyce deserve special mention for their reading and editing of the manuscript at various stages and for their suggestions and discussions. My collaboration with my co-researcher and co-editor, Susan Hood, has been a constant source of stimulation as well as personal pleasure over a number of years.

Thanks are also due to Alison Sharpe of Cambridge University Press who greatly encouraged me at an early stage to consider that the book could be a reality and to Mickey Bonin who took over from Alison and kept me going at just the right point in the process. Julia Harding, who edited the manuscript, brought a fresh editorial eye to my writing and made many useful suggestions.

As always, my patient and uncomplaining family have supported and encouraged me throughout the entire enterprise. It is to them that I affectionately dedicate the book.

The publishers and I are grateful to the following copyright owners for permission to reproduce copyright material. Every endeavour has been made to contact copyright owners and apologies are expressed for any omission.

Goswami, D. and P. Stillman. 1987. *Reclaiming the Classroom: Teacher Research as an Agency for Change*. Boynton/Cook Publishers, a subsidiary of Reed Elsevier, Inc., Portsmouth, NH on p.16; Kemmis, S. and R. McTaggart. 1988. *The Action Research Planner*. Geelong, Victoria: Deakin University Press on pp.33, 51,112; Somekh, B. 1993. *Quality in*

Acknowledgements

Educational Research - The Contribution of Classroom Teachers. In Edge, J. and K. Richards (Eds.). *Teachers Develop Teachers Research.* Macmillan Heinemann Ltd. on pp.33 and 34; McNiff, J. 1988. *Action Research: Principles and Practice.* Routledge on p.51; Allwright, D. 1993. *Integrating 'Research' and 'Pedagogy': Appropriate Criteria and Practical Possibilities.* In Edge, J. and K. Richards (Eds.). *Teachers Develop Teachers Research.* Macmillan Heinemann Ltd. on p.52; Kemmis, S. and R. McTaggart. 1982. *The Action Research Planner.* Geelong, Victoria: Deakin University Press on pp.54 and 55; Hitchcock, G. and D. Hughes. 1995. *Research and the Teacher.* Routledge on pp.71, 72, 136 and 137; Somekh, B. 1994. *Inhabiting Each Other's Castles: Towards Knowledge and Mutual Growth Through Collaboration.* In *Educational Action Research* 2. Oxford: Triangle Journals on pp.72 and 73; Kebir, C. 1994. *An Action Research Look at the Communication Strategies of Adult Learners.* In TESOL *Journal* 4. Copyright © 1994 by Teachers of English to Speakers of Other Languages, Inc. on pp.73 and 177, used with permission; McKernan, J. 1996. *Curriculum Action Research.* London: Kogan Page Ltd. on pp.89 and 94; Brophy, M. 1995. *Helena's Perspective.* In C. Riddell (Ed.). *Journeys of Reflection. ESL Action Research in TAFE.* Office of Training and Further Education and Western Metropolitan College of TAFE, Melbourne, Victoria : Australia, on pp.133 and 134; Koster, P. 1996. *In the Mood.* In *Investigating the Teaching of Grammar. Reports from a Collaborative Action Research Project Conducted by NSW AMES.* NSW AMES Occasional Papers Volume 1 Sydney: Program Support and Development Services on pp.141, 142 and 143; Allan, L. 1994. *Reflection and Teaching: Co-operative Workshops to Explore Your Experience.* Sydney: Adult Literacy Information Office, on pp.147 and 148; Elliot, J. 1991. *Action Research for Educational Change.* Open University Press on p.186; Winter, R. 1989. *Learning from Experience: Principles and Practice in Action Research.* The Falmer Press on p.186; Erickson, F. and J. Wilson. 1982. *Sights and Sounds of Life in Schools.* Research Series 125. College of Education, University of Michigan, on pp.198 and 199; Mazillo, T. 1994. *On Becoming a Researcher.* In TESOL *Journal* 4. Copyright © 1994 by Teachers of English to Speakers of Other Languages, Inc. on p. 201, used with permission; Calhoun, E.F. 1994. *How to Use Action Research in the Self-renewing School.* Alexandria, VA: Association for Supervision and Curriculum Development, on pp.209, 210, 211 and 212; Burns, A. and S. Hood (Eds.). 1995, 1996, 1997. *The Teacher's Voice Series* and *Prospect: A Journal of Australian TESOL.* National Centre for English Language Teaching and Research, Macquarie University: Sydney.

Preface

> ... the challenge and stimulation from sharing the energy
> and professionalism of other teachers on the research team,
> and particularly collaborating with another teacher researcher
> from my college, was very enjoyable.
>
> (Vivienne Campbell, Queensland)

Recently, the notion of the 'teacher as researcher' has received much attention in the second language teaching literature. However, this attention is typically from the perspective of academic researchers rather than teachers themselves. We still know little about how second language teachers view and carry out action research, what kinds of support structures or information are needed as they conduct research as well as carry out regular classroom activities, and what conditions promote or hinder the doing of action research. The last few years have seen a proliferation of publications on classroom-based and teacher-initiated research and reflection. However, few of these publications have focused specifically on action research as it is practised and perceived by teachers and researchers working together to conduct it. The majority of these publications draw on the professional research literature to illustrate their descriptions of and recommendations for teacher research, rather than on the work of teacher researchers themselves. Much of the literature on action research in second language teaching has also had a tendency to characterise and discuss action research as 'collaborative', but then to go on to represent and promote it as a somewhat individualistic enterprise. Few discussions explore how action researchers can link their investigative work to that of other colleagues and in what ways such collaborative processes can make an impact upon whole-school changes and priorities.

The rationale for this book arises from my collaborative work over a number of years as a teacher educator and researcher with ESL teachers in the Australian Adult Migrant English Program (AMEP). Much of the research carried out within this national programme has adopted an action research stance for investigating teaching and learning practices and classroom processes. The aim has been to apply the perspectives gained from this particular approach to organisational curriculum and resource development. The approximately 150 teachers within this organisation with whom I have worked closely on various projects have strongly supported the notion of collaborative involvement in action research and have seen this approach both as a way of strengthening their own research skills and as a powerful route for their own professional development.

Areas for action research have been identified through a process coordinated by the Australian government's Key Research Centre for the AMEP, the National Centre for English Language Teaching and Research (NCELTR), at Macquarie University where I work. All AMEP providers across Australia are invited to have input into the identification of possible research areas. These are then prioritised for their broad relevance to the development of curriculum theory and practice within the organisation nationally. Once research areas are determined, teachers from different states are invited to express their interest in participation as practitioner researchers in investigating this area. During their involvement in the research, the teachers receive paid release time to attend workshops and write up their findings, but data collection activities are conducted in their own time. My own role has been to work together with my co-researcher, Susan Hood, to collaborate with participating teachers and to develop a linked network of teacher researcher groups across the country. For each project we have conducted a series of workshops with these groups over a period of approximately six months, providing input on research and research processes and data collection methods, identifying focal areas for research on an individual or partnership basis and enabling members of the group to report and reflect critically on their research findings and insights.

This book aspires to add to the growing literature on classroom-based action research, but it has, perhaps, a more modest aim: to provide an accessible overview of theoretical perspectives on action research and, especially, to provide a practical introduction from the teacher's, rather than the researcher's, point of view. To this end, the majority of the illustrative accounts in this book are drawn from the work of teacher action researchers and result from my experience of collaborating with them. I also draw to some extent on my collaborations with teachers in a high school, as well as from the work of some of my students and other Australian teachers in further education contexts. In general, these accounts aim to illustrate the kinds of collaborative processes which were set in place in order to carry out the research, as well as the decisions and actions undertaken by the individual teachers within these groups as they directed their research efforts towards change, not only at the classroom level, but also at the broader institutional level. It is to be hoped that this perspective complements existing publications by offering a straightforward account directed towards groups of teachers who wish to test out assumptions of educational theory in practice and to promote a cooperative teaching environment which values critical reflection and informed change. I believe that if teacher action research is to flourish, it needs to be advocated by teachers themselves. It is because of this conviction that I have chosen to use the voices of the teachers I have worked with as a major resource for articulating my arguments.

The authentic voices of teachers in this book, then, are represented by Australian teachers, who are primarily involved in English as a second language in adult immigrant programmes. Readers in other contexts may find themselves working in very different types of English language programmes, in EFL classes, for example, where there are dissimilar class sizes and groupings and learners of very different age groups and cultural backgrounds. You may wonder what relevance the Australian case studies have for you. I would argue that, while the specifics of the research context and the action strategies may turn out to be very different, the kinds of practical questions and issues and daily concerns encountered by teachers of English as a second or foreign language are likely to be broadly recognisable across many educational settings and will, therefore, contain many areas of relevance for teachers in other countries. The same kinds of problems – how to motivate learners, how to teach grammar effectively, how to improve classroom dynamics, how to select and sequence tasks and activities for particular learner groups, how to encourage learners to develop better learning strategies – come up again and again and are researchable issues for teachers anywhere. The purpose of the book is not, therefore, to focus on the Australian scene, but to sketch out issues and possibilities for collaborating in teacher research in any context. However, in order to contextualise the great majority of the studies in the book, it is worth sketching out a broad picture of the AMEP, its learners, programmes and the teachers who work in it, so that readers can gain a sense of the scope and nature of the context that frames most of the teacher researchers' experiences and extracts.

The AMEP is a large-scale national ESL programme established by the Australian government as part of its immigration policies since 1948 and funded by the Department of Immigration and Multicultural Affairs (DIMA). Approximately 1,500 teachers work in this programme in adult teaching centres across the different states and territories.

The major objective of the programme is to respond to the settlement English language needs of adult immigrants coming to Australia from countries all over the world. In general, AMEP classes are characterised by groups of students from many different countries of origin, who will have widely divergent experiences of immigration, ranging from business migration to intake as refugees or as part of a family reunion programme. Students will have a range of very different formal learning backgrounds and differing exposure to the English language, either through formal instruction or informally. Some classes cater for students who may have had little or no previous education or who may have very limited literacy skills even in first language. Others focus on preparing fast-learning students with well-developed learning skills for further education or employment. These various courses are generally taught over a 10–15, or, in fewer cases, a 20-week period. This means that teachers see particular groups of students for very limited periods of time and their timetables may change rapidly as they are scheduled to teach different kinds of classes. In this situation, teachers have to be able to address different learning needs and plan different courses very flexibly.

Over the fifty years of the AMEP's existence, its programmes have diversified at various times to include shipboard classes en route to Australia, on-arrival courses offered intensively at major teaching centres, short community-based programmes and evening classes, on-site and off-site workplace programmes, distance/correspondence education, self-access and independent learning provision and a 'home tutor' support scheme. Because of government policy changes, since 1992 the major focus of the programme has again been narrowed to the settlement language needs of immigrants within their first three years of arrival in Australia. Recent government policy in relation to adult education more generally has also placed great emphasis on vocational education and training and, at the same time, there has been a widespread move to competency- and outcomes-based curriculum development. As part of the AMEP response to these changes, since this time AMEP teachers have found themselves teaching beginner to intermediate level ESL learners within a nationally accredited competency-based curriculum framework, *The Certificates in Spoken and Written English*. In addition, because of the move towards vocational training, some AMEP teachers have been employed in other government-funded, labour market English language programmes aimed at enhancing literacy and numeracy skills in order to increase employment opportunities. For many teachers this has meant rapidly diversifying their teaching from the more 'traditional' adult ESL programmes for newly arrived immigrants to courses for mixed groupings of longer-term immigrant and native speaker learners. Student attendance in labour market programmes was linked to receiving unemployment benefits. Thus, teachers were frequently faced with learners whose attendance in class was involuntary, accompanied by negative responses to learning from previous education, and who may have experienced various social or personal problems associated with long-term unemployment in addition to their language learning needs.

Readers will find the impact of these educational changes on AMEP teachers reflected in several of the case studies in this book. For many readers employed in very different ESL/EFL contexts, some of the AMEP teachers' concerns may seem distant or unreasonable, even bizarre. The idea of second language teachers having to teach mathematics or literacy in mixed group classrooms may strike you as bewildering or unrealistic. The cultural and social ambience of the Australian classroom reflected in the nature of the student–teacher relationships may also be in contrast to your own experiences. However, for the Australian teachers featured here, these were precisely the kinds of new directions they were required to take as second language teachers. Nor, I would argue, is this require-ment to adjust to new classes, new learners and new working conditions, so remote from the experiences of many second language teachers in other multicultural countries where, in the 1990s, similar rapid changes are occurring in government and educational policy, such as in Britain, the United States and Canada. What is illustrated by these examples is not so much the specific classroom subject or content areas to be taught, as these will always differ from teacher to teacher, but the processes and decisions that a second language teacher went through in addressing an action research issue of practical significance in his or her educational situation.

In the chapters that follow, then, action research is exemplified from studies in the Australian context, one that, perhaps more than many others, has been particularly conducive to large-scale collaborative action research in the field of language teaching (McDonough and McDonough 1997; Roberts 1998). Despite some of the very recent shifts in government policy surrounding immigration and adult ESL educational provision, and in contrast to almost all other countries, Australia has had a relatively long and stable history of well-funded national support for adult ESL programmes, resulting in a high level of teacher professional development and specialisation and a coherent large-scale programme of curriculum development and research (see, for example, Nunan 1988; Tudor 1996). At the same time, the increased awareness of and focus on action research arising from the experiences of the 1973–6 Ford Teaching Project in Britain found substantial expression in Australia at Deakin University, which became a major centre of activity from the late 1970s onwards for educational action researchers working from a critical perspective, such as Stephen Kemmis, Wilfrid Carr, Colin Henry and Robin McTaggart. This work undoubtedly provided fertile ground for transposing action research approaches into the adult ESL field so that it could be integrated into curriculum and professional development in a fairly large-scale and cohesive way. While some readers may say that, compared with their own situations, this is an indulgent, or even a provocative, position from which to portray a picture of collaborative action research, it seems to me that the main point is that the AMEP experience has been a fortunate and productive one, which has provided a strong argument that second language teachers can and should have a major, and empowering, presence in research in their own field. It has also provided a critical framework for exploring teachers' responses to involvement in research, for analysing processes for supporting collaborative teacher research institutionally and for highlighting the value of integrating curriculum enquiry with the normal patterns of practitioners' work.

It is teachers' voices, then, drawn from the daily realities of their specific settings that are foregrounded in this book. Most of the teachers whose work is featured have been my colleagues over a number of years. Each chapter is prefaced by suggestions, reflections and evaluations made by some of them during the course of their research. With the teachers' permission, I have also drawn substantially on their work to provide practical illustrations which we hope will be helpful to other collaborative groups. In almost all instances, it was the teachers' choice that I should refer to them by their own first names to reflect the close collegiality that grew within our groups during the various phases of the research. The discussion tasks at the end of each chapter include many of those that we tried out at various points in the different collaborating groups.

Action research has achieved something of a 'flavour of the month' characteristic in recent discussions of teacher education. However, it makes demands of time and energy on teachers, who are not typically encouraged to do research. It can be confronting and unsettling in its requirement that we look at our practices critically. In my experience, it is made more feasible, professionally exhilarating and relevant when conducted with a collaborative and supportive group of colleagues. This book does not make any claims to offer definitive models or theories of action research, but it is hoped that by offering realistic accounts of the personal experiences of classroom teacher researchers and those who have worked closely with them, it will inspire other teachers, teacher educators and researchers to incorporate collaborative action research processes into their own professional activities as a systematic way of theorising and reflecting upon their classroom and organisational practices.

1 Why should teachers do action research?

> Collaborative action research is a powerful form of staff development because it is practice to theory rather than theory to practice. Teachers are encouraged to reach their own solutions and conclusions and this is far more attractive and has more impact than being presented with ideals which cannot be attained.
>
> (Linda Ross, New South Wales)

1.1 Action research: a case study

Linda Ross is an experienced ESL teacher who has worked for several years in the Australian Adult Migrant English Program (AMEP). In 1995, because of changes in government funding arrangements, she found herself teaching a class of adult students with very diverse needs, who were quite unlike the kinds of immigrant groups she had previously encountered. Her class consisted of both first and second language English speakers and it focused on the development of literacy and numeracy skills. Linda describes her class (this and the following quotations are from Ross 1997: 133–7):

> a boisterous, enthusiastic group of ten students in a class funded by the Department of Employment, Education and Training. [The class met] for 20 hours a week, four hours a day for 15 weeks and was for people who are long-term unemployed to assist their entry or re-entry into the workplace. The students' ages ranged from 17 to 42 and many had a somewhat chequered educational history.

Linda became part of a collaborative research group of teachers from different teaching centres within the same organisation who found action research a transformative means of responding to the changing profiles of their classes and developing new teaching strategies and approaches to meet their students' heterogeneous needs:

> At the time I had very little knowledge of how action research works but the focus intrigued me. Surely we have all struggled with groups that are disparate to varying degrees. Could there be any answers? . . .

> On the whole I felt adequate in the area of literacy. However, I felt inadequate in the area of numeracy. It was a new field for me and I was aware that the students' abilities varied widely . . . In the numeracy sessions I handed out worksheets or selected areas from the textbook and then gave assistance as required. These sessions felt hectic, chaotic and generally unsatisfactory.

At the beginning of the project, Linda felt uncertain as to how to find a specific focus for her research, so she began by simply observing her lessons:

> noting what [I] saw and so start focusing on the issues . . . I began jotting rough notes immediately after lessons. On 22/3/95 I noted: 'In a half hour session the stronger students only got a few minutes attention . . . and how can I be sure that the weaker ones are in fact gaining the skills and concepts that they lack?'

> On 27/3/95 I wrote: 'A typical numeracy lesson – hectic! We revised fractions. The stronger ones know immediately that $\frac{1}{4}$ is half of $\frac{1}{2}$. The weaker ones look completely mystified. I need to go much further back for the weak students. How will I find time?'

> A few days later I added: 'A support teacher would help – and more graded materials – and more expertise!'

Through these notes and other observations it began to become clearer to Linda why she felt so dissatisfied with these sessions:

> - Despite expending considerable energy, my efforts were piecemeal.
> - I needed a far clearer picture of the strengths, weaknesses and progress of each student.
> - I needed to develop the basic skills of the weak students but at the same time extend the strong students.
> - My classroom activities were both a time management and a course design issue.

Having analysed some of the problematic factors in her classroom, Linda developed a number of practical action strategies to address them. She proceeded through a series of research phases, each of which enabled her to discover more about her students and how to meet their needs. First, she set about gaining a clearer picture of the students' strengths, weaknesses and skills and developing ways of tracking their progress:

> I developed a checklist of skills so that I could monitor the progress of each student . . . I include a small section below:

	Lillian	Warren	Chris	Kerin	Mike	George	John	Barry	Peter	Kelly
Uses place value up to 5 places										
Uses decimal point appropriately										
Can read numbers from calculator										
Can 'round up'										

The checklist proved extremely useful and the numeracy session felt far more focused. The checklist became the basis of my lesson planning.

Linda was still worried about the amount of time she was able to give to each student. She decided to find out how the students felt:

> I began to discuss some of my concerns with the students ... I mentioned to some of the stronger students that I felt I was neglecting them. They were surprised and assured me that they liked the present system. One of them told me in her usual direct manner:

> > We don't want a teacher breathing down our necks. We don't like to be treated like kids. We like it when you give us the sheet and we can just get on with it. Don't worry – we'll yell if we need you.

> I felt an incredible sense of relief! Why hadn't I spoken to them earlier.

Aiming to improve the classroom management problems she had identified, Linda decided to divide the class into ability groups:

> I prepared worksheets at two levels and gave them out – as discreetly as possible – according to the ability of the student. The students did not actually move into groups. The aim was to allow the weaker students to develop skills at a much slower pace, while extending and challenging the stronger students.

> ... I abandoned this approach very shortly after introducing it as it

was more destructive than constructive. Despite my efforts, the students immediately compared their sheets and there was a subtle change in the group dynamics. Two of the weaker students began to come late, did not bring pens, had not done their homework and so on.

I had made the mistake of 'labelling' some students as under-achievers and realised that I had undermined their morale. This was interesting since they had always found it quite acceptable to label themselves ... It seemed it was quite different if the teacher did the labelling.

Linda reflected on the outcomes of these strategies and decided on a new course of action:

I realised that in my enthusiasm for greater efficiency, I had undermined the self-esteem of the students who required the greatest support. I decided on a new strategy ... I took graded materials into the classroom and explained that the first worksheet was to be done by everyone and was compulsory. After that it was up to the students how much they completed.

I found this method successful. Even though I had feared that the stronger students would complete the compulsory sheet in a few minutes and then simply chat, this was not the case and they were keen to go on with the extra work. The weaker students seemed to gain satisfaction from the fact that they were able to complete the compulsory work successfully.

Using the checklist as the basis of my ongoing assessment, I felt that I was now far better able to monitor progress. At the end of the course it was apparent that all the students had made good progress.

A further step in the research, and additional insights into her students' needs, came when Linda enlisted the cooperation of one of the two researcher coordinators with whom her action research group worked.

This last step should have come much earlier in the process as it gave me so much insight into the students' perceptions and needs. One of the research coordinators, Sue Hood, visited the class and asked the students questions concerning their preferred learning styles and past learning experiences. The students responded very positively to the fact that their views were being sought and valued.

Sue: Is it a problem in the class ... that you have different
         things you want to do? (General agreement from students
         that this is not a problem.)
Chris: The one thing is we're all learning. That's the main
         factor.

Sue: Do you prefer to do all the same work ... so that you're
         doing the same activity? (General agreement from
         students that they prefer this.)
Stephen: I reckon it makes it easier for everyone to learn that way
         and that's the best way to learn instead of teaching say
         three one thing and three another and somebody else
         different ...

Linda drew a number of conclusions from the research she had
conducted:

> As a result of this project I realised that I needed to reconsider a
> number of issues which had concerned me ... When faced with
> disparate levels in a class, it would seem practical to divide the
> class into groups according to their ability. However, in a class
> where the development of self-esteem is crucial to learning, this
> arrangement may serve to undermine the confidence of the weakest
> members. The students in this particular class clearly favoured a
> system where they participated as equal members of the group,
> supporting one another as necessary.
>
> I had viewed the class as a teacher and educationalist and I had
> focused on the negative aspects of being in a group of disparate
> learners. I had been worried that I was not giving the students
> equal attention and that I would not be able to assist all of them to
> achieve the course competencies. I discovered that the students did
> not expect to get equal attention, but that they only wanted help
> when they had a problem, and while they were keen to progress,
> they gave equal importance to factors such as belonging to the
> group. In fact, the students were very positive about the class. They
> did not see themselves as a 'disparate group' but as a cooperative
> group who supported one another in achieving their goals.

Linda had this to say about collaborative action research:

> I would strongly recommend action research to all teachers. The
> process is rewarding because it validates classroom observation and
> encourages you to value your own judgements. The sessions with
> other teachers help to shape your ideas and challenge you to
> rethink many issues. In my case it reminded me of the value of
> asking the opinions of the students. Finally, while traditional forms
> of professional development can be very stimulating it is sometimes
> difficult to relate the theory with which teachers are presented to
> the reality of the classroom. Action research is refreshing as it is
> concerned with the classroom as it really is.

Linda Ross's report (see Ross 1997 for a full account) provides an
example of how a teacher who was part of a collaborative action
research group developed a critical perspective on her practice and
observed systematically various influential factors operating in her

classroom by using action research as a powerful medium of reflection. This is not to suggest that teachers such as Linda are deficient in what they already do; it is rather to propose that reflective analysis of one's own teaching develops a greater understanding of the dynamics of classroom practice and leads to curriculum change that enhances learning outcomes for students.

Doing action research collaboratively is the focus of this book. It is based on my experiences over a number of years of working with several groups of second language teachers in the AMEP, as well as with teachers in schools and organisations elsewhere in Australia. These teachers have been interested in working collaboratively to put into practice the principles of action research in order to investigate and reflect critically on their own teaching situations. Overwhelmingly, the teachers with whom I have worked as an action research collaborator have indicated that they greatly value doing action research. Based on my experiences, I therefore take the position that researching one's own classrooms and teaching contexts is something which can, and should, be considered by language teachers, as a realistic extension of professional practice. The book aims to provide both a theoretical and a practical guide for teachers who wish to extend their role in this way in order to include a research focus. In presenting such a guide, I acknowledge that teachers may not always have the opportunity to work in a collaborative relationship with teacher educators/researchers and with other teachers. However, I also make the assumption that second and foreign language teachers have an increasing number of reasons for wanting to conduct action research – their own professional development, a desire to develop research skills, a wish to present systematic evidence for change to their schools or teaching organisations, or completion of a university course with an action research component.

1.2 A collaborative perspective on action research

Action research, as it is now more typically portrayed in the second language literature (e.g. Nunan 1989, 1992), has tended to take on an individualistic focus, of teachers investigating teaching and learning in the isolation of their own classrooms (Richards and Freeman 1992). However, that view of action research is counter to its original goals, which were to bring about change in social situations as the result of group problem-solving and collaboration. This perspective implies that the main purpose of individual classroom investigation is to reinforce the broader goals of the group, as Kemmis and McTaggart (1988: 5) suggest:

> The approach is only action research when it is *collaborative*,
> though it is important to realise that the action research of the
> group is achieved through the *critically examined action* of
> individual group members [emphasis in original].

While not denying the relevance, and even the necessity, of individual classroom research in certain contexts, this book aims to expand current portrayals of action research in language teaching. Collaborative action research processes strengthen the opportunities for the results of research on practice to be fed back into educational systems in a more substantial and critical way. They have the advantage of encouraging teachers to share common problems and to work cooperatively as a research community to examine their existing assumptions, values and beliefs within the sociopolitical cultures of the institutions in which they work. Policies and practices within the organisation are more likely to be opened up to change when such changes are brought about through group processes and collective pressures. Collaborative action is potentially more empowering than action research conducted individually as it offers a strong framework for whole-school change.

In presenting a collaborative perspective as the motivation for this book, I draw on action research studies which have been undertaken by teachers working within groups rather than by individuals. These case studies and examples are used to provide practical guidance to other practitioners interested in knowing more about collaborative processes of action research. They also aim to strengthen the position of practising teachers' own voices in the second language literature on action research, voices which provide realistic accounts for other teachers of what it is like to conduct action research, and which can hopefully provide other teacher groups with suggestions about what is feasible and valuable within the constraints of other classroom pressures.

There is a further point to be raised briefly in relation to the collaborative aspect in action research which is only rarely touched upon in the 'teacher as researcher' literature. In a recent discussion, Golombek (1994: 404) criticises traditional research on teachers' knowledge about teaching as paternalistic, suggesting that 'the knowledge that is close to science of a theoretician is more highly valued than that of a practitioner'. She cites feminist research which indicates that women's ways of constructing knowledge are more context-dependent and personally orientated (Belenky *et al.* 1986), and suggests that this is likely to have particularly negative implications for women within the more dominant research approaches. Similarly, Freeman (1991, cited in Golombek 1994) has pointed out that women's ways of knowing have been discredited in the positivist paradigm. In a teaching profession which is largely populated by women, the inherently supportive and contextualised nature of collaborative action research may well provide an important avenue for language teachers' (and particularly female language teachers') voices to be strengthened. In addition, the increase in individual and collective knowledge about teaching, as it occurs through teachers' own experiences, has the potential to bring research and practice closer together in productive ways.

1.3 Teachers' responses to action research

In language teaching, as well as in the broader educational community, a strong distinction has often been made between academic research and classroom practice. Academic research conventions have created a separation between theory, research and practice (Hopkins 1993), with the result that many teachers regard research, at best with suspicion and at worst with contempt, as the province of academic researchers who know little – and understand less – about the day-to-day business of life in the language classroom (Beasley and Riordan 1981; McDonough and McDonough 1990). Even when teachers are interested in research and research findings, they may believe that they do not have the skills, training or knowledge to carry out research according to empirical requirements.

In recent years, it has become increasingly commonplace in the field of English as a second or foreign language to hear or read about the 'reflective practitioner' and the 'teacher as researcher'. But why should English language teachers become researchers? After all, teachers already lead busy classroom lives. Why should they wish to add research to all their other classroom responsibilities?

Teachers with whom I have worked have pointed to what they see as the benefits of involvement in action research. A group of twenty ESL teachers, who participated in a recent Australian collaborative project exploring the impact of the introduction of a new competency-based curriculum on teachers' course design, suggested a number of reasons why they viewed action research in a positive light (A. Burns 1997: 107–8). First, teachers highlighted the capacity of action research to enable them to engage more closely with their classroom practice as well as to explore the realities they faced in the process of curriculum change:

> It made me evaluate what I was doing in my classes. I think I have become more methodical in the way I approach assessment and in my explanation to the class, not in *what* I do (which is much the same) but *how*.

> It gave me an opportunity to *undertake* action research and to learn about this method as it related to my teaching.

> It gives teachers an opportunity to reflect on the decisions behind what they do. As well it helps provide a foundation for further developing the curriculum.

Second, collaboration with other teachers was seen as a significant benefit personally and as a key factor in generating solutions to changes in institutional demands:

> It gave me an opportunity to meet with others outside the centre, to listen to their ideas and their methods of solving problems which seem to be common to all.

> Collaboration: discussion was most worthwhile – broadening perspectives, feedback, reinforcement and support.

Other comments related to the sense of personal and professional growth teachers had experienced:

> It felt good to be part of a project again. I liked having the time and direction to reflect on what I was doing and why.

> It was fun! When you're feeling pretty jaded by college and state bureaucracy, it's nice to stretch the brain a bit.

> Writing up – time for reflection, depth of perspective.

> I felt a degree of personal satisfaction once I collected the data and completed the write up – a feeling that I had challenged myself and was able to meet the challenge to a certain extent.

Increased self-awareness and personal insight were also valued:

> Self-analysis – examining strengths and weaknesses – reaffirming commitment to principles of teaching.

> I was surprised by the responses from a questionnaire I gave the students and it was interesting for me to write this up.

Some teachers also suggested that they could now understand the reasons and need for institutional curriculum change more clearly:

> It clarified important issues from outside the classroom.

> It gave me a great feeling of being part of a progression, rather than just fulfilling the teaching requirements of a particular Stage.

> More sensitive now to the demands made by industry on students and teachers. Able to accommodate those that are useful – discriminate those that aren't.

These comments suggest that collaborative action research has the capacity to initiate and enhance teachers' research skills as a natural extension of teaching practice. They also suggest that action research is what Linda Ross, the teacher whose comments are presented at the beginning of this chapter, described as 'a powerful form of staff development'. The teachers' responses indicate that, from their point of view, classroom enquiry and self-reflection are important components of professional growth, providing a sound source for pedagogical planning and action and enabling them to frame the local decisions of the classroom within broader educational, institutional and theoretical considerations. They saw collaborative critical enquiry as a source of teacher empowerment, as it develops the ability to evaluate curriculum policy decisions and to exercise professional judgement and it affirms the role of the teacher.

The views expressed by these teacher researchers are echoed by Goswami and Stillman's (1987: preface) persuasive account of what happens when teachers experience research as part of their teaching role:

> 1 Their teaching is transformed in important ways: they become theorists, articulating their intentions, testing their assumptions, and finding connections with practice.
> 2 Their perceptions of themselves as writers and teachers are transformed. They step up their use of resources; they form networks; and they become more active professionally.
> 3 They become rich resources who can provide the profession with information it simply doesn't have. They can observe closely, over long periods of time, with special insights and knowledge. Teachers know their classrooms and students in ways that outsiders can't.
> 4 They become critical, responsive readers and users of current research, less apt to accept uncritically others' theories, less vulnerable to fads, and more authoritative in their assessment of curricula, methods and materials.
> 5 They can study writing and learning and report their findings without spending large sums of money (although they must have support and recognition). Their studies while probably not definitive, taken together should help us develop and assess writing curricula in ways that are outside the scope of specialists and external evaluators.
> 6 They collaborate with their students to answer questions important to both, drawing on community resources in new and unexpected ways. The nature of classroom discourse changes when inquiry begins. Working with teachers to answer real questions provides students with intrinsic motivation for talking, reading, and writing and has the potential for helping them achieve mature language skills.

In a similar vein, Kemmis and McTaggart (1982: 2–5) list a number of benefits which can accrue from involvement in action research processes. They include:

- thinking systematically about what happens in the school or classroom

- implementing action where improvements are thought to be possible
- monitoring and evaluating the effects of the action with a view to continuing the improvement
- monitoring complex situations critically and practically
- implementing a flexible approach to school or classroom improvement through action and reflection
- researching the real, complex and often confusing circumstances and constraints of the modern school
- recognising and translating evolving ideas into action.

Over twenty years ago, Stenhouse (1975: 143), a major proponent of action research in the context of mainstream education, summarised some of the central arguments for teachers carrying out research. These are now gaining greater currency in the field of second language teaching:

> The uniqueness of each classroom setting implies that any proposal – even at school level – needs to be tested and verified and adapted by each teacher in his [*sic*] own classroom. The ideal is that the curricular specifications should feed a teacher's personal research and development programmes through which he is increasing his own understanding of his own work and hence bettering his teaching ... It is not enough that teachers' work should be studied; they need to study it themselves.

According to these accounts, then, action research offers a valuable opportunity for teachers to be involved in research which is felt to be relevant, as it is grounded in the social context of the classroom and the teaching institution, and focuses directly on issues and concerns which are significant in daily teaching practice.

1.4 Summary

In this chapter I have suggested that action research has a number of personal and professional benefits for second language teachers. These arguments are drawn from the perceptions of teachers who have undertaken action research as well as from the professional literature. In particular, the chapter has aimed to present a case for a move away from the current predominantly individualistic versions of action research to more collaborative and critical interpretations.

I have presented action research in a positive light, with the aims of presenting a rationale for teachers to engage in action research and building a case for critical reflection on practice as integral to teachers' personal and professional development. However, like Linda Ross, many teachers with whom I have worked have initially been uncertain about what action research involves and how to do it. The aim of this book is to draw on their experience and to present practical guidelines for teachers who want to work together to explore their classrooms through an action research approach. In the chapters that follow, the central themes of the book are taken up and extended in greater detail. Chapter 2 discusses the nature and origins of action research and outlines phases in the action research process, while Chapter 3 considers starting points for research, and particularly how a focus for research can be developed. It also reviews the ethical issues to be considered. Chapters 4 and 5 look at procedures and techniques for data collection, using practical illustrations from case studies of collaborative projects. Chapter 6 is concerned with analysing data and drawing out implications for practice. In Chapter 7, ways of reporting on action research and maintaining the impact of action research processes at the classroom and organisational levels are discussed. Chapter 8 aims to illustrate further the realities of conducting action research by presenting excerpts from case study accounts written by teachers and research coordinators who have participated in collaborative projects. Reports by teachers who have conducted collaborative action research are still relatively rare in the second language literature. Readers who are impatient to read accounts of action research in practice may wish to begin with this chapter before working through the more detailed discussion of processes contained in the previous chapters.

In my experience, a helpful first step is often made when teachers gain an overview of different approaches to educational research and the various research processes and methods related to these approaches; this allows for a better understanding of what action research is and what it is not. The next chapter, therefore, considers briefly different approaches to conducting research in the field of English as a second language education and discusses how action research fits into these perspectives. It goes on to discuss the origins of action research and to draw out the relevant phases and processes which can be expected to occur in an action research cycle.

Group discussion tasks

1 To what extent do you agree with the idea that teachers may find academic research findings unrelated to their daily classroom work? Consider reasons for your responses.
2 To what extent do you draw on research in your own teaching? Do you, for example, consult the professional literature? If so, what kind of articles or books do you read and how do you use them in your teaching?

3 What reasons for carrying out collaborative action research can you suggest other than those listed in Section 1.3?

4 What difficulties or constraints might present themselves for teachers wishing to form a collaborative research group?

5 Based on the brief account outlined in this chapter, develop your own working definition of action research.

6 List what you understand at this point to be the main characteristics of action research.

7 What arguments are there for conducting collaborative action research rather than individual action research?

8 What would be the advantages of conducting individual action research?

2 Definitions and processes

> My experience of action research is that it is difficult to grasp or
> explain the concept until one is in the process of doing it. It is in
> the doing that it starts to make sense and become clear.
>
> (Jane Hamilton, Victoria)

2.1 Introduction

In the first sections of this chapter, we shall look very briefly at major
approaches to research in second language education. The discussion
aims to provide a very basic framework for examining more generally
the place of action research within a broad range of research approaches. In providing this overview, I do not in any way claim to
provide anything more than a simplistic outline of different research
approaches. There is now a large number of publications dealing
extensively with research which can be consulted by readers wishing to
know more about these approaches and how they might apply to
research in the second language field (for example, see J. D. Brown
1988; Chaudron 1988; Cohen and Manion 1994; Johnson 1992;
Nunan 1992; Seliger and Shohamy 1989; van Lier 1988; Wiersma
1986).

In his book, *Research Methods in Language Teaching*, Nunan (1992)
points out that a binary distinction is commonly made between two
major contrasting research paradigms: qualitative and quantitative
research. Although there are many other ways to classify differences in
research approaches, in this section we shall consider the major
distinguishing characteristics of these two broad types of research. We
shall also consider how action research relates to these two broad
classifications and then discuss some of the arguments that are made for
considering action research a valid form of research. The chapter will
then continue with a brief overview of the emergence of action research
as a research approach. This is followed by a discussion of various
definitions of action research and the phases and processes involved in
constructing collaborative action research.

2.2 Quantitative approaches to research

Until relatively recently, educational research has tended to favour the more established scientific or experimental approaches which have characterised research in general. Hitchcock and Hughes (1995: 21) describe the dominance of the scientific model of social research in the following way:

> From about the late nineteenth century onwards the scientific model employed by the natural and physical sciences, such as biology, physics and chemistry, quickly became defined as the most appropriate model for investigating the social world ... [This model] is based on the view that the natural sciences provide the only foundation for true knowledge and that the methods, techniques and modes of operation of the natural sciences offer the best framework for investigation of the social world.

The methods employed by a scientific approach to enquiry are aimed towards objectivity and control. Quantitative researchers adopt a structured and standardised approach towards their enquiries. This approach involves forming research hypotheses which are then subjected to controlled testing and statistical measurement procedures. Hypotheses are 'preconceived', or, in other words, they are based on previous evidence which provides the rationale for considering the hypothesis worthy of testing. The researcher intervenes in the research context with a view to detecting cause and effect relationships between the phenomena they wish to investigate. In order to identify these relationships objectively, the researcher controls or eliminates variables in the research context which may affect the outcomes; quantitative researchers work with a limited number of variables which are specifically identified as part of the research procedure.

Another important aspect of quantitative research is the operationalisation of terms; this means defining terms used in the hypothesis in accordance with the steps or tests that will be used to measure them, so that there is no confusion about their exact meanings. For example, if a researcher wanted to investigate the effects of anxiety on student test scores, he or she must first define what is meant by anxiety. Stating, for example, that anxiety refers to a score in relation to criteria on an anxiety scale provides a clear definition of what the researcher means in the context of the study.

In quantitative research, establishing the internal and external reliability of the results obtained is vital. Internal reliability involves asking questions such as: Were the methods for collecting, analysing and interpreting the data consistent? Would the same results be obtained by other researchers using the same analysis? External reliability, on the other hand, raises the following question: Could an independent researcher reproduce the study and obtain results similar to the original study?

The strength of quantitative approaches to research lies in the clarity and rigour of the procedures adopted. They offer ways of testing hypotheses that are widely accepted and standardised. Another advantage is that because an experimental approach offers clear definitions and controls of variables, studies can be replicated and comparisons made across different studies and sites. However, increasingly in the latter half of the twentieth century, social scientists argued that in social situations, where events can be viewed as 'intended, motivated actions on the part of reasoning actors' (Reynolds 1982: 44), what is to be counted as 'true' or 'factual' rests on different interpretations or assumptions. The concept of arriving at external 'truths' or facts which can be verified has come under intense scrutiny as interest has grown in understanding the relative meanings and interpretations of events that are given by the participants in the research context.

2.3 Qualitative approaches to research

Researchers who have adopted a qualitative perspective within the social sciences have argued that a scientific approach is too mechanistic. They have critiqued it for its failure to take into account how human situations, experiences and behaviours construct realities which are inherently subjective. Qualitative researchers, therefore, argue for an alternative frame of reference, one that involves understanding the research context from the inside, that is, from an *emic* perspective, rather than from an outside, or *etic*, perspective (Watson-Gegeo 1988). This viewpoint holds that 'social facts' cannot ultimately be seen as fixed and that quantification glosses over the diversity of multiple and socially constructed meanings.

The aim of qualitative approaches is to offer descriptions, interpretations and clarifications of naturalistic social contexts. Thus, in contrast to formulating, testing and confirming or disconfirming hypotheses, qualitative research draws on the data collected by the researcher to make sense of the human behaviour within the research context. The researcher treats the context as it occurs naturalistically and no attempt is made to control the variables operating in the context as these may be the very sources of unexpected or unforeseen interpretations. Observation and description and the gathering of data from a range of different resources are the main methodological tools. The process of observation and the emerging descriptions and insights of the researchers themselves become an important aspect of the research findings. The emphasis is on

Table 2.1. *Comparisons between quantitative and qualitative research*

Quantitative research	Qualitative research
• values objectivity through the discovery of facts or truths	• encompasses socially subjective and relative interpretations of phenomena
• tests pre-established hypotheses through the collection and measurement of data	• draws on data to develop and refine hypotheses
• establishes cause and effect relationships	• interprets human behaviour from participants' perspectives
• intervenes in the research context and controls variables	• explores naturalistic cultural settings without controlling variables
• reduces data to measurable quantities	• gathers 'rich' data and interprets them through 'thick' description and analysis
• ensures reliability through the consistency and replicability of methods	• ensures validity through multiple data sources
• generalises beyond the research population	• does not seek to generalise beyond the research context
• focuses on research outcomes that confirm or disconfirm hypotheses	• focuses on the processes as well as the outcomes of research

'rich' data collection with extensive explanations and details being provided on the contexts and participants in the research, which are sometimes referred to as 'thick' descriptions. Unlike quantitative approaches, qualitative research does not set out to follow a predetermined research procedure. Rather, the data are used to develop insights and implications which may then become the basis for further research or which may work to sharpen or shift the research questions. Because the data obtained from qualitative research is usually extensive and detailed, qualitative studies typically involve a small number of research contexts or subjects. They do not attempt to make claims about generalising the findings of the research to large populations.

Table 2.1 (based on R. B. Burns 1994) provides a comparison of quantitative and qualitative research approaches.

Some writers have argued that qualitative and quantitative approaches are essentially incompatible (e.g. Smith and Heshusius 1986) as they rest on fundamentally different views of the status of knowledge and truth and the nature of social behaviour. However, more recently, others (Bailey, 1998; Cronbach *et al.* 1980; Firestone 1987) have depicted them as complementary, suggesting that each approach can supplement and complement the other. Brindley (1990: 9), for example, suggests that from the point of view of those involved in TESOL research:

> it makes sense to view research pragmatically and to employ methods which address the issues of concern in the most effective way possible. Thus a teacher who does not wish to generalise the results of a classroom study beyond the classroom in question may collect data solely through participant observation and diary accounts. On the other hand, research aimed at revealing general patterns across large populations (e.g. studying the learning styles of ESL learners) would normally employ quantitative methods to obtain as precise an idea as possible of the distribution of certain kinds of behaviour, possibly supplementing the data thus obtained with more in-depth information from individuals via interviews or observations.

I would argue that neither of these two broad approaches should be seen as superior to the other. They each take a different view of the nature of knowledge and have different goals and functions. The key point is that different methods and procedures need to be selected according to the different kinds of purposes for undertaking the research.

2.4 Action research

The major focus of action research is on concrete and practical issues of immediate concern to particular social groups or communities. It is conducted in naturally occurring settings, primarily using methods common to qualitative research (Nunan 1992; McKernan 1996) such as observing and recording events and behaviours. Its approaches are essentially 'participatory', in that they are conducted by and with members of the actual community under study (Bailey 1998). Because of its practical nature and focus on immediate concerns, it holds particular appeal for classroom teachers and a promising direction for the building of theories related to teaching and learning.

In the view of some researchers, however, action research holds a somewhat fragile status as a research methodology (for example, Brumfit and Mitchell 1989; Jarvis 1991). This may be partly because of the strong claims that are generally made about action research as a process for enhancing reflective practice and professional growth and development. However, supporters of action research put forward a number of reasons why it should be considered as more than just a procedure for professional development.

First, it requires systematic data collection and analysis, and therefore it differs significantly from the more intuitive introspection and reflection that may be part of professional development programmes. Nunan (1992: 18), for example, argues that action research fulfils basic research requirements in that it encompasses a researchable question/ issue, data and interpretive analysis. Action research also parallels the directions and approaches of qualitative research, such as 'grounded theory' (Glaser and Strauss 1967). An essential feature of grounded theory is that theories of practice are generated from observed behaviours or phenomena and are therefore closely related to their supposed uses. Grounded research enables the researcher to adopt interpretations that are motivated by data derived from the actual social situation, in this case teachers' own classrooms, rather than by theoretical constructs alone. As action research is a highly flexible research process, it can also respond rapidly to emerging political, social and educational questions as they impact on practice.

Another argument which is made in favour of considering action research as viable research is that the data collection methods adopted by the researchers can be triangulated. 'Triangulation' involves gathering data from a number of different sources so that the research findings or insights can be tested out against each other. This increases the reliability and validity of the research. Additionally, since collaborative action research encompasses the different perspectives of several participants and researchers, as well as a variety of data collection tools and methods, the findings of collaborative researchers are likely to be more valid and reliable and, therefore, potentially more generalisable than the findings in individual action research.

In comparison with experimental, or even naturalistic, research, action research is still at a stage where some academic researchers would question that it qualifies as research at all. As a result, it suffers from a lack of prestige compared with more established forms of language education research. However, I believe there are several points to be considered in its favour as a research method. It addresses questions of real practical and theoretical interest to many educational practitioners. Where these are reported through workshops, staff meetings or short papers, they have the potential to be replicated by other teachers working in similar situations. Furthermore, teachers are involved in a genuine research process of data collection, analysis and interpretation, which contrasts with intuitive reflection. Unlike traditional research, which tends to leave the implementation of research to the practitioner, in action research, putting findings into practice is an integral part of the research process. Where the research is undertaken collaboratively, the reliability of the findings and the implementation processes are also strengthened. Finally, experimental research has, itself, a history of contradictory and inconclusive results and, increasingly, it is seen as less suited to investigating complex social interactions in situations such as language classrooms.

2.5 What are the origins of action research?

The seeds of action research are to be found as early as the late nineteenth century in the Science in Education movement and a variety of other social reform initiatives (McKernan 1996). It also grew out of the moves by progressive educators, such as John Dewey, in the early part of the twentieth century, to challenge the orthodoxy of the scientific research methods current in the field of education. Dewey argued for demystifying the approaches towards educational research derived from the natural sciences, and for including in research processes those directly involved in the practices of education. Dewey's ideas were essentially democratic in nature, based on the idea that researchers, practitioners and others involved in the educational community should address their efforts toward educational enquiry collectively in order to confront common educational problems. Dewey's propositions for educational research are captured in the following statement:

> The answer is that (1) educational practices provide the data, the subject matter, which form the problems of enquiry ... These educational practices are also (2) the final text of value and test the worth of scientific results. They may be scientific in some other field, but not in education until they serve educational purposes, and whether they really serve educational purposes can be found out only in practice.

> (Dewey 1929, cited in Hodgkinson 1957: 138)

Dewey's ideas on progressive education were extremely influential in educational research in North America. However, whatever practitioner research emerged was rapidly overshadowed by the more powerful claims of educational scientists, particularly the behavioural psychologists. It was not until the late 1970s and early 1980s that calls for practitioner enquiry, which were influenced by publications such as Schön's *The Reflective Practitioner* (1983), were renewed and strengthened in the North American educational context.

In the USA, an important contribution to action research came from Kurt Lewin. Lewin was not an educator, but a social psychologist who had fled Germany in 1933. His early years in North America coincided with a period of immense political, social and ideological upheaval.

McTaggart (1991: 6) outlines the sociopolitical conditions which formed the backdrop to Lewin's initiation of a challenge to the traditions of 'objective' social scientific research:

> Social life in post-war United States was abundant with practical and theoretical problems for the social sciences. The empirical discipline of psychology found a rich vein for the articulation of theory. But for Lewin ... it provided an environment for investigating practical and theoretical problems together, indeed in some respects as if they were one.

In the mid-1940s, Lewin proposed a mode of enquiry that comprised action cycles including analysis, fact-finding, conceptualisation, planning, implementation and evaluation. He proposed that the stimulus to enquiry should reside in group social problems investigated within their own practical environment and involving the players within those environments in developing action and theory in tandem. Lewin's own research, for example on the improvement and change of intergroup relations, led him to acknowledge the need for support and training of participants in the development of new skills:

> We should consider action, research and training as a triangle that should be kept together for the sake of any of its corners.

> (Lewin 1946: 42)

Lewin saw action research as a spiralling process of reflection and enquiry with the potential to become emancipatory and empowering because of its group structure. The more recent interpretation of educational action research as an individual enterprise has moved away from Lewin's original focus on collaboration between researcher and researched and between practitioner and professional researcher. This interpretation is unfortunate as it reduces the possibility that organisational constraints on good teaching practice can be changed, as they are more likely to be by collective research. It also runs counter to the cooperative principles which are key elements of teaching practice in learner-centred programmes and the growing trend towards collaborative and team teaching approaches.

Although attempts were made to legitimise action research in educational contexts in the United States in the 1940s, through the work of educationalists such as Stephen Corey, as a research methodology action research suffered from comparisons with positivist paradigms and methods. In particular, it was criticised for its inability to test hypotheses or to establish cause and effect relationships, for its resistance to the basic techniques and procedures of research and for its lack of generalisability. As a result, action research began to be judged against criteria which were inimical to its central principles of action and reflection within practical social situations. In an attempt to offset these criticisms and to justify it as a research methodology, Corey's writings (e.g. 1953) focused increasingly on the technical procedures for action research, losing in the process the reflective and dynamic elements of group understanding and action. Other accounts of action research by advocates such as Taba and Noel (1957) followed a rationalised six-step procedure: identifying problems, analysis of problems, formulating ideas or hypotheses, gathering and interpreting data, implementation-action, and evaluating the results of action. They described this as a sequence which 'it is not wise to reverse' (page 12), thereby effectively removing from the equation the flexible spiralling and recycling of further action which had been emphasised by Lewin.

The theoretical and methodological arguments which were levelled against action research in the 1940s and 1950s (see, for example, Hodgkinson 1957) meant that it was judged and found wanting by prevailing educational research standards. Its supporters' failure to argue on alternative grounds – such as the inability of professional research to address pressing practical problems or the extent to which scientific research models were relevant to education and the social sciences – resulted in the virtual disappearance of action research as a viable proposal for research in the United States by the late 1950s.

McTaggart (1991) points out that, ironically, an understanding of the need for action research in other countries emerged from the decline of action research in the United States. Criticisms of the 'research and development' movement in curriculum development, and the work of educational philosophers such as Schwab (e.g. 1969, 1970), who argued that practitioners were central to curriculum enquiry and development, underlined the limitations of the scientific model in bringing about educational reform. The centralised and 'teacher-proof' curriculum material of the 1970s did little, in Schwab's view, to initiate the exchanges between teachers and curriculum developers, which he believed were critical for improvements in educational practice. Schwab did not himself engage with teachers and students in the practical realisations of the curriculum or make any suggestions that teachers should themselves be classroom researchers, although he did believe that the key to educational improvement lay in the improvement of teaching. However, the impetus for a renewed interest in action research was linked to the emergence of curriculum development as a field of educational enquiry in its own right.

This interest manifested itself most distinctively in the British educational context in the 1970s, through the work of Lawrence Stenhouse and his successors, John Elliott and Clem Adelman. In his influential book, *An Introduction to Curriculum Research and Development,*

Stenhouse (1975) argued for new approaches to curriculum development which involved the testing of educational theories, as they manifested themselves in curriculum specifications, through their application in practice. He saw action research undertaken by teachers as a key component in the testability of curriculum concepts or as Stenhouse (1975: 142) himself expressed it:

> The crucial point is that the proposal is not to be regarded as an unqualified recommendation but rather as a provisional specification claiming no more than to be worth putting to the test in practice. Such proposals claim to be intelligent rather than correct.

Stenhouse's work in Britain through the Schools Council Humanities Curriculum Project (1967–72), as well as the work of his successors, Elliott and Adelman (e.g. 1973) in the Ford Teaching Project (1972–5), had a major impact on the acceptability of action research as well as on the development of the concept of the 'teacher as researcher'. As the tendency increases in many countries towards centralised curricula, accompanied by an emphasis on school-based curriculum development and renewal, quality assurance and review and teacher appraisal, Stenhouse's model of an autonomous and experimental approach to curriculum implementation, based on the critical judgements of practising teachers, provides a particularly powerful rationale for the role of collaborative action research in contemporary professional teaching practice.

2.6 What does action research involve?

Of the innumerable definitions of action research that have been proposed over the last forty years, a small selection is set out in the box.

Action research ... is a direct and logical outcome of the progressive position. After showing children how to work together to solve their problems, the next step was for teachers to adopt the methods they had been teaching their children, and learn to solve their own problems co-operatively.

(Hodgkinson 1957, cited in Cohen and Manion 1994: 190)

Action research aims to contribute both to the practical concerns of people in an immediate problematic situation and to the goals of social science by joint collaboration within a mutually acceptable ethical framework.

(Rapoport 1970: 499)

Action research is a small-scale intervention in the functioning of the real world and a close examination of the effects of such intervention.

(Halsey 1972, cited in Cohen and Manion 1994: 186)

Action research is the systematic collection of information that is designed to bring about social change.

(Bogdan and Biklen 1982: 215)

Action research is simply a form of self-reflective enquiry undertaken by participants in social situations in order to improve the rationality and justice of their own practices, their understanding of these practices and the situations in which the practices are carried out.

(Carr and Kemmis 1986: 162)

Action research is the application of fact finding to practical problem solving in a social situation with a view to improving the quality of action within it, involving the collaboration and co-operation of researchers, practitioners and laymen.

(R. B. Burns 1994: 293)

It is done by systematically collecting data on your everyday practice and analysing it in order to come to some decisions about what your future practice should be. This process is essentially what I mean by the term *action research*.

(Wallace 1998: 4)

These definitions suggest a number of common features which can be considered to characterise action research:

1 Action research is contextual, small-scale and localised – it identifies and investigates problems within a specific situation.
2 It is evaluative and reflective as it aims to bring about change and improvement in practice.
3 It is participatory as it provides for collaborative investigation by teams of colleagues, practitioners and researchers.
4 Changes in practice are based on the collection of information or data which provides the impetus for change.

The definitions by Burns, Bogdan and Biklen, and Carr and Kemmis also suggest a further purpose of action research. Inherent in these statements is a critical dimension which involves reflecting on the social structures and orders which surround classrooms. A critical dimension implies going beyond investigating the immediate practices of the individual classroom to analyse critically how these practices are mediated by the unexamined assumptions of the educational system or institution (cf. Crookes 1993). This view holds that educational processes are necessarily political and are based on certain, often implicit, ideological positions, beliefs or values. A major part of the process of action research within this perspective implies 'denaturalising' these values and examining the taken for granted assumptions or presuppositions that lie beneath them.

Definitions which include critical perspectives on action research also place emphasis on its participatory and collaborative nature; they stress that less may be achieved by a single teacher researcher investigating and changing practice. Collaborative communities of action researchers are in a stronger position to contribute to broader school or curriculum reform as their collective findings can point to institutional or system level changes that will facilitate better practice. Hill and Kerber (1967, cited in Cohen and Manion 1985) comment:

> Action research functions best when it is co-operative action research. This method of research incorporates the ideas and expectations of all persons involved in the situation. Co-operative action research has the concomitants of beneficial effects for workers, and the improvement of the services, conditions, and functions of the situation. In education this activity translates into more practice in research and problem-solving by teachers, administrators, pupils, and certain community personnel, while the quality of teaching and learning is in the process of being improved.

In broad terms, then, action research applies a systematic process of investigating practical issues or concerns which arise within a particular social context. This process is undertaken with a view to involving the collaboration of the participants in that context in order to provide evidence that can point to change. In contrast to some other forms of research which seek to test out theoretical ideas and to validate them independently, action research is driven by practical actions from which theories about learning and teaching can be drawn. Action researchers initiate an exploratory and interpretive process in which data in and about the social context is documented and collected. This is done so that issues or concerns in that context can be examined in order to enhance the way they are currently addressed. R. B. Burns (1994: 301) states that:

> The action researcher argues that it is the responsibility of practitioners, in contrast to investigators, to take new findings into account.

In this respect, it can be said that the findings and insights that are gained through action research are driven primarily by the data collected by the participants within their specific teaching situations, rather than by theories proposed through investigations which are external to the teaching context, but which may attempt to generalise to that context.

According to Kemmis and McTaggart (1988), action research occurs through a dynamic and complementary process, which consists of four essential 'moments': of planning, action, observation and reflection. These moments are the fundamental steps in a spiralling process through which participants in an action research group undertake to:

- develop a plan of critically informed action to improve what is already happening,
- act to implement the plan,
- observe the effects of the critically informed action in the context in which it occurs, and
- reflect on these effects as the basis for further planning, subsequent critically informed action and so on, through a succession of stages.

(Kemmis and McTaggart 1988: 10)

Kemmis and McTaggart's concept of action research is set out in Figure 2.1. In their explanation of this model, Kemmis and McTaggart are at pains to point out (page 15) that its purpose is to flesh out in a simplified way Lewin's abstract descriptions of action research, but because it is individualistic, it does not capture their notions of action research as an essentially collaborative undertaking.

The Kemmis and McTaggart model has been criticised by Ebbutt (1985) and Elliott (1991) on the grounds that it appears to assume in advance a fixed sequence of procedures which are self-contained, and that it glosses over the complexity and 'messiness' of the action research process. Both Ebbutt and Elliott offer alternative and more complex models which attempt to capture the dynamic, unfolding and mutually reinforcing processes of action research. Ebbutt, for example, suggests that action research is more accurately represented by a series of successive cycles, which allow for interaction and feedback within and between these various cycles. In a critique of educational research, Hopkins (1993) goes even further, by warning of the danger of action research models presenting in a prescriptive and prespecified way what should be essentially free and open courses of action.

Other writers have also suggested that flexibility is central to action research, which must be able to respond to the unpredictability of the social and political situation in which it is used. Somekh (1993) portrays action research as 'chameleon-like', as the plans, actions and observations through which action researchers proceed should be able to be transformed by their social, educational and political settings as well as by their personal and professional values, beliefs and histories. Somekh

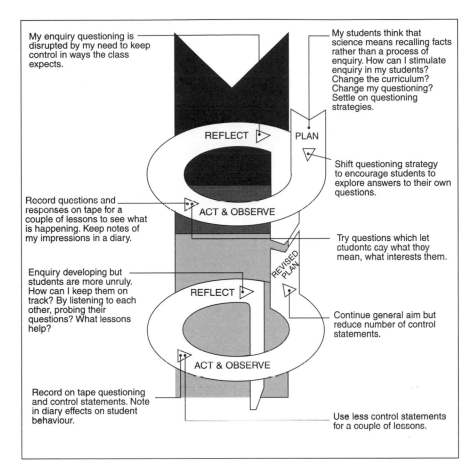

My enquiry questioning is disrupted by my need to keep control in ways the class expects.

My students think that science means recalling facts rather than a process of enquiry. How can I stimulate enquiry in my students? Change the curriculum? Change my questioning? Settle on questioning strategies.

REFLECT ▷   PLAN

Shift questioning strategy to encourage students to explore answers to their own questions.

Record questions and responses on tape for a couple of lessons to see what is happening. Keep notes of my impressions in a diary.

ACT & OBSERVE

Try questions which let students say what they mean, what interests them.

REVISED PLAN

Enquiry developing but students are more unruly. How can I keep them on track? By listening to each other, probing their questions? What lessons help?

REFLECT ▷

Continue general aim but reduce number of control statements.

ACT & OBSERVE

Record on tape questioning and control statements. Note in diary effects on student behaviour.

Use less control statements for a couple of lessons.

Figure 2.1   *The individual aspect in action research*

suggests that in broad terms action research can be seen as a research methodology which includes the following features:

- the research is focused on a social situation;
- in the situation participants collaborate with each other and with outsiders to decide upon a research focus and collect and analyse data;
- the process of data collection and analysis leads to the construction of theories and knowledge;
- the theories and knowledge are tested by feeding them back into changes in practice;
- to evaluate these changes, further data is [*sic*] collected and analysed, leading to refinement of the theories and knowledge which are in their turn tested in practice, and so on and so forth ...;

33

- at some point, through publication, these theories and knowledge are opened up to wider scrutiny and made available for others to use as applicable to their situation. This interrupts the cyclical process of research and action, but is useful in bringing the research to a point of resolution, if only temporarily.

(Somekh 1993: 29)

As already suggested, the focus of action research is on specific practical areas which are investigated within their social context. To begin our exploration of how action research is actually put into practice, in the next section we will look more closely at the kinds of phases that may occur in the action research process.

In describing these phases, I am adopting a view which is essentially collaborative and participatory. It is important to bear in mind that action research may be carried out through different combinations of people working together: by groups of teachers working with university researchers; by teacher–researcher pairs or groups working together; by teachers working in partnerships with administrators, students, parents or community members. Cohen and Manion (1994: 189) outline the range of possible roles which can be adopted by action researchers as follows:

> First there is the single teacher operating on her own with her class. She will feel the need for some kind of change or improvement in teaching, learning or organization, for example, and will be in a position to translate her ideas into action in her own classroom ... Second, action research may be pursued by a group of teachers working cooperatively within one school, though of necessity functioning against a bigger backdrop than the teacher working solo ... And third, there is the occasion ... where a team of teachers work alongside a researcher or researchers in a sustained relationship, possibly with other interested parties like advisors, university departments and sponsors on the periphery ...

Different combinations of researchers may be engaged in an individual project or may be a part of a larger scale project involving the whole school or even groups of schools or institutions working towards a common curriculum change. Teachers may also be involved in national projects, as in the Australian Adult Migrant English Program projects referred to in this book or the National Writing Project carried out in the United States in the 1980s. This is not to suggest, of course, that teacher–researchers should not work alone where there is no possibility or inclination to work with others. However, in this book the overall focus is on collaborative groups working together.

2.7 What are the processes of doing action research?

In a discussion of the processes of action research, it is important to stress again that action research should be seen as flexible (cf. McNiff 1988) and that different combinations of researchers in different situations will need to make their own interpretations of what are appropriate processes for the circumstances of the research. In Section 2.6, I outlined the four major steps in the action research process presented by Kemmis and McTaggart (1988): planning, action, observation and reflection, and suggested that some commentators have seen models such as these as too prescriptive. McNiff (1988), for example, states that they are too systematic and do not allow researchers to accommodate spontaneous, creative episodes. In addition, she argues, they are not 'intrinsically educational' (page 35); models appear to imply only that teachers apply a system of action research, without at the same time recognising the role of the teachers' own theorising and personal development in the action research process (see Chapter 1).

In the Australian studies in which I have been involved, the reality of the research process was perceived by the participants not so much as a cycle, or even a sequence of cycles, but as a series of interrelated experiences involving the following phases:

1 exploring
2 identifying
3 planning
4 collecting data
5 analysing/reflecting
6 hypothesising/speculating
7 intervening
8 observing
9 reporting
10 writing
11 presenting

In addition to identifying these features, which are not necessarily clearly delineated and separate points in the research, the majority of the participants reported that a crucial aspect of their experiences were the collaborative discussions that occurred regularly throughout the process. These discussions provided points of reference which enabled both their thinking and the subsequent changes in their teaching practices to go beyond what could be achieved through their own individual reflection and action. The collective and social nature of the collaboration was a key factor in the theory-building that occurred in relation to teaching practice. As one teacher commented:

> It's absolutely invaluable ... to have someone to be a sounding
> board in the process of trying to clarify what you are already doing
> and to move into new teaching practice.

What follows, then, is not so much a 'model' as general pointers
which provide a schema or framework for the processes of action
research from which teacher groups can guide their own action research
work. They are based on the key phases outlined above, which emerged
from the Australian action research work, and they reflect the kinds of
issues which became significant for teachers along the way.

Each phase is illustrated by examples from a recent project (based on
Harmey *et al.* 1996) I carried out with teachers in an Intensive English
Centre (IEC) in Sydney. Intensive English Centres are specialist ESL
schools set up by the New South Wales Department of Education and
Training to cater for the needs of newly arrived immigrant students of
high school age, who are given intensive English instruction for up to
three 12 week school terms as preparation for entering high school. For
the project that framed this example, the school had received funding
support from the government through a 'Disadvantaged Schools
Program'. As a result, release time was available for teachers to
participate in daytime meetings and staff development sessions. The
school executive had also agreed with the staff to move towards a team
teaching approach with a focus on groups of teachers working together
to develop students' language outcomes at beginner and intermediate
levels in different language skill areas. The whole staff became involved
in collaborative action research as a way of monitoring school-based
changes in programming and class organisation (see Section 8.4 for a
fuller account of this project).

PHASE I: EXPLORING

This is a very open-ended and uncertain phase where teachers 'feel their
way' into the research questions. It involves identifying and agreeing
upon a general idea or issue of interest to the group. It is a starting point
for undertaking some initial action, such as documenting your general
observations of the situation, in order to clarify your understandings
about the issue or problem and to bring these back to the group. It may
also involve doing some reading of recent articles or books to obtain
ideas for research.

Here are some examples of general areas for research identified by the
ESL teacher researcher teams working at the IEC. Not all areas will be
as well developed as these at this stage, as you may recall from Linda
Ross's account in Chapter 1.

(a) In our class, students seem very reluctant to speak English. What can we do to elicit more oral responses from the students and increase their oral interaction in class?

(b) Our students don't listen well to classroom instructions. Why is this happening and what teaching strategies can be developed to improve listening skills?

(c) We have students in our class who are very withdrawn and are making slow progress. What factors may be impeding their progress and what teaching strategies can we develop to increase their confidence and motivation?

PHASE 2: IDENTIFYING

This involves a 'fact finding' process which enables the researchers to refine their ideas about the general focus area and to prepare for more systematic investigation. At this stage, a short period of time is spent recording or documenting observations which relate to the research area in a broad and relatively unfocused way. This process helps to clarify the nature of the situation and to suggest further action.

We shall use research area (c) above to provide examples of the kind of decisions that are made during this and subsequent phases. This research involved a team of three teachers who all taught the same group of beginner level students, between the ages of 11 and 15. The teachers realised after a short period of general observation that:

- a small number of students were more withdrawn than the others
- these students seemed more fearful, nervous and distressed than the others
- although these students were not complete beginners they were not using the English they knew because of lack of confidence
- they were students who had experienced very recent migration
- their pre-migration situation had involved separation from family, or war experiences.

PHASE 3: PLANNING

This phase involves developing a viable plan of action for gathering data, and considering and selecting a range of appropriate research methods. The plan is aimed at trialing a particular course of action and collecting data on the outcomes of this action.

We shall follow through our research example. As a result of their preliminary observations of the class the research team realised through discussion that the learning environment and the individualised activities they had set up for the students were not meeting their affective needs.

In their meeting, they decided to observe the progress of the four most withdrawn students very closely and at the same time to develop group, rather than individual, student activities which they hoped would improve the classroom dynamics and relationships between all the students. They saw this as a way of increasing their confidence and encouraging them to communicate and participate more. They decided to collect data on the results of their new teaching strategies.

PHASE 4: COLLECTING DATA

During this period, the procedures selected for collecting data are developed and put into action. These might not be the only data gathering events, but this period begins the process of going more deeply into the issue being researched.

The teachers in our example developed a number of new activities for the students. They set up what they called 'an enrichment programme' of communicative activities, using games such as Monopoly, Alphabet Snap, Happy Families and Bingo, and 'fun' excursions with shared activities and a shared lunch. In all these activities the focus was on students interacting much more in groups than would normally have occurred. They employed a number of methods to collect data on the students' interactions:

• they held a weekly programming and assessment meeting where formal and informal observations on progress were shared
• they observed each other teaching and noted the students' classroom behaviour
• they videoed the group of four students in the first lesson where games were introduced
• they transcribed a segment of the video recording in order to compare subsequent oral interactions.

PHASE 5: ANALYSING/REFLECTING

In Kemmis and McTaggart's model, analysing is not treated as a separate component of action research. However, in our experience, close analysis of data is often the stimulus for reflection so that these two elements become conflated. This phase is therefore considered as a combination of both analysis and reflection. At this stage, the data are analysed using a systematic process of analysis and interpretation according to agreed criteria.

In our example, the research team carried out the following analyses during a team meeting. They:

• scrutinised the short transcribed segment of the video recording and noted the quantity (e.g. number of turns, length of utterances) and type of the language (e.g. asking questions, responding appropriately to questions or instructions) each student had produced

- reviewed the video to relate their analysis of the transcript to the visual data of the recording
- compared their analysis of the transcript with their informal observations of each student.

This analysis led them to the following insights:

- one member of the student group (A) had produced no turns and had used only gestures, such as pointing
- one member (B) had produced only one-word utterances (mainly, *no*)
- one student (C) had produced mainly numbers (e.g. *three hundred twenty*)
- one member (D) had asked the most questions and had challenged other students over their playing of the game (e.g. *Is not your money . . .*).

PHASE 6: HYPOTHESISING/SPECULATING

In this phase, teachers may be in a position to draw out hypotheses or predictions about what is likely to occur, for example, in students' learning, classroom behaviour or progress. These hypotheses are based on the data that have been collected to this point, on their analysis and on the reflections that have arisen from the analysis. The hypotheses may form the basis for further action to test them out.

In our case study, the team of teachers made two predictions as a result of their analyses and interpretations. They predicted that:

- student A would remain withdrawn and would need additional time in the same class
- student D would make rapid progress and would soon be amongst the top students in the class.

PHASE 7: INTERVENING

This phase involves changing classroom approaches or practices in response to the hypotheses one has made. It may involve some further deliberate experimenting with different or non-usual teaching methods or testing out developing hunches or predictions by more formal means, such as giving students a test or repeating an activity previously administered to compare the results.

The teachers in our example worked through this phase in the following ways. First, they carried out formal assessments on all their students' oral and written skills. This was, in any case, part of the whole school procedure for monitoring student achievement, but it was a useful check on their students' progress at this stage. These assessments involved spoken and written tasks which were assessed on a number of competency-based criteria. On the basis of these assessments, the out-comes of their predictions were the following:

- Student A was relocated to another class with a slower learning pace. However, the teachers' observations indicated that her behaviour had changed as a result of her increased participation in classroom games and other activities and she began smiling more and initiating conversations.
- Student D, who had participated well in early interactions and who had originally received strong assessments, began to show less improvement. She had major problems with sentence structure, word order and punctuation in written composition, such as recounts and descriptions.

In the case of student D, the teachers in the research team developed a new prediction and decided on further intervention. They speculated that the student had problems in production in her first language, Portuguese, that affected her second language production.

They decided to test out their assumption by arranging for the student to be interviewed by a bilingual aide. The aide administered the same tasks in Portuguese that the student had carried out in her English assessment. She confirmed that these problems existed also for the student in her first language. This information helped the teachers to focus on giving her writing tasks which would develop her skills in these areas.

PHASE 8: OBSERVING

This phase involves observing the outcomes of the intervention and reflecting on its effectiveness. This involves a new set of teaching strategies and activities and a recycling back into a period of further data collection.

The teachers continued to develop new strategies for teaching and to collect data systematically on the outcomes of their interventions. These included the following:

- One teacher in the team focused on developing the skills of all the students in giving short oral presentations. She focused particularly on two oral tasks: bringing to school and talking about an item of personal interest, and giving a demonstration of a procedure, such as 'how to clean your glasses' or 'how to use a walkman'. Both sets of presentations were videoed and the team analysed the students' progress in one of their meetings. The teacher also documented the list of presentations and wrote field notes on the students' presenta-tions and the language they used.
- The two other team members continued to monitor all their students' writing with a particular focus on students B, C and D. They developed

a series of writing tasks, in particular focusing on the skills of student D which they had identified as needing improvement. They introduced written texts such as recounts of past events and collected samples of the student's writing for analysis. When all three teachers later compared a writing task on 'My weekend' completed by student D in August, when they had first identified her writing problems, with one she completed on the same topic in November, they noticed the following:

- the student was able to produce a much longer piece of writing
- the structure and progression of the whole text had improved
- the student was now forming complete sentences rather than using isolated phrases
- the student was using the correct form of the past tense such as *I went*, *I watched*, to refer to past events
- the student was beginning to use complex sentences with conjunctions such as *because*
- the student was beginning to use adverbs such as *after* to indicate time sequence.

Outcomes for students B and C showed similar results, but interestingly one student in the class had shown less improvement in writing than they would have predicted and another student showed unexpectedly rapid progress. The team identified these outcomes as areas which would have been of interest to follow up in further research, although they were not able to do so because of the close of the academic year.

PHASE 9: REPORTING

This phase involves articulating the activities, data collection and results that have come out of the research process within the research group. Verbalising these activities through discussion results in 'problematising' the analyses and observations by extending and critiquing them with other members of the research community.

The teachers in the school who were all involved in action research held regular team meetings (approximately six over the course of the project). Some of these were timetabled as part of the team-based approach to teaching adopted in the school; others were set up specially for the research and sometimes included myself as the university researcher with whom the teachers worked in partnership. Reporting to other team members and from team to team within the school was, therefore, interspersed across the whole period of the research.

PHASE 10: WRITING

This is a 'summative' phase where the research questions, the strategies developed, the process of the research, and the analyses and results observed are drawn together by writing up an account in a report or article. This is a very important phase as it aims to ensure that the research has a chance of being disseminated to others, rather than remaining as a private or isolated activity. It makes the research accessible to other teachers or researchers who wish to read about teaching issues similar to their own or to find out what teachers can do about particular classroom problems.

In the school our example is based on, each team of teachers wrote up a short account of the research they had conducted. This was sometimes undertaken by the whole team or sometimes by combinations of people within a team. The reports were bound together into a single volume and copies were distributed to all staff members as well as to district consultants and other personnel from the Department of Education and Training. In the case of the team of teachers whose research we have followed in the examples, they made the following decision when writing their reports:

- The two teachers who had worked on writing skills agreed to write about the whole project and to focus particularly on the results of the writing strategies they had introduced. They included samples of student writing in their report.
- The teacher who had focused on oral presentations complemented the first report by giving a detailed account of how she had taught these activities and presenting the documentation she had collected.

PHASE II: PRESENTING

This phase also aims at ensuring that the research is presented to a wider audience. It involves giving more formal presentations about the research than those that take place in group discussions. These talks can be given to a number of interested audiences, for example at staff meetings or to professional association workshops.

After the action research was completed, the staff in the school we have discussed were involved in the following presentations:

- They set aside a morning during their first staff development meeting of the term. Each team was allocated time to present their research, to answer questions and to discuss issues the whole staff felt were important for the changes they had been introducing into their programme. The presentations were videoed for future reference.
- Three of the teachers were invited to present at a national professional development workshop for language teachers, which focused on classroom research.

In the instance of this school, the staff development workshop represented a new starting point where some of the teachers decided that they would become involved in a new cycle of research. They intended to build further on their own work across the coming year. At the time of writing this book, this research was still proceeding and being reported to other teachers in the school.

The phases outlined here are based on the collaborative action research experiences of language teachers in the Australian context. It is important that they should not be seen as prescriptive steps which must be carried out in a fixed sequence, but rather as suggestive of various points in the research process. Many of these phases will overlap or will occur simultaneously. Some phases may occur in a different order from the way they are listed here. They may also be recursive and cycle back into each other. In practice, action research turns out to be much more 'messy' than commonly presented models suggest and the processes should be adapted to suit the needs and circumstances of the particular participants who are involved in it. These will vary from teacher to teacher, learner to learner, classroom to classroom, school to school and country to country.

2.8 Summary

In this chapter I have introduced some of the central themes and processes of action research. In presenting these themes, one intention was to situate action research within broader approaches to research in education. A purpose of the brief historical overview was to stress the original collaborative intent of action research, that is, to enhance and develop group processes which aim to address social issues relevant to the community of researchers. This overview has also traced the origins and the development of the action research movement and the different perspectives from which it has been viewed within educational research paradigms.

A further aim of this chapter was to begin to provide a fuller picture of the realities of an action research process. The example from the Sydney high school involving teams of teachers conducting school-based action research is intended to give readers some concrete instances of how these processes may be carried out in practice. Various aspects of the action research process will be taken up in the rest of the book and treated in more detail. They will be discussed through two dimensions; the existing literature on action research which, in the absence of an extensive ESL literature, draws substantially on research in the broader educational context; and practical examples using teachers' accounts of how these processes have been realised within collaborative research groups.

Group discussion tasks

1 Discuss some of the advantages and disadvantages of quantitative and qualitative approaches to research.
2 Look back at the working definition of action research you developed in Chapter 1. Would you now wish to modify this in any way?
3 What features could be said to distinguish action research from teacher reflection?
4 With others at your teaching institution, begin a list of possible themes or focus areas for collaborative action research.
5 What possible research team combinations could be initiated in your current teaching context? What support would you need?
6 In relation to the particular curriculum followed by you and others at your teaching institution, what aspects of this curriculum could, to use Stenhouse's term, be further 'tested through practice'?
7 Consider the list of action research phases presented in Section 2.7. Which of these phases seem to you to be the most difficult to implement in your current situation? What kind of support might help?
8 Which of the three research areas in Phase 1 identified by the staff in the Intensive English Centre are of most interest to you? To what extent are any of these three areas of current concern with your present learners?

3 Getting started

> The early advice of other project members was invaluable –
> namely, to narrow my area of enquiry.
>
> (Anne Fowler, Queensland)

3.1 Introduction

Teachers new to action research frequently comment that finding a focus and developing a research question is difficult. In fact, for many this may be one of the most difficult points in the research process. You may feel uncertain both about the kinds of questions that can be asked and about how to focus the questions sufficiently to make them manageable.

This chapter looks at what is involved in getting started on the action research process and provides some suggestions. However, in order to avoid assuming that conducting action research is simply a question of teachers deciding to do it, and to frame this discussion within the realities of most institutional contexts, I first acknowledge some of the obstacles that may be experienced by teacher researchers. I discuss the organisational constraints and personal impediments that may be placed in teachers' way and suggest some strategies through which these might be, if not eliminated, at least minimised or addressed. I then go on to look at ways of developing a focus for institutional and group research. The chapter also suggests some practical questions which could be used for exploring different areas of language teaching and learning, drawing on the research conducted by Australian teachers. Finally, questions and issues related to the ethics of conducting action research are considered.

3.2 Constraints and impediments

It would be unwise to begin any discussion about getting started on action research without acknowledging that the institutional circumstances and conditions in many schools make it very difficult for

45

teachers to carry out any form of classroom research. Teachers are not, after all, given academic credit for conducting research in the way that researchers in universities are (Jarvis 1980; Myers 1985); time is not set aside for research activities; teachers' writing is not acknowledged for employment or promotion purposes; and, in general, schools operate in a climate where research may be viewed as either peripheral to classroom goals and practices or even downright wrong. In some circumstances, teachers may experience active resistance to the idea of doing classroom research, where they may be appearing to be a threat to accepted school norms and conventions. Similarly, some colleagues may deride teachers' attempts to investigate their classrooms critically, criticising it as pointless or, perhaps, fearing that this will cast them in a bad light for not doing the same.

McKernan's (1993) survey of constraints on action research conducted amongst 40 project directors in educational settings in the USA, UK and Ireland is telling. Most frequently ranked amongst the constraints were:

- lack of time
- lack of resources
- school organisational features
- lack of research skills.

These were followed by:

- obtaining consent/support to research
- language of research
- pressure of student examinations
- disapproval of principal.

At the other end of the ranking scale were human factors:

- disapproval of colleagues
- beliefs about the role of the teacher
- professional factors (union policies, contract)
- student disapproval.

Although such an extensive survey has not, to my knowledge, been conducted in the second language field, various commentators have suggested that these kinds of constraints are similarly a reality for most TESOL teachers (e.g. Allwright 1993; Brindley 1991; Burton and Mickan 1993; Nunan 1993; van Lier 1994). Comments on the constraints they experienced from my own teacher researcher colleagues placed time well ahead of other factors:

- Time factors

> I felt pressured for time both during the process of data collection and in the writing of the report.

> This piece of action research was, as is often the case for busy teachers, carried out under the pressure of time constraints.

> What disadvantages are there in being involved in an action research project? Time, time, time, time, time, time, time ... What are the major problems in doing research and teaching? Time, time, time ...

Other comments reflected some of the constraints highlighted by McKernan's research, while yet others pointed to different pressures:

- Additional work

  > There was pressure from the extra workload.

  > Teachers are often already on overload and such an involvement best happens when it is not viewed as an onerous chore.

- Limited local support for continuing or recognising the research

  > My latest challenge is how to continue with the process of collaborative action research in my centre – where do I go next?

  > A major problem is the recognition of the importance of research.

- Limited local support for publicising the research

  > There didn't seem to be any opportunities to tell other teachers about our research. Not many people seem to be aware of it.

- Anxiety about revealing teaching practices

  > There's a certain degree of vulnerability in sharing classroom practices.

  > Turning the spotlight on one's teaching practice tends to reveal all, good and bad, which can be an uncomfortable process.

- Anxiety about research skills

  > It worried me that I was doing the right thing, that my data collecting methods became a bit slapdash and less thorough than they should have been.

- Scepticism about the usefulness of practitioner research

  > The conclusions reached in this small project are neither new, nor I suspect particularly useful for many teachers.

  > There is a danger of developing trivial / narrowly focused projects that do not have a broad applicability to others in the profession.

- Timetable pressures

  > At the end of a semester courses and evaluations were winding up also.

  > My timetable had to be adjusted and course planning still had to be done.

- Tensions between researching and teaching

> There's an amount of class time eaten up which could be used to consolidate teaching.

> It is essential that the project / research does not determine the delivery of the course. The research should slot into the course as originally planned.

- Anxiety about divisions being set up between colleagues

> We need to guard against division within the staffroom between those doing research and those not doing it.

- Anxiety about producing a written account of the research

> I felt a lack of experience in writing up the final research findings (but it was a great learning experience).

Given the many personal and organisational constraints identified by these comments, teachers may well feel that attempting to investigate changes in practice through action research is not worth the effort. However, apart from the personal benefits also noted by the same teachers and listed in Chapter 1, there are a number of educational arguments which provide a very strong rationale for teacher research. The central theme of these arguments is the key role that teachers can play in the promotion of English language teaching as a professional enterprise.

1 In most national contexts, second and foreign language teaching suffers from low status in broader educational settings. If TESOL is to enhance its status as a real profession, a stance is needed by ESL institutions which encourages practitioner research. This provides a base for strengthening the relationships between theory and practice in relation to actual contexts of pedagogy.

2 If the field of second and foreign language teaching is to make claims to be a recognisable professional field, practitioners within this field will need to be able to make principled statements and judgements about teaching. These judgements need to be based on concepts about curriculum practice which are shaped by classroom enquiry and critical reflection. Otherwise teachers are reduced to being simply the unthinking deliverers of curricula which are developed by bureaucrats or 'experts', whose expertise may be based on notions of traditional research rather than knowledge of classroom practice.

3 In many national settings, rapid change means that education is becoming increasingly centralised, placing greater demands for accountability on educational institutions and teachers. One result of this climate of accountability is that teachers' scope for decision-making and autonomy becomes eroded (Apple 1982) and the danger

of teacher 'deskilling' is increased. Language teachers need to develop practical activities and strategies for self-reflection and critical enquiry to resist this trend.

4 In tandem with increasing centralisation, in many countries, schools are, paradoxically, being required to undertake local restructuring initiatives which involve measures such as teacher appraisal, local curriculum evaluation, local responsibility for professional development and school improvement. These requirements may result in piecemeal and fragmented activities which amount to no more than 'tinkering at the edges' of schooling, unless improvement in teaching is integrated with research into classroom practice. There is growing evidence that the most successful school-restructuring initiatives are those that link teaching to whole-school activities (Hopkins 1993).

5 Quality measures introduced by government requirements in a number of countries, including Australia, are placing schools and other teaching institutions in insecure funding situations which often involve competitive tendering processes. In such situations, institutions which have a strong professional development and curriculum research base are likely to be in a stronger position to compete successfully for programme delivery.

Van Lier (1994) suggests that while ESL teachers may feel a general 'malaise' about their status in adult educational institutions or school districts, they generally wish to do the best by their students. Many teachers develop creative ways of circumventing institutional constraints and directing their activities towards reflective practice. Van Lier advocates a critical approach towards the theories of practice that teachers develop about their classrooms. This involves conceptualising the classroom as a part of the 'wider institution and social contexts in which our work and our students' world unfolds' (page 6).

What, then, can be done in practical terms by teachers who wish to become involved in critical reflection on their classrooms and see action research as part of these initiatives, but who may be working in situations where professional development is not encouraged or not available? Several writers have made some useful suggestions for alleviating these problems.

Crookes (1989: 51–5) identifies situations where teachers are given minimum opportunities for professional support by managers and administrators as 'alienation'. He states that these circumstances often involve (a) mandated and centralised curricula; (b) large amounts of administration related to accountability demands; (c) limited interaction, because of timetabling arrangements or physical location; (d) large classes and lack of resources. He lists the following ideas for 'grassroots action' by teachers to reduce their professional alienation in such circumstances, in a way that might begin the process of critical enquiry and reflection on practice.

1 **Peer observation** Pairs of teachers can arrange to observe each other's classes in order to begin a dialogue about common assumptions, teaching problems, the demands of the curriculum, teaching philosophies or other issues of mutual interest. Where observation is too difficult to arrange, recordings can be made and used as the basis for collegiate discussion.

In respect of Crookes' first suggestion, there is widespread evidence that many teachers rate peer observation highly as an activity which assists their own professional development.

2 **Time** Most teachers are 'time-poor' and administrators may take the attitude that a teacher's function is to be in direct contact with students. Lobbying administrators for time for professional activities and demonstrating what improvements can be achieved with time, such as collaborative work to improve materials or curriculum, should be used by teachers as a bargaining strategy.

3 **Curriculum committees** Teachers can use existing in-house curriculum committees to change 'taken-for-granted' curriculum practices. One example is moving from the use of published materials to developing collaborative teacher-made resources, preferably using available desk-top publishing facilities. This increases a feeling of professional growth, and a commitment to undertaking shared projects.

4 **Local workshops** Teachers can develop a commitment to lifelong professional learning. This implies availing themselves of whatever faculty development activities occur. Ideally, these would involve presentations by teachers themselves and not only by visiting experts. They should also involve a series of workshops on the same topic, rather than single sessions, as well as opportunities for 'peer coaching' so that teachers can be supported as they take on and try out new ideas.

5 **Professional networking and availability of relevant professional information** Teachers could form study circles where written versions of speakers' presentations can be discussed. This allows for a more thorough and critical probing of the ideas presented in workshops. It also allows for technical writing and complex ideas to be discussed in a more digestible form. Where visiting speakers can be retained for discussion, this is also helpful. Alternatively it may be possible to argue for a local teacher to take on a position as a resource person.

Other suggestions by Crookes for 'action in the face of a lack of cooperation' include larger-scale issues to do with increased professionalism, such as pushing for professional standards and official programme recognition through local ESL professional organisations, or working through teacher organisations or unions.

Kemmis and McTaggart (1988: 25–6) provide a number of 'observations from experience' for getting started on action research. Amongst those that would lay the groundwork for action research in school settings where conditions are less than supportive are:

1 Get an action research group together and participate yourself – be a model learner about action research.
2 Be content at the start to work with a small group. Allow easy access for others. Invite others to come when topics that interest them will be discussed.
3 Get organised; get things started by arranging an initial launching, identifying a nucleus of enthusiasts, negotiating meeting times, and the like.
4 Start small – perhaps offer simple suggestions to get people started. (For example, about who talks in your classroom and who controls the development of knowledge in your classroom group.) Work on articulating the thematic concern which will hold your group together and establishing agreement in the group that the thematic concern is a shared basis for collaborative action.
5 Establish a time-line – set a realistic trial period which allows people to collect data, reflect and report over two or three simple cycles of planning, acting, observing and reflecting.
6 Arrange for supportive work-in-progress discussions in the action research group.
7 Be tolerant and supportive – expect people to learn from experience and help to create conditions under which everyone can and will learn from the common effort.
   . . .
9 Plan for the long haul on the bigger issues of changing classroom practices and school structures. Remember that educational change is usually a slow social process requiring that people struggle to be different. Change is a process not an event.

In a similar vein, McNiff (1988: 144–5) offers the following hints for maintaining enthusiasm for action research in the face of discouragement from other colleagues or the school system in general:

1 Don't give up.
2 Enlist the help of colleagues.
3 Keep a positive attitude.
4 Be prepared to compromise.
5 Be generous.
6 Go public.

7 Join a local action research group.
8 Establish a reputation for success.
9 Publish reports in journals.
10 Have faith in your own personal knowledge.

Other writers, Allwright and Bailey (1991) and Allwright (1993), concerned that the current calls for teacher research may add an unacceptable pressure on teachers and a burden to daily teaching, advocate the notion of 'exploratory teaching'. By this is meant 'fully integrating research into teachers' normal pedagogic practices' (Allwright 1993: 125), so that the way research is carried out becomes an integral part of classroom teaching. Allwright proposes a set of criteria that can be taken into account in this approach to teaching. These are presented below with an accompanying gloss (based on Allwright 1993: 128–9):

1 Relevance
   [This relates to teachers exploring 'puzzles' relevant to themselves.]
2 Reflection
   [Integrating research and pedagogy should ensure that reflection by both teachers and learners is promoted.]
3 Continuity
   [Integrating research and pedagogy should be a continuous enterprise and not one involving 'mini research projects' that take over teachers' lives, thereby discouraging them from further research.]
4 Collegiality
   [The integration of research and pedagogy should aim to bring teachers together and to bring teachers closer to learners. Ideally, it should also break down the rift between teachers and academic researchers.]
5 Learner development
   [Questions asked should be relevant to learners as well as teachers. 'Exploratory learning' should also be seen as a goal of integrated research and pedagogy.]
6 Teacher development
   [The research should contribute to the teacher's own development as well as to a more general development of the professional field. It should also ultimately contribute towards building theories of language teaching.]
7 Theory-building
   [Gaining a greater understanding of classroom teaching should involve the research of those most closely involved, teachers and learners.]

Hopefully, not all second and foreign language teachers will find themselves in situations where opportunities for action research and critical reflection on practice are actively discouraged. Crookes (1989: 47) suggests that 'most teachers want to see our programmes improve and so generally seek an element of change over time'. In line with Crookes' sentiments, one of my own teacher colleagues wrote the following to me on concluding her research:

> I like teaching – I like the classroom context and interaction with the students very much. I'm not a theoretician or an analyst but looking at research findings and being part of the research project will, I hope, contribute to my effectiveness in the classroom. ESL is a wide field and there is so much left for me to 'conquer' that any research which leads to a better delivery/presentation helps.

In my view, collaborative action research is a stimulating direction for curriculum change and professional development. There is now increasing evidence that, despite the constraints, it integrates productively into second language curriculum and professional development programmes for many teachers (see, for example, Freeman 1998). Reports of action research (for example, Strickland 1988) also suggest that it works best for teachers when it is collaborative and framed by supporting structures, such as a school or teaching centre decision to integrate action research within a professional development programme, or research which is undertaken as part of a higher education course such as a Master's or Bachelor's programme. However, given the very real barriers faced by practitioner researchers in many educational settings, the question of how a collaborative research orientation can be integrated and sustained institutionally within professional teaching practice is a crucial and complex one and it is taken up again in Chapter 7.

3.3 Finding a focus

Although it may be self-evident to suggest that the kinds of questions asked in action research are different from those which emanate from other forms of research, Cochran-Smith and Lytle (1990: 5) assert that this is 'not a trivial issue'. Teachers' questions are likely to emerge from a mismatch or gap between what is planned for the classroom and what actually happens; they can, therefore, be said to arise from an intersection of theory and practice. They are likely to be 'highly reflexive, immediate, and referenced to particular children and classroom contexts' (page 6). In these respects, they are unlike more traditional academic research, which reflects theoretical and empirical concerns.

These observations are borne out in a small-scale study conducted by Brindley (1991) with six language teachers who were undertaking research as part of a course of study. His aim was to investigate their perceptions of the research process and to explore the relationships between teacher-conducted research and professional growth. Brindley (1991) suggests that in identifying a focus for their research, all the teachers began with a concrete or practical teaching concern which was generated by questions they had already been asking themselves about aspects of their own teaching and its effect on learners. As 'Teacher 3' in Brindley's study expressed it:

> It was an area I felt the need to do something in anyway. I had been teaching for some time a very low level group, illiterate in L1 mostly and some of them had become good readers and others not. So that was the question and it's also a question that I had felt that I needed to answer for some time so it wasn't as if I had much difficulty with finding the question.

Brindley suggested that an initial focus for teacher research could arise from the following factors:

- Teachers' research questions may begin with concrete teaching interests.
- Particular incidents may highlight a researchable issue.
- Teachers may wish to validate experiential knowledge or beliefs.
- Research may arise from issues that teachers have puzzled about for some time.

(adapted from Brindley 1991)

One way to begin the process of identifying more specific focus areas is to pose to oneself a series of questions such as the following:

1 What is happening in my classroom that am I concerned about?
2 What makes me concerned about this issue?
3 What could I do to get more information about what is happening?
4 How will I go about collecting this information?
5 What could I do to change what is happening?

(adapted from Whitehead and Barratt 1985, cited in McNiff 1988: 57)

Alternatively, generating a series of statements relevant to your practice might suggest possible research areas. Kemmis and McTaggart (1982: 18) suggest the following starting points:

- I would like to improve the ...
- Some people are unhappy about ... What can I do to change the situation?
- I am perplexed by ...
- ... is a source of irritation. What can I do about this?
- I have an idea I would like to try out in my class.
- How can the experience of ... be applied to ... ?
- Just what do I do with respect to ... ?

Other statements proposed by teachers in the Australian studies with which I am familiar have been:

- I don't think I know enough about . . .
- My students don't seem to . . . What can I do about this?
- I'd like to change the way the students . . .
- I'd like to integrate more . . . in to my class. How can I do this?
- A colleague and I would like to try out . . . What would happen if we did?
- Why do some students in my class . . . and others . . . How can I find out what is happening here?

In the Brindley study referred to above, it was noted that one of the problems teachers experienced was developing a research question where the focus was narrow enough to be manageable. Here, it is worth taking into account a number of considerations.

First, avoid questions you can do nothing about. As Kemmis and McTaggart 1982: 18) point out:

> Questions like the relationships between socio-economic status and achievement, between ability and tendency to ask questions in class, may be interesting, but they have tenuous links with action. Stick with issues in which you do something which has potential for improvement.

In many language teaching situations, teachers may, for example, have to work with a set syllabus or course book or with large classes. It may not be possible to change these circumstances, but it may be feasible to try out different ways of using the materials or of grouping student activities in the classroom.

Second, limit the scope and duration of the research. This could mean setting a realistic timeframe for the research and focusing on a small issue. Having achieved some success with a small-scale initiative, the individual researchers or the group can then make decisions about where to go next with the research. For example, setting yourself a natural time-limit based on how programmes operate in your school or teaching centre (one course, semester or term) and, for example, documenting all the written materials you use during this period, would get you started on a critical analysis of your selection of materials with a sense that there is an end in sight.

Third, try to focus on one issue at a time. Even though there may be a number of possible factors which are of interest to you, it is probably unwise to try to link them all into one investigation. It is more useful to focus on one issue and to investigate it through a number of different methods so that different perspectives emerge. For example, exploring the teaching of writing to beginners through the use of different approaches, materials or methods, and documenting your own and the students' responses, may reveal successful new strategies which can be shared with other teachers.

Fourth, choose areas for research which are of direct relevance and interest to yourself and to your school circumstances. This makes the focus for the research more motivating and is potentially of interest to others in the same educational organisation. For example, if your school has recently adopted new ways of placing students in programmes, or a different approach to teaching writing, keep a journal of what impact this has on the kind of lesson planning decisions you now have to make.

Fifth, if possible, link questions for your research with broader changes in school curricula or professional development priorities. This ensures that your research aligns with the wider context of school restructuring or curriculum renewal and you will be in a better position to suggest realistic and relevant changes to practice, especially if the research is carried out collaboratively.

Essentially, action research questions are an attempt to capture insights about the gap between curriculum specifications or ideals and what actually happens in classroom practice. The following examples of starting points for research questions are all drawn from different aspects of second language teaching and learning practice. They were identified by Australian teachers who used them to begin focusing their research.

AFFECTIVE FACTORS

> My students don't seem to concentrate well in class and are making slow progress. What physical or emotional problems are affecting their ability to learn English?

> My students come from very different language backgrounds and have had different immigration experiences. How do these individual factors affect their learning?

> My students have been placed in a literacy class but really need help in improving their confidence and motivation. What 'non-language' focused tasks can I introduce and will these help?

CLASSROOM GROUPINGS

> I'm teaching a very diverse group of students with different levels of proficiency. This seems to be a problem to me, but what are my students' perceptions about being in this class?

> I'm always keen to use group work in my class and I usually take the responsibility for organising how the groups are formed. I wonder what my students think about group work and the way I group them?

I want to organise groups for students with similar learning speeds. Is my current way of grouping students effective?

COURSE DESIGN

I'm worried that I am not really meeting my students' needs. What would happen if I asked the students to share decisions about the planning and teaching process according to their perceptions rather than mine?

My classes feel chaotic and disorganised because of different language learning needs. How should I select and sequence common materials and activities in order not to disadvantage individual learners?

I've never thought consciously about how I plan my courses. Can I learn anything from observing how I make decisions about content, topics and materials in the course I'm teaching this term?

EXPLOITING MATERIALS AND AVAILABLE RESOURCES

I have found a course book I like to use with my beginner learners. How can I personalise the tasks in it so that they are more interesting and relevant to them?

I teach students in a workplace situation where they have very limited time in class. How can the students become resources for each other in order to speed up the learning process?

I am fortunate to have a bilingual aide to help my students with computing skills. Will having this support help more with computing skills or language skills?

LEARNING STRATEGIES

Some of my students have never been to school before. What strategies do I need to teach them to help them organise materials and understand classroom instructions better?

My students don't seem to use English outside the classroom. What tasks can I develop to raise their awareness about the importance of practising in real-life situations?

My students are too dependent on me for their learning. How can I involve them in more activities to promote their own learning and what kinds of language tasks would support this?

CLASSROOM DYNAMICS

My class is a mixed-level class and sub-groupings don't seem to be working. Is it possible to develop whole-group activities that will improve class interaction?

My students seem hostile towards each other. Why is this happening? Are cultural factors having an influence here?

3 Getting started

Teaching grammar:

> A colleague and I have decided to offer extra grammar support for weaker students. What kinds of activities will best supplement what they learn in their regular classes?

> I want to offer tutorial assistance in grammar for students with limited formal educational backgrounds. What grammar items should I select and what kinds of grammatical terms should I introduce?

Teaching literacy:

> My students are still making mistakes in writing even when I teach them the same structures and grammatical points several times. How can I encourage them to self-correct more effectively?

> My students say they want to improve their writing. What are their perceptions about their needs and the progress they are making in writing?

> I teach beginner learners. Is it possible to develop 'critical literacy' skills at this level?

> My students have all expressed different writing needs. How can I develop a writing programme that will provide a common focus and motivate them to write?

Teaching speaking:

> I've just read an article that suggested that speaking often involves using set 'formulas' or 'chunks' of language. What kinds of chunks do my students use on a set task and can I exploit this idea in teaching speaking?

> In a workshop I just attended, we studied samples of everyday spoken conversations and I was amazed at how different they really are from dialogues in course books. Can I introduce more natural speaking samples into my teaching and how will my learners react?

ASSESSMENT

> My students now have to be assessed using competency-based criteria set out by my teaching organisation. What kinds of classroom tasks can I develop for assessment and how should I explain them to my students?

> It's time-consuming developing separate teaching and assessment tasks for different skills areas. Is it possible to integrate assessment tasks across a number of skills?

> I have heard about using portfolios of students' writing to assess

their progress. How can portfolios also be used for self-assessment by my students?

I have already suggested that action research can be conducted through a variety of researcher groupings. Cohen and Manion (1994) point out that the scope of action research is 'impressive' as it can range from, at one extreme, an individual teacher trying out new teaching approaches in his or her classroom to a large study of organisational change, at the other. In all situations, however, the evaluative frame of reference is the same, that is, adding to the practitioners' functional knowledge base for practice. In the sections that follow, I present Australian case studies which illustrate how areas for research were identified. These examples encompass research undertaken in large-scale national research projects involving collaborative networks of teachers as well as group-focused initiatives and individual investigations. In each instance I will consider how the starting points and focus questions for the research were reached.

3.3.1 System level projects

In a large-scale collaborative process, the responsibility for finding a focus is generally not solely individual, even though the investigations carried out by each group member may ultimately be undertaken individually. Individual investigations, however, usually emerge from a predetermined collective theme and may take shape gradually during the course of a series of activities and group discussions in which other colleagues make suggestions, problematise the research situation and assist each other to pinpoint the focus for research. In this situation, teachers effectively find a starting point when their search for a focus is directed towards similar concerns and issues.

At the beginning of a recent Australian AMEP project, 'Investigating the teaching of disparate learner groups' (Burns and Hood 1997), the common theme for research was already established through a national process of identifying research priorities for the whole programme. Teachers in this project had volunteered to be research participants, in partnership with the two academic researchers, because the theme reflected a major issue they were currently attempting to address in their own classes, that is, how to teach mixed-ability adult language classes effectively. At the New South Wales Collaborative Group Workshop 2 (7 April 1995), as one of the researchers I outlined the identification of the project theme to the participants in the following way:

> one of the topics or areas that came up very strongly last year when
> people were nominating different areas for research was the issue
> of the growing number of disparate groups which are now

> occurring in ... the AMEP. Partly that's because of changes in the funding area and changes in the policy area of language provision in Australia for adults.
>
> And what teachers are finding is that whereas in the past they had ... what I guess could be loosely described as slightly more homogeneous classes, now what's happening is that there are many more heterogenous classes with people presenting at those classes with a range of factors affecting the learning process.

I then went on to summarise some possible starting points that had been generated by the group in a brainstorming activity in the previous workshop, which had been the first for the project:

> What we did last time was to start discussing what those various factors might be. We asked you to collect some data for us in an initial way before you came to the workshop, looking at various areas such as what were the features of these disparate learner groupings, what did multi-level groups of learners look like, what were their characteristics, what were some of the difficulties in teaching these groups and also what solutions could be found to cope with these difficulties?
>
> And we've been thinking about that in terms of different levels of the organisation, so ... what could a teacher do at the classroom level, what could be done at a teaching centre level and what could be done at an organisational, system level to assist some of those factors? And then finally we looked at what the advantages might be of teaching this type of disparate level group.

A programme of activities negotiated in the first workshop provided a structure for timetabling the research and for setting out a framework of research activities. This proved helpful to the members of the group as a way of limiting the scope of the research and setting up some agreed timelines. The activities are set out in Table 3.1.

By this second workshop, the research focus for each individual was still relatively open-ended and individuals were at an exploration phase. The workshops provided a reference point where teachers could bring back their reflections and any initial data they had collected from the classroom, which might provide them with ideas for taking the research further. These were my comments (as leader of the workshop) at this point:

> So this is the second workshop in a series of five and between each workshop we'll be developing, in a sort of spiralling and ongoing way, particular questions to focus on in terms of methodology. At this point we don't expect that people will have fully focused research questions that they'll want to pursue.
>
> We see this very much as an open-ended process and as the group

Table 3.1. *The timeframe and structure of the project*

Event/process	Timeframe	Purpose
Workshop 1	1 day	• introducing research context and model • discussing issues • focusing research and data collection techniques
Research	approximately 3 weeks	• reflecting • collecting and documenting data • clarifying focus • discussing with colleagues
Workshop 2	$\frac{1}{2}$ day	• reviewing focus for research and data collection methods • discussing early reflections
Research	approximately 4 to 6 weeks	• collecting data • reflecting and interpreting • intervening and collecting more data • discussing with colleagues
Workshop 3	1 day	• presenting interim report • discussing each other's research • interpreting, problematising findings
Research	approximately 3 weeks	• collecting additional data to confirm interpretations or identify other issues
Workshop 4	$\frac{1}{2}$ day	• planning final written report
Report writing	approximately 3 weeks	• drafting final report • discussing with colleagues
Workshop 5	$\frac{1}{2}$ day seminar	• presenting written reports • presenting short informal seminar on research

comes together on these different occasions the areas for research will become much more focused. So, we're starting off in a fairly open-ended way ... sharing our ideas and our perceptions and then moving on more clearly into specific research areas ... we hope (laughter).

Even though the collective theme for this project had already been identified, each teacher was still working towards finding a focus area based on an issue of relevance in his or her own teaching centre and classroom. During this second workshop, individuals were given time to describe to others the activities they had undertaken since the first meeting. This was a very important step in helping to delineate and refine possible areas that could be taken further as more focused questions.

We will consider the case of Linda Ross, whose research study we encountered at the beginning of Chapter 1, as an example of how this process unfolded. During the workshop session, the group collaborated in supporting Linda to refine the next phase of her research further.

Linda described what she had done since the previous meeting. She had:

1 documented her general observations (notes, personal observations, anecdotes, occurrences, steps and procedures in lessons)
2 focused on what she saw as problems:
   • not feeling confident in teaching numeracy and in meeting the students' needs
   • having very different student levels (wide gaps in skills, knowledge)
   • not being sure 'how to manage timewise'
   • not having a clear sense of the students' feelings and perceptions of the above areas.

In discussion with the other participants, Linda identified the following further areas to focus on:

• the time management issue ('I need to think of more ways to cope with that')
• the problems of very low level students and their desire to go on to higher level work before Linda felt they were ready ('I'm not sure what I should do about this')
• the need to work out a system of documenting her students' skills and needs in more detail ('I need to work out a way of documenting what concepts they've actually got').

Further discussions gave rise to possible solutions which were arrived at collaboratively:

• Lenn suggested that Linda might develop an answer key for student self-correction, which would eliminate her feeling that she had to give each student individual attention.
• Linda began to say that she might forget about having different perceptions about class disorganisation from her students. ('It doesn't seem to worry them as much ... hopefully, as it's worrying me.')
• Sue suggested she consider streaming or offering additional models to lower level students. This was identified as an issue relevant to the whole teaching centre ('that's a centre problem thing').
• Linda suggested she could talk to the principal of the centre to find out what was possible.

At the end of Linda's presentation of her concerns about her class, one of the other participants was able to summarise and clarify several possible areas for her research:

Sue: There's the preparation issue and finding the resources to cope with the different levels. There's the operational management during the lesson of sharing your time around and making sure you're not devoting ... you know ... you *are* sharing your time around and there's the issue you just raised then of monitoring what's going on and recording the outcomes.

Linda: And I realise you know that I haven't been systematic enough about that.

Although the workshop did not result in the formulation of a specific question for Linda's research, she felt she had clarified a number of possible directions. She decided to work on devising a system for documenting her students' skills and needs as the next focus area for her research. As the case study presented in Chapter 1 shows, the three areas summarised above were interrelated in Linda's teaching situation. By developing a strategy to document her perceptions of her students' skills, Linda was subsequently able to devise activities which would meet their needs and also overcome the problem of different levels of students within the same class. This also led to a feeling that she was better able to manage the classroom activities.

The data from this workshop discussion demonstrate that finding a focus for action research often occurs as a gradual and evolving process rather than as an instantaneous decision about a specific question. The area for research may only become more clearly focused after the teacher has tried out several different practical strategies, tasks or materials, and so on in the classroom. In my experience, in these initial phases teachers can often feel frustrated, that they are 'in a fog', that they don't know what they are doing and that 'this doesn't feel like what I know about research'. It is important to realise that these are common experiences.

This way of going about finding a focus represents one of two possible approaches. Hopkins (1993: 67–8) refers to this approach as an 'open' or 'evolutionary' way into research question formation. He states that an open approach is characterised as:

- take a broad area of enquiry
- carry out the initial enquiry
- gradually focus the enquiry.

The other possibility for formulating a question is a more 'closed' or 'sequenced' approach, which follows the pattern:

- take a specific issue
- derive research questions
- choose an appropriate methodology.

This more 'closed' approach can be illustrated in the work of a group of six teachers from South Australia. Unlike the New South Wales teachers in the national project described above, they were all colleagues who worked at the same teaching centre and knew each other well. The processes they took towards question formulation are outlined in the next section.

3.3.2 Group focus

Clearly, not all action research experiences occur within large-scale or national projects, but may arise from a variety of group processes or needs. Some examples are given below:

1 Teachers working on the same high school staff in New South Wales undertook action research as part of a school restructuring process. The inclusion of action research in this process was negotiated with the staff by the lead teacher. Restructuring had involved developing a team approach to programming and teaching, and the teachers identified a common action research focus within each team.
2 Teachers within the same adult ESL teaching programme in New South Wales enrolled for a professional development programme which featured action research as an option. They decided on a common focus of investigating ways of teaching grammar with beginning and intermediate learners. This focus was relevant to a new curriculum which had recently been introduced within the programme.
3 A group of adult ESL teachers in South Australia began to discuss the theoretical concept of 'critical literacy'. Some of them had read about this concept in recent articles and others had attended conferences or courses where it had been discussed. They were interested to try out some strategies for teaching critical literacy and worked together to develop and discuss activities and materials.
4 A group of Adult Literacy and Basic Education teachers in Victoria came together through a state-based teacher research network. They wanted to evaluate the impact of a new competency-based curriculum framework on their teaching programmes and practices.

I will elaborate on the case of the group in example 3 above to illustrate the 'sequenced' approach to identifying a research focus, which was referred to at the end of Section 3.3.1. However, it is important to stress that it is not the general rule that large-scale projects adopt an open approach whereas groups adopt a closed approach. As example 4 above implies, collaborating groups can also arrive at a focus through a more 'open' approach. Similarly, large-scale projects may have a precise teaching issue to investigate, as in the case of an

Australian project which investigated how genre-based approaches to teaching writing developed in primary schools could be applied to the teaching of adult ESL literacy (Hammond *et al.* 1992).

In the South Australian situation in example 3 above, the teachers had already identified a specific area when the group came together. This was: How can we integrate the concept of critical literacy into our teaching? Critical literacy, and more generally the notion of critical language awareness, referred in this project to developing a way of teaching that specifically drew attention to how language is used to construct and promote particular ideologies, viewpoints or positions within written and spoken texts. At the time of the research, this was an area that was being increasingly highlighted in ESL teacher journals in Australia and debated in professional development workshops on literacy development.

The group's research question had surfaced spontaneously before the action research process formally began: first, through the attendance of one of the members at a professional development workshop and her subsequent reporting back to her colleagues; then, through informal discussions amongst interested colleagues at her teaching centre; and finally, through a study circle set up by the group where they exchanged, read and discussed articles focusing on this topic. Having decided to formalise the action research process as a collaborative investigation, the group then worked in partnership with myself and another AMEP researcher experienced in facilitating action research (see Burns and Hood 1998). They developed a timeline for their investigations similar to the one presented in Section 3.1.1. This took into account institutional necessities, such as the fact that the teachers worked with the same group of students for short courses of only 10–15 weeks. During the first workshop, the members of the group exchanged the following information:

- The teachers each described the level of class they were teaching and gave a profile of their learner group.
- The research facilitators outlined the action research process and suggested methods for collecting data and discussed these with the teachers.
- The group exchanged views on their understandings of the concept of critical literacy and critiqued these ideas.
- The group discussed approaches to teaching critical literacy outlined in the articles they had read and brainstormed ideas about how these could be implemented or adapted.
- The group exchanged ideas on the kinds of texts that could be selected as classroom materials.

By the end of the first session, the teachers were able to outline some preliminary research questions, drawing on the discussions and the preparations they had made before the project began. Although these changed somewhat over the course of the research, at this early phase the teachers felt sufficiently focused to be able to formulate individual questions:

- What resources and activities can be used to develop a critical literacy perspective in a low level class?
- Can I develop a set of discussion questions which would help students to raise their critical awareness of a range of written texts?
- What decisions do I make in selecting different types of texts for students?
- How do I incorporate a critical literacy perspective into my current approach to teaching reading?
- Can I apply a similar critical literacy approach to teaching both reading and writing?
- How can I prepare learners for becoming critically literate through oral activities at low levels?

Judy Perkins, the teacher who formulated the first question, worked with a group of 12 post-beginner level students who had all arrived in Australia within the previous 18 months. The students were from Vietnamese, Bosnian, Chinese, Hungarian and Polish backgrounds and their ages varied from the early 20s to late 40s. They had all had between 8 and 12 years of education and their goals were to find jobs as soon as possible. Judy had been intrigued by the concept of critical literacy for some time and had already done some reading and thinking about this issue while working with students of a more intermediate level. She was curious to find out whether a critical perspective could be adopted in the development of literacy skills with students at a more beginning level. (Perkins 1998 gives a full account of Judy's research.) Judy describes her thinking on this issue in the following way:

> It seemed to me that if a critical literacy perspective was an important aspect of literacy development then it must be incorporated into teaching at all levels. And although I use authentic, real-life texts with learners at all levels, I felt that discussion about texts and closer analysis of texts would be more difficult with [post-beginner learners]. I wondered what kinds of texts would be both interesting and accessible to the learners and also provide a rich resource for discussion. What kinds of classroom activities would encourage critical analysis? Is there a clear progression of skills? To attempt to answer these questions, I formulated my research question as: What resources and activities can be used to develop a critical literacy perspective in a low level class?

Having settled on her question, Judy set about devising classroom actions and monitoring their impact. She collected texts which were on the same topic, but written from different sources and viewpoints. While assisting her readers to develop the reading skills she would normally focus on, she added 'an extra dimension to the kind of reading programme I would normally plan' by encouraging her learners 'to look at any texts with a critical eye'. In order to do this she devised sets of 'before reading' and 'after reading' questions such as the following:

Before reading

- Where might you find these texts?
- Who wrote them?
- Why were they written?
- Why are there pictures in the text? Is this helpful?
- Do you have similar texts in your country?

After reading

- Do these texts give you enough information?
- Is there anything else you would like to know?
- Are the texts difficult to read? Why?
- Can you get good reliable information from these texts?
- Which texts are more reliable?

Throughout her research, Judy collected data through the use of a journal and by setting aside short periods of time to write brief notes during and immediately after each lesson (see Chapter 4 for further discussion on techniques for note-writing). This enabled her to monitor the effectiveness of the activities she had designed in relation to her class goals and the reactions of her students to these activities. Her observations include the following:

> It was clear that in experimenting with activities that might not be successful, it would be important to embed these activities into others which would be interesting, enjoyable and immediately relevant.

> [In this activity], I considered aspects of classroom dynamic, such as the physical setting, group structures, where I stood or sat ... I deliberately downplayed my role as a teacher ... This was a useful activity in terms of establishing both teacher and learner as sources of knowledge and expertise.

> The main part of this lesson consisted of typical reading development activities. It was primarily in the 'before reading' and 'after reading' section that I added new questions ... The learners were not used to discussing texts in this way and were at first unsure what they were supposed to be doing. However, after some

discussion they had little difficulty in answering most of the questions. The one question which caused problems was the language analysis of the Medicare brochure 'Thinking about the writing'. Even after talking through it, some of them were still unsure what I was talking about and we abandoned the question. I think that if I had raised the question in general class discussion rather than write it on the worksheet for the learners to answer in groups, it would have been more successful.

Two approaches to question formulation have been described in this and the previous section. One is an 'open' or evolving approach where a question or area for research may not be immediately obvious, but may emerge through a group or a teacher's own critical reflection or by 'nosing about in the field of events' (Dillon 1983). The 'closed' or sequenced approach assumes that a question is more or less determined in advance, although the teacher may refine it further before proceeding with a plan of action. My aim in providing these two examples has been to illustrate that collaborative action research can legitimately be initiated through either approach.

3.4 The role of theory in question formulation

Bound up with processes of research question formulation at this early reconnaissance or exploration stage will be issues of theory. In the process of arriving at researchable topics, two theoretical dimensions are likely to inform the thinking and reflection that occur. The first relates to the teacher's current knowledge and understanding of curriculum or learning theories that have been generated through research and may be current in guiding and shaping practice within the field. Examples of such 'grand' theories in the second language teaching field are the role of task-based activities in learner-centred instruction, the place of authentic materials in communicative language teaching, or process-writing approaches to classroom composition. A second dimension of theory is the personal assumptions, values and beliefs that the researcher may bring to the research. Davis (1995: 436) puts it this way:

> Contrary to the often-held belief that qualitative researchers have no preconception about the area under investigation, they bring particular theoretical and experiential frames of reference to the research task. The first step in conducting a qualitative study is to determine the theories and views that are likely to affect the study.

Davis goes on to suggest that 'to gain an understanding of the meanings of research participants, we have to be keenly aware of the ways we interpret meanings from our own sociocultural frameworks' (page 437). Engaging in classroom research involves theorising one's practice, not only from the point of view of assumptions about starting points, but, as the research proceeds, from more systematic examination and critical analysis of what emerges. Hopkins (1993: 73) suggests that when this kind of critical reflection occurs, teachers 'a) stand in control of knowledge rather than being subservient to it and b) by doing this they are engaged in the process of theorizing and achieving self-knowledge'.

An example of how this form of theorising may be embedded in the initial research processes can be drawn from the action research work of Jan Phillips (1996), conducted as an individual project for a Master's programme. Jan found that once the general thematic concern of her research, the teaching and learning of pronunciation in an intermediate English for Work class, had been formulated, a period of reflection was needed before she embarked on her research plan. Her reflection involved theorising in order to make more explicit:

- an understanding of the present situation and its theoretical basis
- an examination of the researcher's own values
- a relating of the course to the wider context of education and work.

(Phillips 1996: 56)

Jan's analysis of the first area led her to clarify two major intersecting dimensions within her research:

1 The teaching of pronunciation was not featured in the syllabus of the English for Work Program, which assumed that literacy skills were the major area for development. However, her analysis of her students' needs and progress unearthed a different issue, student intelligibility, as a problem. A key question for further theorisation and review became: Is it important to teach pronunciation in an English for Work programme?

2 There were a number of focal questions that needed to be directed towards Jan's exploration of the theoretical base of pronunciation teaching. They included:

- How important is pronunciation for communication?
- How has the teaching of pronunciation changed?
- Can pronunciation be integrated with other skills and activities?
- How can pronunciation be assessed?
- What are the main problems for learners?

Jan also examined her own personal and educational values as they related to her research question. She listed them as including:

1 Her commitment to personal and professional development. She believed it was important and relevant to her teaching to understand educational theories and that these would help to improve her class-

room practice. She also believed that personal satisfaction could be gained through changing and improving her teaching methods and receiving feedback from her students.

2   Her belief in the explicit teaching of pronunciation. She had begun teaching in the 1970s using audio-lingual methods and felt that students gained a sense of mastery from repetition, drills and memorised phrases. However, her observation of changes in methods led her to feel that these techniques could be successfully combined with contextualised and authentic listening and speaking activities, more common in communicative language teaching.

3   Her preference for criterion-referenced assessment procedures. She 'rejected' global judgements and preferred to attempt to specify criteria for judging pronunciation performance. She saw this as related to issues of fairness. A key question was: How can we be sure the teacher is judging on performance only and not on personality or other factors?

In relation to the wider context of education and work, she examined 'the needs of different stakeholders' and considered what possible tensions might be present:

1   She identified the programme she worked in as part of a wider government agenda to prepare immigrants for the workplace. However, she regarded programme time factors as unrealistic.

2   She recognised that her immigrant students were in a work-related programme. However, she considered that many have motivations for learning other than gaining employment.

3   She acknowledged that the students needed to see progress towards seeking work. However, she believed it was likely that they would progress better if their learning experiences and time in an educational context were positive.

Gaining greater clarity about one's practice is at the heart of the kind of theorisation that goes on in action research. Attempting to be more explicit about the theoretical assumptions guiding the research provides a useful point of reference as the research proceeds. Although this framework may change in the course of the research, it acts as a navigation point for the investigation and a means of making sense of and questioning the data that emerge. It is also part of an awareness-raising process that provides the basis for change.

3.5 Ethical considerations

Ethical considerations are an important part of any research enterprise. Questions relating to the conduct of research are issues inevitably confronted by teachers early in the research process. In my experience, these are the kinds of questions that emerge:

- Should I tell my students about my research?
- What should I do if the students don't understand my explanations because of limited proficiency in English?
- Do I have the right to 'experiment' on my students?
- What happens if students refuse to be part of the research?
- Do I have to ask my supervisor for permission to do research?
- Should I get written permission from the people I interview?
- What about using students' names?
- Should I tell other teachers what I am doing?
- Should I present samples of what people have said or written, such as student writing or interview responses?

Winter (1989: 23) rightly points out that the data gathering methods employed in action research 'involve[s] the professional practitioner in new sets of relations with colleagues and clients'. Central to these relationships are questions of whether data gathered during the research compromise professional relationships or exploit colleagues and students who may be the subjects of research. Key principles in the ethical conduct of action research are *responsibility, confidentiality* and *negotiation*. Confidentiality ensures that the identities of those involved in the research are not made public, thus reducing the likelihood that they may be judged negatively by colleagues or supervisors. It is also important for researchers to negotiate what access to their data is made available, giving those who are subjects of the research the right to veto release of the data. Teachers who work in a collaborative way also need to negotiate agreed 'codes of practice' on the ethical principles that guide their research.

Hitchcock and Hughes (1995) propose three areas which should be subject to ethical consideration: professional integrity; the interests of the subjects; and responsibilities and relationships with sponsors, outside agencies, academic institutions or managements. They elaborate the following ethical rules for these three areas (adapted from Hitchcock and Hughes 1995: 51–2):

Professional integrity

1 Ensure that the research you propose is viable, that an adequate research design has been established and appropriate data collection techniques chosen.
2 Explain as clearly as possible the aims, objectives and methods of the research to all of the parties involved.
3 If using confidential documents, ensure that anonymity is maintained by eliminating any kinds of material or information that could lead others to identify the subject or subjects involved.

Interests of the subjects

1 Allow subjects the right to refuse to take part in the research.
2 Build confidentiality into the research.
3 Gain the permission of the parties involved if the research is to be published.
4 Ensure that all researchers adhere to the same set of ethical principles where research is conducted jointly or collaboratively.

Responsibilities and relationships with sponsors, outside agencies, academic institutions or management

1 Ensure you are clear on the terms of reference and on your own and your subjects' rights in relation to the finished research, where the research is 'sponsored'.
2 Ensure you are aware of the possible uses to which the research may be put.

Where collaborative groups work in partnership with academic researchers, it is preferable to negotiate working guidelines. Some academic researchers who have collaborated with teachers have been concerned about the possible power differentials which may emerge and have evolved agreements aimed at ensuring greater equality. Somekh (1994: 360), for example, outlines extracts from a 'Code of Confidentiality' which governed relationships in the Pupil Autonomy in Learning with Microcomputers (PALM) project in which she was an academic coordinator:

1 It is understood that the use of any evidence or data collected by teachers will be fully negotiated with the individuals concerned.
2 It is also understood that the discussions of formal or informal meetings remain confidential to participants in the meeting until they have given permission for more general release (but see 3 below).
3 It is understood that students will have the same rights as teachers to refuse access to data that they have provided (e.g. notes taken of interviews with them).
4 Pupils' anonymity will normally be safeguarded at all stages of the research. Individuals will be mentioned by name only with their prior agreement or, where appropriate, with that of their parents.
  . . .
9 Wherever possible PALM teachers will share the outcomes of their investigations, first with their school and cluster teams and with the central team, then across the participating LEAs [Local Education Authorities], and finally more widely where appropriate.
10 All reports produced by teachers will be published under their

names in order to give full credit to them for their work. All such reports will be subject to negotiation with the sponsor and the three LEAs. The central team will assist teachers with this work as and when required.

In second language learning contexts, conforming to some ethical procedures, such as explaining the research to learners, can be difficult when their English proficiency levels are not high. There are a number of strategies that have been used by AMEP teachers to address this problem:

- explaining the research in language appropriate to the level of the students and encouraging the students to ask questions about it
- providing written information and discussing it in class
- arranging for bilingual information or explanations through aides or other more advanced students
- explaining the research to family members with higher levels of English.

Catherine Kebir (1994: 28), a teacher from South Australia, outlines how she went about explaining her research to her post-beginner students:

> I needed to collect data and then identify what sort of communication strategies my learners used in classroom tasks. I explained my intentions to the group and asked permission to tape them. I told them I would be recording their spoken language as part of a project on how to improve my teaching of oral skills. However, because their proficiency level was elementary, I had some difficulty in getting my message across. It became clear that this would be an ongoing problem, so I relied on bilingual assistance to translate the consent forms and ensure that my students understood what was happening. I discovered that for many immigrants the idea of having their conversation recorded was quite threatening, and I had to be sure that their fears were allayed.

While Catherine's students felt anxious about being involved, other teachers have reported that their students are eager to be involved and often feel 'special' to have been chosen. Vivienne Campbell (1995: 125) notes that:

> In the first week of the project, I discussed my research with the students, explained the purposes for it and asked them for their involvement. I also handed out simplified written summaries of the project for their information and so that they could ask me for further explanations of it if they needed to.

Far from feeling anxious, for Vivienne's learners 'participating in the project gave them a sense of being valued and listened to ... They were treated as respected adults with important contributions to make' (page 129).

A simple information and consent form, such as the following (adapted from Campbell 1995 and Carroll 1995), can be useful in setting out clearly for learners what their participation will involve and how the results of the process will be used.

Information and consent form

This project is being conducted by: _____ with Class: _____

Description/Title of project
Some teachers in my organisation want to find out more about how students feel about the things they are learning and the ways they are learning. This is so that the information can be used by people who write the courses for learners in this programme.

What I will ask you to do in this project
I am interested in finding out more about how you see yourself as a learner and how you learn. Each week in class we will spend some time thinking, talking and writing about the work you have covered in class and the techniques you use to learn English. I will ask you to:

- Write down what you have learned in class. We will do this for 5 minutes at the end of each day.
- Write in a journal about how you learn English. We will do this for about 15 minutes twice a week.

Once a week on Thursday we will discuss your ideas for about 15 minutes.

I need your help. I am interested in your honest opinion, so that we can all know more about the best ways to learn English.

What will happen to the information I get
I will use the information to help me plan new classroom activities that students find the most useful. My organisation will also use this information to improve the English courses and students' opportunities for learning. The result of the project will be written in a book of reports for other teachers.

Your agreement to take part in the project
If you agree to be part of this project:

- you can ask me questions about the project at any time
- you are free to withdraw at any time
- you do not have to give a reason for withdrawing
- you will be asked if the information you write or say can be used in the written report
- your real name will not be used in the report
- you will be able to get copies of the report if you wish.

I, _____, agree to be part of the project.

Signature: Date:

Dilemmas occasionally arise when there are concerns about how the research might affect already sensitive classroom dynamics or when informing the students might alter the nature of the data. In these rather more unusual situations, some teachers have used the strategy of informing their students on completion of the research, giving explanations for their reasons and asking their students' permission to report on the research. In cases where individual students or other colleagues state that they would prefer not to be part of the research, it is important that data about these individuals are not included in any final reporting. Research reports should, in any case, keep the identities of research participants confidential and use pseudonyms when referring to individuals.

3.6 Summary

This chapter has attempted to map out ways of beginning the action research process and finding an initial focus. Although there are obvious impediments which may stand in the way of teachers carrying out research, I have suggested ways of obviating or, at least, reducing them so that a reflective stance on classroom practice may be facilitated. Accounts of practitioner research suggest that identifying researchable areas and questions for teacher research is not necessarily straightforward. One aim of this chapter has been to provide some guidelines and pointers for arriving at curriculum issues or questions to investigate. Case study examples taken from the experiences of teacher researchers have, hopefully, illustrated that there is no one fixed means of clarifying research questions and that both evolving and sequenced processes are legitimate ways to begin.

Having worked through the exploratory phases of reconnaissance and reflection, the action research group should be at a point where a framework for further action will have emerged. This framework may comprise:

- an idea of the general area for research, which may include a refinement or clarification of the focus of action
- an account of the areas or issues of classroom practice that are considered to require change
- a plan to act on these proposals, by introducing new teaching strategies, activities or materials
- a consideration of the discussions one needs to have with others, such as academic research partners, supervisors, colleagues or students
- a clarification of the resources that may be needed to undertake the proposed changes, e.g. materials, equipment, classroom settings, colleagues

- an agreement about the ethical principles that will guide the research process
- a timeframe or schedule for carrying out the research
- a proposal about methods and techniques for collecting data and monitoring the changes to be implemented.

In the next chapter we shall look in more detail at the last of these features. We shall consider various methods for gathering evidence and monitoring classroom research activities. These accounts will be accompanied by illustrations showing how teachers who have conducted collaborative research have used them.

Group discussion tasks

1 Get together with others in your school or teaching centre who are interested in doing action research. Discuss what constraints or impediments you may encounter and brainstorm ways of addressing these problems. Identify those you can do little or nothing about as opposed to those that are potentially open to change.
2 With your colleagues, develop a list of areas that could be starting points for research that relates to your institution or teaching centre.
3 Pilot one of these areas. Observe your class closely over a week and document your observations. What more specific questions or focus areas for research do your observations suggest?
4 Meet with your colleagues again and compare your observations. In particular, identify any common areas of practice you would like to change. Formulate some more specific questions or areas for research by the individuals in your group.
5 Develop an initial plan of action for getting started on data collection. Consider:

    who will be involved
    who will need to be informed
    what strategies you will put into action
    what resources, human and otherwise, you will need.

6 Develop a sample timetable for a group cycle of action research, such as the one in Table 3.1. Consider:

    a logical duration for the complete cycle;
    an appropriate number of group meetings;
    the length of time required for data collection between each meeting;
    the length of time required for reporting and writing up the research.

Monitor the cycle and adjust it according to your group and institutional requirements.

7 Develop an agreed 'code of practice' for your group that takes into account the ethical considerations discussed in this chapter.

8 Adapt the sample consent form to develop one suitable for your own research.

4 Observational techniques for collecting action research data

> Taking field notes has led to a greater self-awareness in the classroom. It has enabled me to formulate more clearly my teaching aims, methods and results.
>
> (Helen Hanrahan, Victoria)

4.1 Introduction

In this chapter and the next, I outline a number of methods and techniques for collecting data in action research investigations. What is presented here is by no means an exhaustive account of all the methods that could be used. My aim in these two chapters is to emphasise accounts of selected methods which teacher researchers have found both feasible and practicable and to set these out as examples for others who may be interested in undertaking collaborative action research.

Techniques for collecting action research data are generally qualitative in nature (Nunan 1989), reflecting the primary purpose to investigate practice critically and to work towards changing it within the context of the teaching situation. This does not necessarily mean that quantitative methods are irrelevant to action research; there may well be cases where quantitative methods will be used to complement or extend the findings of collaborative or individual action research projects (Brindley 1990). It is more the issue, however, that action researchers are actively concerned to conduct their investigations on themselves and on their own individual or group practices, rather than on other people. Therefore, they have less need or reason to adopt the kinds of quantitative measures which would enable them to make statistically generalisable conclusions (see Chapter 2).

Action research, then, relies on exploratory and interpretive methods, which, for a number of reasons, are likely to be more appealing to the classroom teacher. These methods allow teachers to explore the realities of practical circumstances without the requirement to control the variables of their classroom context or to set up and allocate subjects randomly to experimental or control groups. The flexible and eclectic nature of action research also means that teachers are able to change the questions or issues guiding their research, to adopt different research methods or to take their interpretations in new directions as the need arises, a variation which would not be appropriate in quantitative research.

Pam McPherson, a teacher who worked on the research project investigating the teaching of disparate adult groups outlined in Section 3.3.1, touches on the appeal of action research methods for teachers:

> The action research model is probably the most versatile method of research for a teacher, and for me it included the development of both research skills and teaching expertise. It allows for a systematic examination of the effects of teaching practice but at the same time it can change direction in response to emerging needs, thus promoting teacher and learner satisfaction. Importantly, it can be self-managed by the teacher. Collaborative action research is a concept for me which exponentially increases the value of the cyclical research process.

> (Burns, Hood, Lukin and McPherson 1996: 21)

Chapters 4 and 5, then, focus on a range of interpretive and qualitative methods which can be used to collect data in action research. For convenience, I have categorised these methods into the two broad groupings of observational and non-observational methods. However, these categories are not mutually exclusive; for some methods a degree of overlap inevitably occurs.

In this chapter an overview of observational approaches is followed by a more specific focus on various techniques for data collection. These include:

- notes: descriptions and accounts of observed events, including non-verbal information, physical settings, group structures, interactions between participants
- diaries/journals: regular dated accounts of teaching/learning plans, activities and events, including personal philosophies, feelings, reactions, reflections, explanations
- recordings: audio or video recordings providing objective records of classroom interactions
- transcripts: written representations of recordings, using conventions for identifying speakers and indicating pauses, hesitations, overlaps and non-verbal information
- diagrams: maps or drawings of the classroom indicating physical layout and/or student–teacher interactions or locations.

Some observational methods used in classroom research I have not included, perhaps most noticeably, formal observation schemes composed of predetermined categories of teacher and learner behaviour. I have omitted them because most teachers with whom I have worked have regarded them as too complex and time-consuming or unrelated to the specific issues they have chosen to research. Useful as many of these schemes may be for certain kinds of classroom-based research studies, for many teacher researchers they represent an 'add-on' which makes demands beyond the kinds of observations which may be more naturally aligned with routine classroom activities. For readers interested in observational schemes, excellent reviews are provided by Long (1980), Allwright (1988) and Chaudron (1988), while Malamah-Thomas (1987), Nunan (1989) and Wallace (1998) provide accessible introductions and make suggestions for the use of such schemes in classroom research. Spada and Fröhlich (1995) provide an extensive account of the coding conventions and applications for COLT (Communicative Orientation of Language Teaching), which, to date, offers one of the most sophisticated observation schemes for interaction analysis in communicative language classrooms.

Because this book has been written with a teacher researcher audience in mind, the focus in the description and discussion of each method is very firmly on teachers' accounts of how it can be used. With a very few exceptions, each method is reviewed and then illustrated from the perspective of teacher researchers who have used it during collaborative action research. Teachers' descriptions and suggestions are presented so that readers interested in conducting their own classroom investigations can gain a sense of how these methods work in practice from the perspective of other teachers.

4.2 Observation

Observation is a mainstay of action research. It enables researchers to document and reflect systematically upon classroom interactions and events, as they actually occur rather than as we think they occur. The term observation is being used here in the sense of taking regular and conscious *notice* of classroom actions and occurrences which are particularly relevant to the issues or topics being investigated. It also refers to using *procedures* that ensure that the information collected provides a sound basis for answering research questions and supporting the interpretations that are reached. Observing students' classroom behaviours and actions is a common event for most teachers, but in the action research process the daily personal experiences of 'just looking' are made more systematic and precise. This gives us a basis for examining underlying assumptions, sharing them with others, and opening them up to alternative viewpoints.

Schools and classrooms are complex and dynamic social settings. They are also familiar and routine working environments and their very familiarity can mean that it is often not immediately obvious what aspects of the research situation to observe. One helpful strategy for refining the focus of observations is to spend some time 'just looking', but taking conscious notice of the situation in a fresh and more objective light.

Annabelle Lukin, a teacher from New South Wales, highlights how observing classroom practices more consciously began for her the identification of a specific area of her teaching that was then pursued in greater detail.

> [My group of teachers] began with a general observation and documentation of our course design practices rather than with a specific focus issue in mind. The general objective was to consider any changes we experienced in the process of course design working within the context of a competency-based curriculum framework and to document any issues which arose ...
>
> (Lukin 1995: 54)

In this way, particular areas or questions for research begin to become more evident. There are some basic factors which should be considered in order to help guide observations and make them more manageable:

1 Decide on a focus for the observation which is relevant to your group's research. Don't try to record everything.
2 Identify a specific physical location in which the observation will be conducted (e.g. playground, coffee area, classroom, reading corner).
3 Consider the group or individual to be observed (e.g. whole class, student groups, a mixed-gender pair, individual student).
4 Record the events as they happen or as soon as possible after they happen.
5 Be as objective and precise as possible in your observations and avoid using attitudinal or evaluative language that makes inferences about people's behaviour or thinking (e.g. 'surly', 'anxious', 'unwilling' and so on).
6 Try to record complete events or incidents. This allows a more inclusive and holistic picture of the situation to emerge, so that ordinary as well as unusual events are observed.
7 Develop a system for recording that fits in with other activities occurring in the context of the observation.

The great strength of observational methods is the new perspectives they offer on familiar situations. Ordinary and habitual occurrences can be given new meanings when they are engaged with more closely and systematically. Observation allows us to see in a relatively unobtrusive way what it is that people actually do compared with what they say they do.

4.2.1 Observation roles: Participant and non-participant observation

The terms *participant* and *non-participant* refer to the differences in the kinds of roles that can be taken up in research observation. Put simply, participant observation involves entering the research context and observing oneself as well as others in that context. The researcher becomes a member of the context and participates in its culture and activities. Non-participant observation, on the other hand, means watching and recording without personal involvement in the research context. In this kind of observation, the researcher's purpose is to remain aloof and distant and to have little or no contact with the subjects of the research. The most extreme examples of non-participant observation are observations that are made from behind a two-way mirror, as in some psychological studies, or through video recordings made in the absence of the researcher.

The very nature of action research, conducted, as it typically is, within a specific school or organisational context, implies that all teacher researchers are participants to some extent, although, in practice, participant observation may mean adopting different levels of involvement in the research situation. These range from completely active involvement, where the teacher is both a participant and an observer, to a more passive form of involvement, where the teacher researcher may be an observer but not a participant. Teacher researchers who take the latter role will need to strike a balance between maintaining their objectivity as observers and finding a place within the social structures of the classroom, particularly when their observations take place over a period of time. Working in collaborative groups means that teachers have greater opportunities to take up either an active or a passive participant observer role. Colleagues may, for example, decide to work together to observe each other's classrooms or use a team teaching approach to exchange participant roles.

The research of Vicki Hambling and Lorraine Hatcher-Friel provides an example of how different participant roles might work in collaborative action research. Vicki and Lorraine worked in the same teaching centre, where a team of three practitioners was involved in a collaborative research project (see Section 8.2, for a fuller discussion of this project). Vicki's classroom of 20 mixed-ability beginner adult students became the location for the research, which involved developing and trialing multi-level materials to meet the different needs of her learners. She describes her research process:

The action research involved a process of teaching, observing,
developing materials, evaluating the materials, adapting and
improving the materials and so on in an ongoing cycle.

(Hambling 1997: 27)

Lorraine adopted the complementary role of passive participant observer in Vicki's classroom and 'critical friend' in their subsequent
discussions.

I became an observer and a consultant, so that together we could
discuss the day-to-day issues that arose for her. My observations
and reflections would add another perspective to her own.

(Hatcher-Friel 1997: 81)

Vicki and Lorraine met at regular intervals and recorded their discussions. They used each other's observations and recordings of classroom
events as a sounding-board for identifying and clarifying different
aspects of the research and for checking perceptions, as they discuss
below.

- **Focusing the research**

  Lorraine: We agreed that the focus for our joint research would be
  to look at using common content rather than teaching
  different lessons to the different learner types. This gave
  us a clear question for our research: *While focusing on
  common content in what ways can materials be adapted
  to engage all the learners in the lesson?* (page 81)

  Vicki: The core resource I used was a course book ...
  Additional materials were developed around this. I
  observed how the materials were used by different
  students and I evaluated their effectiveness. On-the-spot
  reflections and ideas were attached to the materials with
  stickers. I also took 15 minutes at the end of each lesson
  to write down the reactions of the students. (page 77)

- **Evaluating the development and use of the materials**

  Lorraine: Low (1989: 153) suggests that 'designing appropriate
  materials is not a science; it is a strange mixture of
  imagination, insight and analytical reasoning'. As I
  observed Vicki intently involved in the creation of
  graded support materials, I could not help but agree.
  The added dimension of different levels of materials
  being used simultaneously in the classroom also lent
  itself to the image of the teacher as juggler – a balancing
  act of timed tasks. (pages 81–2)

  Vicki: Teaching a mixed-ability class is very time-consuming in
  terms of materials development. However, there can be
  considerable advantages for the students. By pairing

stronger and weak students, the weak students get one to one help and strong students improve their communication skills. It was necessary, however, to teach the stronger students how to help their classmates so that they didn't simply give them the answer they needed. (page 79)

- **Identifying personal teaching style**

Lorraine: Clearly the teacher of this class was a driving force. Her voice was clear and high in volume and her body language very exaggerated, animated and energetic. The confidence with which instructions were delivered was resolute. This is not necessarily a personality thing. Vicki identified this as an explicit teaching strategy. (pages 82–3)

Vicki: The importance of good group dynamics and a supportive environment became clear early on ... I spent a lot of time organising getting-to-know-you activities, including excursions and morning teas as an important part of this process. Students had to move around in pairs so that they met new people. (page 79)

- **Using first language learning strategies**

Lorraine: In particular a 63 year old Bosnian woman became a major topic of our discussions. She was completely withdrawn ... Was it possible to engage her in the learning process?

... The first instance of this was in naming parts of the body, when the learner was asked to give the word in Bosnian. Her response was remarkable. Her posture changed markedly. She made eye contact, her back straightened and the volume of her voice increased. When new language was being introduced, this learner was encouraged to vocalise the translation into her L1. While the oral use of the target language by this learner did not increase dramatically, her participation and involvement in the classroom did. (page 83)

Vicki: I could see she'd drop out ... I just couldn't see she'd make any progress at all ... and I wasn't even sure of her skills in L1. And then I wasn't sure of this personality shift, you know, where if they're very quiet in the classroom ... and can hardly look you in the eye, are they like that normally? Or is it the fear of English? Or the fear of being strange? So to be able to make an assessment on that, I decided to get her, at various points, to use L1, and see if her behaviour was the same, and it was totally different. (page 83)

Working collaboratively in their different participant roles meant that events in Vicki's research could be considered from the perspective of different levels of engagement that offered both 'insider' and 'outsider' observation. As a member of the same teaching institution, Lorraine was able to appreciate the constraints and demands of Vicki's classroom, yet at the same time to offer a more objective, distanced and broadly contextualised viewpoint on classroom interaction. Through Lorraine, Vicki was given a channel for continually rethinking and reanalysing themes and issues emerging from her research, ranging from micro-level analyses of classroom events and student behaviours to macro-level reflections on the meaning of these events and how they linked with personal teaching theories.

4.3 Notes and diaries

Observational note-making of various kinds is a flexible tool for action research data collection, although, of course, it requires additional time during or after teaching. It can be utilised in different ways, for example as a way of documenting and analysing issues and themes already identified as the main purpose of the research, or alternatively, as a useful way of finding a clearer focus for the research in the initial stages. The cumulative effect of recording observations and reflections through notes or journals is very illuminating as over time they build a picture of classroom participants and interactions and provide a record of the processes of problematising and elucidating the teaching and learning issues. Classroom observations can be recorded relatively informally at suitable intervals during the lesson through 'jottings' or stream-of-behaviour records made on the spot as the lessons proceed. Scribblings and jottings taken during the lesson serve as an aid to memory. Classroom events, behaviours and reflections collected in this way can be written up later when there is more time to describe, interpret and reflect upon the events. Events should be recorded as soon as possible after they occur, so that they remain fresh and can be reconstructed more accurately.

The extensiveness of the notes you may wish to record will depend on the time you have available. As both a participant and an observer in the classroom, it can be difficult for a teacher to juggle teaching and note-making. Practical solutions need to be found that fit in with personal preferences and time constraints. Pam McPherson drew attention to this problem during her presentation to other teachers on the approaches she developed to capture observations of her newly arrived immigrant learners as the class was in progress:

> You develop your own systems and your own ways of recording ...
> and I found the best way for me to record what was happening in
> my class was on my program ... as I went through the day, I'd just
> scribble down things that happened in the class or things that I
> noted in my classroom. That's why my [lesson programmes] are
> always a mess because I've got things scribbled all over them, all
> over the back, along here and along here, notes everywhere. But
> that all gets put down somewhere else and it's used ... it's very
> useful. And I can go back through my program to see what I did,
> what happened when I did it, what was the response from the
> students when we did particular things and from all of that data I
> was able to learn a lot about what was going on in that classroom.

> (McPherson 1995)

The issue of how to 'keep fieldnotes while also teaching' is also raised
by Samway (1994), who, in a very helpful and practical paper, sets out
several strategies which seek to minimise the time spent in recording
observations. Samway reiterates Pam's point about developing one's
own system, stating that 'what works for a friend may not work for me
and vice versa' (page 47). While their actual systems might differ,
Samway identifies common elements that have characterised her own
and her two colleagues' data collection and storage schemes:

> (a) We do not want to have to rewrite notes when transferring data
> to students' folders; (b) we need to date our notes; and (c) we need
> enough time to be able to record such details as a conversation
> excerpt or a description of a student's actions or words.

> (page 47)

The three systems Samway and her colleagues have designed to meet
these requirements are summarised below.

1 **Peel-off address labels**   On a label, the teacher records the student's
   name and the date, and observations about that student. The label
   can then be attached to student folders. Students can also be
   encouraged to write their own reflections on the same incidents for
   storage in their folders.
2 **Manila folders with post-it notes**   Into a manila folder, the teacher
   attaches one post-it note beneath the name of each student. Dated
   observations are written on the post-its which are then attached to
   individual students' pages in a three ring binder.
3 **Manila folders with index cards**   Notes about students are recorded
   on index cards which are taped one on top of the other into a manila
   folder in a flip chart arrangement. Students' names are printed on the
   bottom of each card for easy identification. Observations are recorded and completed cards taped into student folders.

Samway's discussion re-emphasises a key point that has been made throughout this book, that data collection tools for action research should be designed as far as possible to be a realistic and manageable extension of classroom tasks. As action research in language classrooms becomes more widespread, as it seems set to do, conventional frameworks for conducting qualitative research are likely to be adapted creatively to fit the constraints of classroom sites.

A combination of observational and note-making techniques has the advantages of enabling the action researcher to:

- identify emerging classroom patterns and themes
- clarify the issues that are central to the classroom investigation.

4.3.1 Notes

Notes, or field notes as they are often referred to in qualitative research, are descriptions and accounts of events in the research context which are written in a relatively factual and objective style. They generally include reports of non-verbal information, physical settings, group structures and records of conversations and interactions between participants. The observations recorded in notes can be oriented in different ways, from overall impressions of the classroom, to specific aspects of the research, to recordings made about one or two students. Note information focuses on answering *who/what/where/when/how/why* questions and can be organised in different categories to record descriptions, reflections or analyses of events (R. B. Burns 1994).

Writing notes means more than simply recording data, as the act of writing provides a first analysis from which research areas can be further refined. Suggestions for producing more permanent notes from initial rough notes, key words or jottings are:

- Write on one side of the page only.
- Number each page of the permanent notes consecutively.
- Start a new page for each new research day.
- Begin the notes with the date, location, or context of the observations and brief biographical information on the main participants referred to (these need only be written once).
- Preferably, write any verbatim quotations in a different colour pen if in long hand, or underline so that they stand out from the main body of the notes if typed.
- Keep at least one copy of the original permanent notes. This guards against loss or damage and makes the process of analysis and writing up easier.

(adapted from Hitchcock and Hughes 1995: 132–3)

The length and detail of the notes will clearly vary according to the time available and the level of formality of the research. You may also find that the level of detail tails off as the research questions and context become more familiar and other data collection techniques take over. Notes, when taken regularly, provide an excellent way of chronicling both ordinary and extraordinary research events, and later help to form the basis of a research report or oral presentation.

One teacher researcher, Judy Goodman, used short notes to document her observations of her workplace-based intermediate students. In a coffee break during one lesson, Judy noted:

> Good conversation generated from Ting's promotion from casual to permanent. We discussed the meaning of these words and what they meant in the workplace.
>
> The usefulness of having a social chat could not be underestimated. This exposed students to everyday language.

(Goodman 1997: 66)

She later observed:

> Sira brought his Amway catalogue. Good conversation generated from discussion of the products at coffee break.
>
> George and Nelson discussed problems in their respective workplaces.
>
> Thong asked Milan to explain something on his pay slip.

(page 66)

Judy used her notes to identify the patterns of social cohesion developing within the group. She noted also that classroom activities that contributed to language learning were not always those that she planned and 'controlled'. As a result, she maximised the 'open-ended' learning activities that arose incidentally, enhanced classroom dynamics and encouraged students to take greater responsibility.

A time-saving alternative to producing written notes is to make oral notes using a small hand-held recorder. Patricia Prescott, a Western Australian teacher, kept a recorder in class which she used for on-the-spot recording of her observations, for example during group work activities or while students completed writing tasks. This allowed her to note significant events or behaviours while they were still fresh in her memory. Pam McPherson, reported that she often 'walked out of the classroom talking into [her] recorder'. She added, 'I can do this quickly and it doesn't take extra time. I then listen to the recordings again as I drive home from work and this gets me thinking'.

4.3.2 Teacher diaries or journals

Diaries or journals are an alternative to field notes, or a supplement, if time permits. They provide continuing accounts of perceptions and thought processes, as well as of critical events or issues which have surfaced in the classroom. Diaries and journals contain more subjective and personal reflections and interpretations than the relatively formalised recordings of notes. Hitchcock and Hughes (1995: 134) provide a neat description of the main difference between diaries and journals and field notes:

> The journal or diary allows the researcher to let off steam, to complain, or to moan. They enable some of the pressures which are inevitably placed upon the researcher in such work to be taken off. But the significance of keeping a journal or diary is not only the emotional security it may afford but also for the researcher to reflect on the research, step back and look again at the scenes in order to generate new ideas and theoretical directions. The fieldwork journal or diary is the place where the researcher in conversations with herself, can record hopes, fears, confusion and enlightenment. It is the place where the personal side of the fieldwork equation can be recorded. These kinds of journals or diaries need to be distinguished from other kinds of fieldnotes.

However, as the diary is a personal document, whether one uses it as a kind of emotional safety valve is a matter of preference. In any event, it needs to be thought of as a flexible personal recording tool, to be used in ways that fit in with classroom tasks. The flexible nature of journals and diaries is stressed by McKernan (1996: 84–5) who categorises them into three types:

1 **Intimate journal**   This is the most personal of documents. It is a set of personal notes, a log of events rich in personal sentiments and even confessions. Entries are usually made on a daily basis, or at a regular interval.

2 **Memoir**   The memoir is impersonal as a document and often written in fewer sittings than the intimate journal. It tries to aspire to being more objective and does not concentrate on personal feelings. The records of war correspondents are good examples ...

3 **Log**   The log is more of an accounts record. It is a running record of transactions and events, such as a list of contacts or telephone calls made during the day, of meetings or of signatures of persons entering a building; or it may be the sort of written log kept by a ship's captain.

Michael Carroll, an ESL teacher from South Australia who has made extensive use of journals, notes that personal reflective writing helps teachers to understand themselves and make sense of their experiences. Michael's own journal-keeping experiences led him to see this activity as a valuable one for his students:

> I found myself thinking about how to involve my students more deeply in decisions about the direction the course should take, and as I considered this in my journal, I found that it was really two questions. The first appeared relatively straightforward. How could my course structure allow for student participation? But at a second glance, the problem was more complicated. Like most English teachers I analyze students' needs by means of application forms, testing, discussion, or questionnaires, followed by mid- or end-of-term evaluations ... Such diagnostic activities are not wrong, but they allow little opportunity for students to give serious consideration to their responses. It seemed there would be considerable advantages both for me and for the students if they were involved at a deeper level. But it was not simply a case of listening to what students had to say. They needed help in saying it. My second question was: How could my students learn how to think about what they were doing so they could contribute meaningfully to curriculum decisions?

> (Carroll 1994: 19)

Bailey and Ochsner (1983), Bailey (1983) and Bailey (1990) provide valuable guidance on procedures for keeping journals. Holly (1984) and Holly and Smyth (1989) discuss how the principles behind everyday practice can be reflected through journals. Teacher research reports from diary studies in the general educational field are contained in Fulwiler (1987), Goswami and Stillman (1987) and Miller (1990).

Depending on how they are used – whether for recording direct observations or for documenting introspective reflections on teaching or learning – diaries are tools that overlap the distinction that has been made between the observational tools discussed in this chapter and the non-observational tools discussed in the next. Student diaries as introspective tools are further discussed in Chapter 5.

4.3.3 Proformas

Separating the descriptive aspects of one's observations from the reflective aspects allows analysis and interpretation to become more focused. One way of doing this, relatively simply and easily, is through the use of a 'proforma', or grid, containing headings that separate objective observations from subjective observations. One example of a 'proforma' was developed cooperatively by a group of teachers involved in a collaborative project. The group investigated the impact on their course planning of a new curriculum, *The Certificate in Spoken and*

Written English, a competency-based curriculum framework which had been introduced into their programme.

The teachers were not enthusiastic about the use of journals or diaries, which required more time than they had available for their research, but they wanted to explore their initial impressions of the decision-making processes of course design. They saw the proforma as a quick way of tracking the more pressing questions or issues they need to deal with on a daily basis. Interestingly, the proforma they developed mirrors some of the stages of the action research process itself. It identifies the day-to-day issues that arose, the action taken by the teachers and the teachers' reflections and evaluations of these issues or actions. The following example is taken from Margaret Carew's proforma. Margaret's observations centred particularly on the progress of two students, Abdullah and Ricarda:

> I decided to make regular notes of my observations. Generally these covered two or three lessons a week as I co-taught the class and did not see much of the students during the early part of the week. My co-teacher, however, was aware of what I was doing and we had some fruitful discussions ...
>
> As far as the notes were concerned I found it best to record small details as they happened in class, if they struck me as somehow significant, and then to reflect on them later. My notes on 20 May, for example, recorded these observations:

Date	Issue/ Question	Action	Reflection/ Comments
20 May 1994	What is the Certificate in Spoken and Written English? Wanted to explain and tell them what the competencies were at Stage 1. I expressed these in simple terms. Now have them written up and displayed on wall. Emphasised that competencies	Class very quiet. Some copied the competencies down, including Abdullah and Ricarda. Explained that some had already passed some competencies. Did not say anything about having to pass all competencies to get to Stage 2. I just said that if they didn't pass them this term,	I felt quite uncomfortable during this. The students had not been told about the Certificate prior to this. Most of the teachers at the lower levels prefer not to, especially with classes such as this where achievement can be so slow and some will never achieve more

involve tasks, so that we can see what the students can do with the language. Talking a bit about assessment.	they'd be able to finish next term.	than one or two [competencies]. I feel that they should know, but that it should be presented to them in as non-threatening a way as possible. Assessment should be as informal as possible within the requirements of the Certificate. Could not be sure what Abdullah and Ricarda made of it.

(Carew 1995: 114)

A variation on this format is provided by Ann Beales (1995), a work-place-based teacher of an intermediate class, who developed a proforma to record decision-making points throughout her course.

Week	Competency-based content	Comments relating to content	Critical incident/ content change	New direction	Useful content but unrelated to CSWE

Dora Troupiotis, a teacher from Victoria, wished to develop greater awareness of how she integrated grammar into her teaching, particularly how she selected and sequenced grammatical items during her syllabus planning and how she responded to students' grammatical needs as the course developed (Troupiotis 1995). Dora used a further variation on the proforma to track the tasks she developed and her reflections on them. The entry shown below occurred toward the last week of the course.

Date	Activity/Task	Language item/ Grammar	Why teach? Why now? What terminology was used to describe the grammar?	Other
Tuesday 24 May 1994

Week 17 | A student from each group read their 'five things for a happy marriage' – wrote them on blackboard.

Tried to create a commonly agreed list for the whole class. | Revision of past perfect v. present perfect. | A lot of vocabulary work and definitions so that students would have the necessary vocabulary to be able to write their essays.

At start of lesson one of the students asked another student 'Did you ever fall in love?' I picked up on this and used it to revise the use of the present perfect – especially its use when we ask about an event occurring in the past and we don't know when. Also to illustrate time starting in the past and continuing up to the present time. Students suggested learners need to know other similar sentences and wanted to check how to say some sentences. | This activity generated a lot of discussion. There were disagreements about the importance of some ideas. Also a lot of cross-cultural similarities and differences to attitudes to marriage. Also differences arose because of marital status and gender. |

Dora reported that she experimented with the format of the proforma until she arrived at a version she felt would allow her to record the information she needed.

> Initially when I was thinking about the project, I thought I would record what was happening in class using the headings: date; content; why?; why now?; and what next? However, on reflection I felt that this would not allow me to record what happened in the class, so I modified it and made it more detailed by adding columns for tasks and grammar items. When I tried to record what was happening in the classroom I felt that I could collapse some of the categories and allow a column I called 'other' for anything else that I felt I needed to record and so finally I settled on this version of the proforma which I subsequently used.

> (Troupiotis 1994)

4.4 Audio and video recording

Audio and video recording are a technique for capturing in detail naturalistic interactions and verbatim utterances. Used in the classroom, they are, thus, very valuable sources of accurate information on patterns of interactional behaviour which may not be obvious during the actual teaching process. They are invaluable in assisting teacher researchers to reflect on the implicit beliefs, classroom scripts or mental schemata which are brought to classroom processes. Recordings can be used to obtain general observations and impressions of the classroom or alternatively to focus on specific concerns such as pairwork interactions, the amount of learner talk generated through particular activities, or the analysis of 'critical incidents'. Teacher researchers in my own context have used video or audio recording, for example to secure learners' responses to discussions of learning strategies; to record small group interactions on different types of classroom tasks; to interview students on problem areas in reading or writing and to analyse the way they provide learner feedback. McKernan (1996: 104) provides a useful checklist for using video to focus in on various aspects of classroom behaviour. Many of his suggestions could be equally applied to audio recording:

1 What do you wish to observe (aspects of behaviour, problems, for example)?
2 What are the positive features of the performance?
3 Are the goals of the lessons clear?
4 What is the role of the teacher (e.g. expository, inquiry)?
5 Are the students involved/interested?
6 Who is doing the talking?
7 What type of utterances are made?

8 What types of questions are asked (convergent/divergent)?
9 What type of pupil involvement is there?
10 Is the pace right?
11 What style of classroom/pupil organisation is used?
12 What negative features of this performance present themselves?
13 What non-verbal behaviour is present?
14 What symbols, icons, rituals or artefacts are observed?
15 Are the voices clear?
16 Is the language formal/informal?
17 What mannerisms are evident?
18 Do any distractions occur?
19 What things have you learned from this analysis?

It is useful to be aware of the relative advantages and disadvantages of audio and video recording. Perhaps the major disadvantage of video recording is that it poses more ethical problems than audio recording. Participants can be easily identified and this may cause embarrassment as well as breach confidentiality in reporting the research. Given this important caveat, it is clear, however, that video recordings can encompass a greater range of both verbal and non-verbal behaviour, such as facial expression, board writing, the seating and grouping arrangements and so on. A broad range of interactional patterns and behaviours are therefore available for constant review, and recorded over time they can build up a distinctive account of typical classroom patterns or rituals that researchers can pinpoint, reflect upon and revise. This kind of close revision also allows for the identification of the possible causes of problems, as well as the areas that are promoting learning, in a more holistic way than is possible through audio recording.

In terms of student participation in the research process, video recordings may be more valuable triggers to discussion as they provide both visual and oral support. However, the presence of the video recorder is intrusive and can cause a distraction in the classroom context which may contribute to substantial changes to regular behaviour patterns. Carmel Brown describes how this type of disruption occurred during her own action research activities:

> What I discovered was that the camera itself dominated
> proceedings through the reactions it precipitated. There appeared
> to be a mixture of interest and anticipation bordering on
> excitement about being on show, for some people, whilst the most
> vocal person in the group was very concerned about appearing on
> screen, and therefore positioned herself out of the camera's eye. As
> a result, I decided to change technical aids and tape record the next
> session.

(C. Brown 1995: 8)

These kinds of problems are sometimes overcome through increasing familiarity with the equipment itself and with its presence in the classroom over a period of time. Arrangements for operating the equipment must also be considered. To some extent these will depend on whether equipment is placed in a fixed position or whether it is hand operated. If it is hand-controlled by an operator other than the researcher, there is the possibility that the operator will determine what is to be recorded and this may or may not accord with what is of interest to the researcher.

As Carmel Brown points out, there may be good reasons for selecting audio rather than video recording as an action research technique. Although participants may still be self-conscious about the presence of the recording equipment, audio recording is clearly less intrusive than video recording and familiarity with the presence of the equipment is likely to occur much more quickly. For many teacher researchers, audio equipment is also more readily available than video recorders. One of the main disadvantages of using audio recording is that it fails to include non-verbal interaction and therefore it may be difficult to distinguish the identity of the speaker or the significant contextual details which surround – and perhaps motivate – the speakers' utterances. Both audio and video recording result in large quantities of data which are time-consuming to review, especially if transcription is undertaken. Unless time is not an issue, one practical approach may be for action researchers to review short segments of the recordings, particularly those which represent critical points in relation to the research issues.

Recordings are invaluable in furnishing researchers with objective first-hand data for analysing individual teacher behaviour. Carmel Brown (1995: 10), for example, describes how recording her classroom interaction enabled her to gain informative perspectives on her questioning techniques, in terms of the kinds of questions she asked, how these questions could be classified, and what she was attempting to achieve by using these questions. Using the recording, she transcribed a segment of her lesson and reported that she:

> read the transcript with a touch of embarrassment. What stood out in [the] initial review was the exertion and over-explanation – covering all possible interpretations of meaning, as well as [the] efforts to encourage students to notice and analyse.

Her initial analysis was followed by 'a refinement of [the] first, almost intuitive commentary', from which she developed a categorisation of seven question types: connection/information, confirmation, eliciting/retrieval, information, eliciting/judgement, knowledge and collaboration. She discovered that 'the major aim of [the] questions, was to assist the provision of information and to draw out analyses/judgements' and it appeared as though she placed 'importance on data and information in the development of students' analyses and judgements'.

Recordings can be invaluable when used collaboratively, for example to review classroom processes through a 'stimulated recall' procedure (Nunan 1989, 1992). In this procedure, video or audio recordings provide the stimulus for articulating the rationale underlying classroom actions. In an action research project where I worked collaboratively with Sarah, a teacher of beginner learners (A. Burns 1996), we used audio recorded data to explore the teaching beliefs and principles underpinning a particular lesson. We reviewed classroom interactions by pausing the tape at various points and discussing our interpretations of the thinking and decision-making that had motivated classroom activities. The following short extract between the teacher and one of the students, Lian, exemplifies some of the early exchanges in the lesson:

Transcript: How was your weekend?
Li: . . . went to Chinatown.
T: So how was your weekend? Lian? What did you do at the weekend?
Li: I . . . went to Chinatown.
T: Oh, great! What day . . . what day, Lian?
Li: Uh . . .
T: On Saturday or Sunday?
Li: Er . . . Saturday.
T: Ah, fantastic. And who did you go with?
Li: Er . . . husband.
T: With your husband.
Li: Yes.
T: Ah, right . . . right. Any friends?
Li: No . . . er . . . husband . . . go.
T: Just the two of you . . .
Li: Yes.
T: Right. Was it good?
(Lian laughs and nods)

Sarah had stated that one of her teaching principles related to learner-centred classroom interaction and that in this lesson she wanted her learners to be able to communicate with others about personal topics. Reviewing this segment of the recording she commented:

> I mean, just listening . . . it's very much teacher–student, teacher–student the whole time . . . and er, obviously it would have been good to try and get them to interact. Possibly this was the problem, I think, with this class . . . was that it was very much, you know one-to-one, teacher–student. I mean it kind of glares at me at the moment . . .

The discovery that she 'controlled' classroom questioning much more than she had realised led us to discuss strategies for developing more communicative and active learner involvement. As the next phase in her reflection process, Sarah devised tasks where this learner involvement could be facilitated through greater use of first language.

A further way of using video and audio techniques for reflection in action research is to record collaborative research discussions. Many teachers have found it useful to review recorded meeting discussions in order to:

- focus their topics for research
- provide additional input into note-taking or journal-writing
- further their individual or collective thinking on research themes
- review the discussion contributions they made from a more objective stance
- revise and reflect further on accounts of their own and/or other teachers' actions or interpretations.

4.4.1 Transcription

One way of handling data collected through audio and video recording is to transcribe it. Transcription allows researchers to scan particular classroom episodes relatively quickly without the need to review the whole recording. Of itself, the process of transcribing produces revealing insights into the data as the researcher becomes closely engaged. Unfortunately, transcription has a major drawback in that it is immensely time-consuming, often requiring four to five hours of transcription for each hour of recorded interaction. As a result, action researchers deciding to use transcription as a tool for data collection need to do so advisedly. However, teachers with whom I have worked have reported that if one is prepared for the extra time and effort that is needed, even short transcriptions are a very valuable way of reevaluating recorded data collected through classroom discussions or interviews. Transcription has the effect of concentrating the mind considerably beyond simply listening or watching and provides a basis for more in-depth analyses, while any length of time spent transcribing also means that the data become very familiar.

Catherine Kebir, a teacher from South Australia, researched the communication strategies used by her post-beginner learners on two-way information gap tasks (Johnson and Morrow 1981). She describes the problems that transcribing can present:

> I recorded six pairs of learners on three different occasions doing three different picture dictation tasks ... However, transcribing the taped classroom interaction proved extremely time-consuming and

difficult mainly because the equipment was inadequate in the trial runs and had to be changed, but also because of the sheer length of the transcripts and the patience required to listen again and again. I also found that the acoustics of the classroom are far from ideal and in future projects would record pairs privately in another room if the focus is on the learner language and not the classroom context itself.

(Kebir 1994: 29–30)

Despite the drawbacks, Catherine reported that transcribing the interaction enabled her to arrive at a detailed analysis of the communication strategies used by her learners for different tasks and to develop a further phase in the research where she used teaching strategies based on similar analyses of native speaker interactions on the same tasks.

Restrictions on time will determine whether transcription is used in action research. One suggestion is to transcribe only small portions of the recordings. Another is to share the task of transcribing with other partners with an interest in the data. Group or individual criteria can be developed to identify which portions are selected. For example, you may decide to focus on student group interactions or segments which highlight error correction, or to record episodes which seem to illustrate 'critical points' in the interaction. Alternatively, it can be useful to transcribe 'routine' episodes as a way of rethinking activities or patterns of classroom interaction that are taken for granted.

Data can be transcribed in many ways using conventions ranging from highly detailed and complex systems to simple orthographic representations (see Ochs 1979; Brown and Yule 1983; Allwright and Bailey 1991). Burns, Joyce and Gollin (1996: 61–62) list the following simple coding conventions and guidelines developed by a group of teacher researchers who collected short samples of everyday spoken language used outside the classroom. The extracts were used by the teachers to explore the authentic use of English in different contexts as a basis for developing classroom activities. These conventions could be easily adapted for action research transcripts:

Coding conventions
[ ]   overlapping turns
...   a short pause (approximately one second)
( )   contextual information accompanying text
(( ))   uncertain transcription
((?))   indecipherable
< >   altered transcription used for confidentiality

Before the data were transcribed, the following points were also discussed by the research group in order to make the process more manageable:

- Keep the transcription as simple as possible and include only what is necessary.
- Decide as soon as possible on the set of conventions you will use and maintain them throughout the transcription.
- Label the speakers using one of the following systems:
  - letters, e.g. A B C
  - first names (pseudonyms, or real names if confidentiality is not an issue)
  - names of positions (e.g. Information Officer, Receptionist).
- Number the lines or clauses for easy reference.
- Insert contextual information to explain essential aspects of the location or topic, and any non-verbal interaction.
- Retain the wording as accurately as possible.
- Avoid making the text look visually disorganised as this may interfere with understanding.
- Use ordinary orthographic transcription, with conventional punctuation where appropriate.

The mechanics of transcription involve a number of procedures, which can be adapted according to how much time is available and how much detail is required.

1 Transcribe as soon after the event as possible, in order to preserve your memory of the context. Field notes can help to provide any additional, non-verbal, information.
2 Listen to the complete tape at least once to remind yourself of the whole interaction and to develop an initial sense of the topic and who is talking.
3 Replay the tape stopping at comfortable intervals to transcribe what has been heard. Pedal-operated transcribing machines can greatly speed up this process. Ordinary cassette players will need to be rewound and paused, often several times. Headphones may make the recording more audible by reducing extraneous noise.
4 On completion of the first draft, relisten to the tape and check your transcription. Make any corrections necessary.
5 If possible, listen to the tape again after a few days and further refine your transcription. This step can be continued until you reach the level of detail required.

There are few short cuts in the process of transcribing and it would be unrealistic to understate the amount of time and effort involved. However, it is worth taking note of Heritage (1984: 238) on the benefits of transcripts:

> ... the use of recorded data is an essential corrective to the
> limitations of intuition and recollection. In enabling repeated and
> detailed examination of the events of interaction, the use of
> recordings extends the range and precision of the observations that
> can be made. It permits other researchers to have direct access to
> the data about which the claims are being made, thus making
> analysis subject to direct public scrutiny and helping to minimise
> the influence of personal preconceptions or analytical biases.
> Finally, it may be noted that because the data are available in 'raw'
> form, they can be used in a variety of investigations and can be re-
> examined in the context of new findings.

In a collaborative practitioner group, it may at least be possible to
transcribe data collaboratively, thus sharing the burden of transcription
as colleagues undertake different segments or check, read and discuss
each other's transcripts.

4.5 Photographs

The use of photographs is under-explored in action research and, indeed,
in qualitative research in general. Kellehear (1993: 75) comments:

> Since George Eastman invented the box brownie back in 1888, the
> photographic image has permeated every aspect of our lives from
> passport, student and drivers' identification cards to family and
> travel home albums. Social scientists have done little to tap this.

Photographic data holds promise as a way of richly illuminating
numerous aspects of the classroom quickly and relatively inexpensively
and providing new angles on the context being researched. Used with
other qualitative techniques, photographs are a way of greatly enhancing classroom analysis and providing visual stimuli which can be
integrated into reporting and presenting the research to others. The use
of photographs is also a technique for data collection that combines
effectively with a range of language classroom tasks and activities
where visual aids are an invaluable support in learning. Amongst their
potential uses are:

- linking sound recordings to action research 'moments' (Walker and
  Adleman 1972)
- personalising the subjects highlighted in the research (Bello 1994)
- eliciting responses or communicating complex messages (Walker
  1985)
- providing reference points for interviews or discussions (Hopkins
  1993)
- illustrating teaching techniques (Erickson and Wilson 1982)
- building up a portfolio of visual classroom images, that are more

instantly accessible than video recordings (Hitchcock and Hughes 1995)

• providing a permanent visual resource for classroom tasks.

Photographic data can be collected spontaneously and intermittently or at pre-determined intervals, for example, taking a frame every sixty seconds. If colleagues or students are recruited to take photographs, this leaves the teacher free for other tasks. Photographs of classroom participants can be complemented with 'artefacts' from the classroom, for example signs and notices, classroom exhibits, student products, materials used for different activities or even 'incidentals', such as items left lying around on desks. Thus, they provide an interesting window on the cultural nature of the classroom as a social context, which greatly extends the analysis of classroom interaction. A series of photographs provides an excellent record, gives people a focus for discussion and stimulates them to talk in detail about their activities.

Somekh (1996: 3) comments on how using photographs in her classroom research enabled her to critique some of the personal theories she constructed around her teaching:

> when I was a school teacher carrying out action research, the data included photographs of myself standing with my hands on my hips. My focus on improving students' learning included trying to establish warm, informal relationships with them, but my posture in the photographs looked rather aggressive. Upon that I based the theory that there were things I could change in my body language which might actually reinforce rather than counter my efforts to develop more intimate relationships with my students. So I made those changes and I could then test out whether there did seem to be any improvement in students' relationships with me.

Photographs can be drawn from two sources: those that already exist as 'archives' in the teaching institution and those taken by the researcher. School-based photographs may be of value in documenting the broader images of teaching and learning promoted by the institution, against which the action research is juxtaposed. They can highlight changes in physical layout, people or teaching resources that have developed over a period of time. Photographs generated by the researchers can focus on classroom or school locations, layouts or interactions and may illustrate organisational patterns, student interactions or elements such as facial expressions, spatial positions and student groupings or pairings.

Teacher colleagues in one collaborative group I worked with studied the photographs shown here of students conducting group tasks. During the ensuing discussion, we suggested that these photographs could be used to identify:

- which students had chosen to work together
- whether students had chosen to work with others who spoke the same language
- what gender combinations had been chosen
- where the students has chosen to work and how and where they had positioned themselves
- what spatial relations or body language were suggested
- who appeared to be taking the lead in the interaction
- what materials the students were employing to complete the task.

A further suggestion was that the photographs could be used with the students concerned as a stimulus for discussions or interviews where explanations of the interaction could be provided, thereby helping to confirm or disconfirm the teacher's observations. They could also be used with different students to stimulate discussion of the purpose of group tasks in learning or to raise awareness of strategies for learning from other students.

One of the problems that arises in using and analysing photographs in comparison with video recordings relates to how representative they are of the situation, that is, how generalised or how selective they might be. Associated with this is the question of authenticity, that is, who or what is included and who or what is left out of the portrayals. The ethical problems found in using video recording also apply in the case of photographs and, clearly, before using photographs publicly, you would need to obtain permission from the individuals concerned. Despite these limitations, photographs provide much useful contextual data and can also trigger personal evaluations of classroom experiences, thereby illuminating categories of beliefs or feelings, or people's priorities and values (Walker 1991).

4.6 Charting the social organisation of the classroom

Diagrams such as layouts, maps and sociograms yield useful information on the way learning situations are socially structured and the impact of this on classroom dynamics. They are also useful in documenting how teachers and students orient to the classroom spaces and physical locations they have available. They can reveal how these movements contribute to particular patterns of classroom interactions or expectations. The spatial organisation of a school or classroom relays messages about the kind of culture and ethos of learning that exists. In second language classrooms, valuable cross-cultural issues for investigation may emerge through documenting spatial and organisational patterns.

4.6.1 Layouts and maps

Hitchcock and Hughes (1995) suggest a number of interesting research questions related to spatial arrangements and organisations. While these questions are not necessarily easy to answer, they promote reflection on the social arrangements operating in the classroom that are usually unstated and taken for granted:

1 What is it that a particular spatial arrangement is actually saying?
2 How do people construct spaces to give off messages and how does this influence the interaction which takes place in them?
3 How do people attend to and make sense of the features of spaces and place?
4 How do people physically conduct themselves in particular spaces and places?
5 How do they act, stand, queue, walk, etc.?
6 How are territories and boundaries developed, maintained and crossed?

(adapted from Hitchcock and Hughes 1995: 270)

Such questions enable action researchers to reflect on how spatial arrangements reflect certain curriculum concepts or personal teaching and learning preferences. For example, implicit theories of learner roles, teacher- or learner-centredness, learning activity types, visual stimuli and teaching approaches are embodied in the way the physical context is set up. Analyses can also be made of how movements around the room result in different kinds of interactions, for example, how a teacher's movements result in attention being given to different students, or which of the areas set out to encourage the use of different materials or activities are used by students and which are not.

Recording spatial and interactional arrangements provides useful information to supplement other kinds of observational data, by explaining how and why people and things are positioned, or position themselves, in the classroom. Layouts and maps can document how the classroom set-up changes over a period of time in response to action research strategies and can reflect the range of different spatial arrangements set up during the research. Recordings may be undertaken formally, for example using carefully scaled measurements to identify exact locations of movable and immovable furniture or more informally, through descriptive accounts focusing on the movements of students and teachers. These data may reveal, for example, who students want to sit next to, what combinations of groups or classroom furniture are preferred, and how male and female students mix in the classroom. The degree of detail required in mapping this information

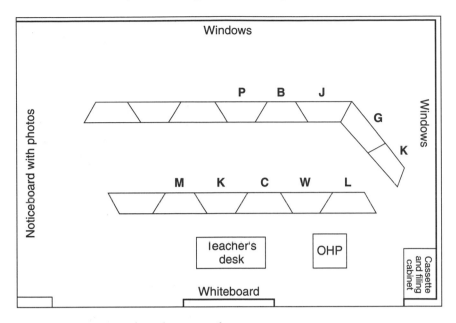

Figure 4.1 *Layout of Linda Ross's classroom*

needs to be considered. This will depend largely on the topic of the research, what the teacher is looking for and how much time can be given to documenting observations. Detail can range from carefully scaled maps to sketchy diagrams that act as *aides-memoire*. Anderson *et al.* (1994) provide a useful and detailed discussion on the use of mapping, as do Hitchcock and Hughes (1995).

Mapping classroom layouts and movements at the same time as teaching a class means that practical decisions need to be made about how data are collected. This is not necessarily an easy task and teachers who use this technique will need to find procedures that blend with other classroom activities. One suggestion is to use colleagues or other researchers, where possible, to map movements over a specified period of time, for example, documenting the teacher's position every three minutes for an hour. Alternatively, the observer can focus on different combinations of individuals or groups, again over a predetermined period of time, for example by shadowing the movements of an individual each day for a week or observing a group every half hour during a day to note who they are with or what they are doing. From time to time, new individuals or groups can be selected and mapped to provide comparisons.

Pam McPherson describes how using a series of classroom diagrams was incorporated into her research procedures. A major issue in Pam's research was her students' reluctance to interact in group or pair activities. Pam used a variety of observational techniques, including monitoring classroom layout, in order to identify and trial strategies to solve this dilemma:

> And the layout, classroom layout too, I think was also very important. The drawings I found very useful for me to document as time went on how the interactions in the classroom changed and whether they changed or not. So at the beginning of the course I had a particular diagram – how the students were laying out their chairs and how they sat together, who they talked with. And by the end of the course the whole layout of the classroom was totally changed. They were using much more of the classroom space itself and were less rigid about where they would sit and they would move about much more. So the drawings documented all that in a much more accessible format to me than writing it all out.
>
> (McPherson 1995)

Linda Ross's documentation of her classroom, described in Chapter 1, also involved a diagram. Rather than showing change over time, this diagram represented the way her class had been set up for the entire duration of her course. Linda used the diagram as a record of the nature of the personal expectations that underpinned her learners' concepts of what a classroom should be like. Linda's diagram is set out in Figure 4.1.

Key

L = Lillian, aged 40. Completed primary school. Many unskilled jobs. Failed First Aid in Health Care course.

W = Warren, aged 35. Completed Grade 9. Butcher. Second term in same course.

C = Chris, aged 33. Completed Grade 9. Factory work. Second term in same course.

K = Kerin, aged 18. Completed Grade 12. Already completed Industrial Cleaning and Hospitality course.

M = Michael, aged 21. Completed Grade 9. Lots of social problems at school.

K = Kelly, aged 19. Left high school due to emotional problems. Had been in course for Intellectually Disabled.

G = George, aged 42. Lebanese, 6 years in Australia. Storeman and Croupier.

J = John, aged 20. Completed Grade 10. Failed Plumbing course.

B = Barry, aged 18. Completed Grade 9. Second term in course.

P = Peter, aged 32. Tongan. Attended school in New Zealand.

The rigid classroom layout selected by her learners challenged Linda's personal theories of teacher–student interaction in an adult classroom. Mapping the layout became a way of understanding the meanings the learners attached to the classroom and the attitudinal factors that motivated their classroom interaction. Linda comments:

> When we first got into the classroom, it had chairs with flip-over lids for writing. The students didn't like these at all. They wrote to the Assistant Principal asking for desks and they were supplied with tables shaped to link together.
>
> I prefer a learner-centred classroom so I wanted the classroom set up in groups or circles so that I could encourage them to work together and introduce a less formal atmosphere – I wanted it to be an adult classroom. I put the desks into a horseshoe shape and they complained – they said the people on the end couldn't see properly.
>
> However many times I changed the desks around the students changed them back into this conventional set-up. They also set out a desk and chair for me every day right up at the front of the class. They made it look like a traditional classroom. They insisted it had to be this way. They liked the desks in rows and they liked the same desk. They got upset if someone else sat in their desks.
>
> (Linda Ross personal communication, 1997)

The classroom layout revealed by Linda's diagram symbolised important underlying factors that she discovered she needed to take into account as the teacher of this particular group of students.

> Most of the students had negative memories about school. I think they liked the security of it being like this. I discussed this with my co-researcher, Lenn, who was teaching a similar class and getting the same reaction. Both of us preferred a more informal arrangement. But then we realised we weren't being fair to the students. I've thought about this since and I think it shows that they took their learning seriously. They had certain beliefs about what a classroom should look like – the classroom has to look like a classroom with desks in rows. Several of them also called me 'Miss' even though I kept telling them to call me Linda, but I think they weren't comfortable with Linda as they had their own ideas about the role of the teacher and what a classroom should be like.
>
> (Linda Ross, personal communication 1997)

Seating arrangements shape classroom expectations and levels of participation in subtle ways. Linda's analysis reminds us that teachers and students come to have personal understandings of the way things get done, with whom and how, within the physical dimensions of the classroom. These understandings are aspects of practice which may need to be renegotiated in some situations if classroom interactions are to operate effectively. Seating observation records can be valuable in recording targeted behaviours such as teacher questioning behaviour and student responses. Readers interested in following up more formalised recording charts should consult Day (1990) on the use of seating observation records to record teacher and student talk, at-task behaviour and movement patterns in ESL classrooms.

4.6.2 Sociometry

Sociometry provides detailed information about the social structures and interpersonal relationships of groups. It may be used as an extension of classroom layouts and maps to develop even more in-depth analyses of the specific nature of learner interactions within a group. It also uncovers the emotional 'climate' of a group by revealing patterns of reciprocity or rejection amongst students. Kemmis and McTaggart (1988: 103) define a sociometric method as:

> A method used to find which individuals are 'liked', 'like' each other or 'dislike' each other within a group. Questions are often posed with a view to finding which peers a student would like to work with on a topic or associate with on a camp or other activities. Questions may also seek to find out with whom students prefer not to work or associate. Results are normally expressed diagrammatically on a sociogram recording relationships with the whole group.

Congdon (1978: 6, cited in Hopkins 1993) describes the following procedures for administering a sociometric process:

> Each child is handed a slip of blank paper and told to write his [*sic*] name at the top. Some teachers prefer to have the names of all pupils in the class written on the blackboard. It is always advisable to write up the names of any pupils who are absent. The test should be meaningful to the pupils, So, for example, the context of the test could be a project. After deciding on a project the pupils could be told that they will be allowed to work in groups and that the groups would be made up according to their own choices.

> On the left hand side of the sheet the pupils are asked to write the name of the person with whom they would like to work in a group. Underneath they are asked to write the name of the one they would like next best, then the next and so on. They can be told to write as many names as they wish or none at all. The pupil is then asked to turn over the sheet and again down the left hand side of the page to write the names of any children with whom they do not wish to work. The teacher again tells them that they may write as many names as they wish or none at all. And what is more important she tells them that the names will be known only to herself, i.e. the choices are made privately and no pupil should be told either who chose him or how many choices he received. In this way no one's feelings are hurt.

Diagrams known as sociograms are a common method of collating the data produced via the use of a sociometric method. Figure 4.2, based on Kemmis and McTaggart (1988: 103), provides an example of a sociogram illustrating the interactional preferences of a group of eight students.

Procedures for drawing up such a diagram are:

1 Identify the student chosen most frequently by members of the group and provide a symbol (for example, first name or number) for that student.
2 Identify others chosen by that student and add symbols for each of them.
3 Add students who chose any of the previously identified group members.
4 Continue until all mutual choices are completed.
5 Begin a fresh group starting with the most chosen student.
6 Identify and add in any students who are not chosen.

(adapted from Congdon 1978: 7)

The sociogram is a useful way of presenting information in a condensed form about the social interactions of the group from the perspective of group members themselves. In Kemmis and McTaggart's illustration, C is clearly popular and therefore potentially a mediator, either positively or negatively, of group interaction. D and G have formed a close pair and may, therefore, be reluctant to be part of other types of group structures. E wishes to be associated with C, who does not reciprocate, and is rejected by B, while F is specifically rejected by three students in the group. H neither seeks out nor is sought out by other students and is a loner.

A number of caveats are in order in the use of this method. Asking students directly about their social interactions with others, as Kemmis and McTaggart and Congdon suggest, could be seen as threatening. This procedure needs to be handled sensitively and adapted to the particular dynamics of the classroom situation. Students also need to be reassured that the information they provide will be treated confidentially by the teacher. A less threatening variation on using sociograms is for the teacher to utilise them without input from the learners as a way of recording diagrammatically the changing structures of the group. In combination with the drawings of her classroom layout described in the previous section, Pam McPherson used her personal version of a sociogram to observe the social interactions of different individuals:

> And drawings I found really, really useful – sociograms. In the particular class I had, the problem was with people not interacting with each other and not wanting to be involved with each other

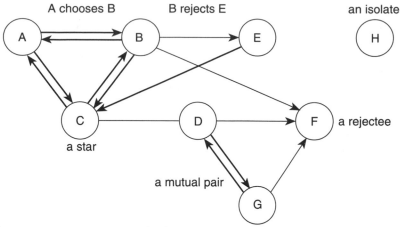

Figure 4.2 *Sociometric methods*

and I found it really useful for me to draw diagrams ... to see who typically worked together and who didn't work together and to try and gain some understanding of why this was going on.

I began to realise that the patterns of interaction that the students were setting up in the arrangement of the desks and who they talked to allowed them to minimise interaction with some students and to barricade themselves into certain groups.

Pam overcame the problem of time constraints while teaching by drawing up a very rough version of her sociogram while in the classroom and then redrawing it more clearly later.

In her sociograms (e.g. Figure 4.3), Pam combined the interaction patterns between students in the classroom with a drawing of the classroom layout. These sociograms highlighted interaction patterns that 'were well entrenched and seemed to be the only lines of communication which were acceptable to the students' (personal communication).

One of the purposes of using a sociometric approach is to enhance student relationships and attitudes towards one another. It is a method that can be employed dynamically to work towards improved interactions. In Pam's classroom, sociograms, used in combination with other methods throughout her research, uncovered patterns of interaction resulting from ethnic and racial tensions within the group which had been heightened by recent warfare within the students' country of origin:

It seemed that for a majority of the class, there were quite deep divisions and tensions amongst them in relation to their ethnicity and the political struggles of their country of origin ...

In particular the self-selection of groups in which to work had been difficult for them. It required decisions about selection and

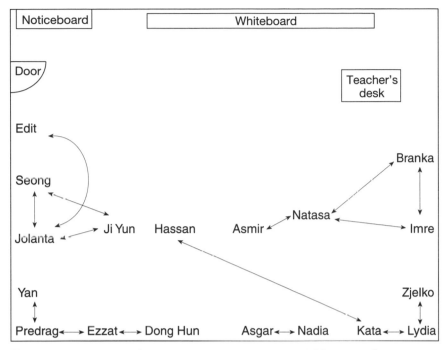

Figure 4.3 *Layout and interaction patterns in Pam McPherson's classroom*

rejection of individuals and some students felt this would cause offence.

(McPherson 1997a: 57–8)

In order to lessen student fears of misunderstanding or causing offence, Pam devised a number of activities, for example games or class excursions, designed to activate 'neutral' interactions. These produced a rapid improvement:

> I was amazed at how quickly the class responded and the atmosphere lightened. In the early part of my research I had drawn up a sociogram of the students' interaction patterns and had found them quite limited. Now interaction was varied and wide-ranging across the class. Students came out from behind their desks and one particularly affected student who had remained barricaded by desks in the corner of the room for 15 weeks, now wandered freely about and was reluctant to sit down at the beginning of the class.

(McPherson 1997b: 29)

From this point in her course Pam decided that gathering data through sociograms was no longer relevant to her understanding of the problem she had encountered as students were now 'interacting quite freely with their classmates in their language activities and the cliques and divisions seemed to have disappeared' (personal communication).

While sociograms are commonly used for sociometric analysis, they are not always essential. Lucy Valeri, a teacher of an intermediate vocationally focused class of adult learners, used sociometrically or-iented questions as part of survey methods to gain data about her learners' attitudes to group work. 'An avid promoter of group work', she had always grouped learners subjectively, without delving into their perceptions of how they wished to be grouped. However, in the initial weeks of her course, she had observed what she saw as a number of interactional difficulties which included: a general reluctance to work in groups; students of the same language background or gender wanting to work together and biases on the part of some students to work only with students of the same educational or employment background. Lucy decided to focus her research on improving student group interaction. She began by ascertaining her learners' views through questions such as:

> How do you like working best (tick one): by yourself
> with a partner
> in a group?

> If you had a choice of five other people to work with in a group, how would you select them and why? (Take into account age, language, sex, nationality, religion, etc.)

The responses indicated that only 38% of the students wanted to work with students from different countries or language backgrounds, while 28% liked to be grouped only with people with higher levels of English. The majority of learners stated they would like to work in groups only if they could select the other members.

In order to explore possibilities for group tasks and interactions further, Lucy discussed the results with her students and throughout the course introduced a variety of group structures. Sometimes these were based on factors of homogeneity such as nationality or language, educational levels, gender, age and so on. At other times, she made the groupings as heterogeneous as possible. A third possibility was student-selected groups. The teacher and the students completed anecdotal observation sheets immediately after group work and Lucy also adminis-tered mid- and end-of-course surveys to determine how perceptions were changing. By the end of the course she noted the following:

- There was a noticeable shift from learners not liking group work to almost demanding it.
- Only 9% of the students still preferred to work individually.
- The female learners who initially wanted to work together now

preferred a mixed-gender group and were more confident in dealing with the males.

- Almost all the learners stated that they preferred to work in heterogeneous groups with others of different languages and language levels, nationality and educational and employment backgrounds.

Lucy comments:

> The learners were themselves astounded at how their perceptions of group work had changed in a matter of weeks. They felt they had taken charge of their own learning and had become more independent in both thinking and classroom management. My co-teacher had also noticed this change. The other revelation was that I had nothing to do with how this eventuated, as the learners had grouped themselves in the last three weeks of the course.

(Valeri 1997: 39)

4.7 Summary

In this chapter I have highlighted qualitative observational methods for conducting action research. In reviewing what are relatively well-documented approaches, a key aim has been to provide a somewhat different perspective from previous accounts associated with action research in the language classroom. This has been offered by focusing on the use of these methods by teacher researchers who have recently conducted collaborative action research. These descriptions of how teachers have gone about drawing on and using the methods described here are intended to provide a stimulus for other potential action researchers. They are also intended to place the teacher's viewpoint at the centre of the question of which data collection techniques are most feasible for action research studies.

The methods highlighted in this chapter include notes, diaries/journals, transcripts, diagrams and audio and video recording. The descriptions of these methods are not exhaustive, but have aimed to highlight general practical considerations which teacher researchers have found to be of use.

Two points remain to be made in relation to these accounts, as in relation to those that follow in the next chapter. The first is that teachers interested in action research methods should draw upon these methods flexibly according to resources of time, support and opportunities for collaboration with others. Action research is above all aimed at offering adaptable and creative avenues for classroom investigation. The second point is that when considering methods for collecting data it is highly appropriate for teachers to select those that can be integrated with regular classroom activities. As some of the descriptions in this chapter have aimed to illustrate, the research process becomes less burdensome for the teacher if the methods used are able to serve the dual purpose of data collection and task development.

The chapter that follows continues the discussion of data collection methods and techniques. It introduces a range of techniques, some of which are relatively new in action research but which have provided interesting alternatives for reflecting upon and interpreting classroom issues.

Group discussion tasks

1 Try out the proforma in Section 4.3.3 to observe in a general way two or three lessons you teach. What issues arise for you and what actions do you put into place to address these issues? What patterns of classroom decision-making emerge from your observations? Compare your observations with those of colleagues in your research group.
2 Select a location in your school which is very familiar to you. Sketch a map of this area. What kinds of teaching and learning activities would the layout encourage or discourage? How is this location currently used by the participants (consider use of space, ways of communicating)? With your colleagues, brainstorm strategies for adapting these locations.
3 Discuss the facilities available for video and audio recording in your situation. How could they be incorporated into classroom research?
4 What are the major advantages and disadvantages of audio recording and video recording in your particular situation?
5 What strategies could be developed to overcome some of the practical disadvantages of recording? How could you involve the collaboration of other action researchers?
6 Which of the strategies suggested for keeping notes or jottings seem most feasible to you? With others in your group, try out some of these strategies and discuss how well they worked. What other ways of keeping records of this sort can your group suggest?
7 Record and transcribe a short segment from one of your lessons. Use or modify the transcriptions conventions suggested in Section 4.4.1. How useful were they? Discuss whether you needed to modify them and how you did this. How long did the transcription take? How valuable did your group find the process of transcription?
8 Share your reflections on the patterns of classroom interaction revealed by your transcript with other members of your group. How similar or different are they from other colleagues' reflections? What common areas for group research do they suggest?

5 Non-observational techniques for data collection

[I] prepared a detailed profile of five of the students. I don't usually intrude into students' personal lives, but these students saw these issues as affecting their learning ability and wanted me to understand them.

(Marie Muldoon, New South Wales)

5.1 Introduction

This chapter continues the discussion of techniques for data collection by overviewing a number of non-observational methods. Non-observational tools result in data that are essentially introspective, that is, they invite personal and individual accounts of events, attitudes and beliefs. They encourage respondents to 'self-report' their perspectives on the phenomena under investigation. The contribution of such data is that they can give rise to issues that have not been anticipated by the researcher, or which take the question beyond what was originally expected. Further and deeper cycles of research can therefore be stimulated. They can also provide rich and in-depth portrayals of groups or individuals and the physical contexts in which they operate.

As in Chapter 4, methods are first outlined and then examples of how they have been used by language teachers in the conduct of action research are presented. The methods described include:

- **interviews and discussions**: face-to-face personal interactions which generate data about the research issue and allow specific issues to be discussed from other people's perspectives
- **questionnaires and surveys**: written sets of questions used to gain responses in non-face-to-face situations; questions are usually focused on specific issues and may invite either factual or attitudinal responses
- **life/career histories**: profiles of students' previous life and learning experiences told from the perspective of the individuals concerned which may be built up over a period of time
- **documents**: collections of various documents relevant to the research questions which can include students' written work, student records and profiles, course overviews, lesson plans, classroom materials.

The chapter concludes with a discussion of metaphor development, a less conventional method for collaborative reflection on practice.

5.2 Interviews

Interviews are a popular and widely used means of collecting qualitative data. If they are incorporated into the lesson, whenever possible, as an aspect of the regular activities of the classroom, they can double as a classroom task and as a way of investigating and collecting data on areas one wishes to explore. Interviews can be conducted through a variety of participant combinations: teacher to teacher(s); teacher to learner(s); learner to learner(s); researcher to teacher(s); teacher to researcher(s); researcher to student(s). Teacher researchers have recounted a variety of situations in which they have conducted interviews using some of the combinations suggested below:

(a) A teacher researcher interviewed other teachers at her teaching centre in order to find out to what extent their strategies for planning course design processes were similar or different from the ones she had documented in her own classroom.

(b) At the request of their teacher, a researcher interviewed students on their perceptions about being placed in a mixed-ability literacy class, which included both ESL students and native English speakers. The teacher wanted to record responses to issues she had already begun to investigate with her learners. The researcher interview provided her with additional data.

(c) A teacher interviewed two selected learners in her classroom on an individual basis in order to deepen her initial observations of the range of learning strategies used by beginner learners with limited literacy skills in English.

(d) A research coordinator worked with four teacher researchers and interviewed small groups of their learners about their responses to competency-based assessment. The teachers organised the interviews so that they could obtain more 'neutral' learner responses.

(e) A teacher interviewed a researcher whom she had just observed teaching her class using a grammar teaching technique which the teacher was finding difficult to use. The teacher did this in order to clarify her own ideas about why this technique was not working and how to go about changing it.

(f) A researcher assisted a teacher by interviewing her students on their current life situations, previous work and current learning experiences. The teacher wanted to record this information as it was recounted to another person in order to gain a more in-depth view of affective factors affecting her students' learning.

(g) A teacher organised learner to learner interviews on their perceptions about group work. The teacher provided a set of interview questions and asked the group to audio-record their responses. She did this in order to increase her own and her learners' understanding of group work and classroom dynamics.

(h) A teacher incorporated regular discussions into his classroom activities in order to investigate his learners' perceptions of a new curriculum approach as well as to clarify his own responses to it.

As these combinations suggest, interviews can be undertaken with individuals or with groups of interviewees. Individual interviews are clearly more time-consuming and a group interview has the advantage of enabling the interviewer to collect more data from a greater number of people on a single occasion. Often the data collected from a group is far richer than that collected from individuals as the various members of the group can trigger additional, and more productive, responses from each other. Individual interviews, on the other hand, have the advantage of enabling the researcher to follow up in more detail particular issues which have been identified, or insights or observations already made but not fully reflected upon.

Action researchers need to consider what kind of interview is most appropriate to the research issues and to the types of learners involved. Interviews are often characterised, according to the degree of control the interviewer decides to exercise over the interaction, as structured, semi-structured or unstructured. For each of these different types of interviews, it is useful to record the interview responses. Audio recording has the advantage of capturing verbal responses verbatim and leaves the interviewer free to participate in a more spontaneous way. Note-taking requires concentration on the part of the interviewer, both on the flow of the interview and on the information that must be recorded. However, note-taking may be more appropriate in situations where interviewees are intimidated by audio or video recording and it is also a useful supplement to recorded data, particularly where significant non-verbal data need to be documented. Issues related to audio and video recording were discussed in more detail in the previous chapter.

5.2.1 Structured interviews

In the structured or formal interview, the researcher works through a list of preplanned questions in a fixed order. This approach has the advantage of standardising the interview and therefore ensuring greater consistency and reliability. However, it represents a relatively closed interview situation in which there is limited opportunity to pursue unpredicted responses or probe more deeply into people's perceptions or beliefs. The structured interview can be valuable where the researcher wishes to follow up particular areas through, for example, survey interviews conducted by learners or other teachers. An example from situation (d) described above shows how the structured interview can be incorporated into collaborative action research. The four teachers involved worked across different teaching centres and wished to standardise their learner interviews in order to compare their results. Nan Dingle, the action research coordinator who conducted the interviews on the teachers' behalf, explains how they took place:

> I ... conducted and audio-taped interviews or discussions with groups of learners from each of the four classes. I attempted to make these sessions as non-threatening as possible and their recorder shyness wore off quickly as those in the groups were volunteers who seemed enthusiastic about talking about their learning experiences. The learners were asked to respond to the following questions:
>
> 1 Are you familiar with the Learning Outcomes of your course?
> 2 Do you want to know when you are being given an assessment task?
> 3 Whose responsibility is it to pass you?
> 4 Could you assess yourself?
> 5 How often would you like to be tested over the course?
> 6 Which assessment tasks have you found hardest?
> 7 Are you always aware of the criteria for assessment?
>
> (Dingle 1995: 134)

5.2.2 Semi-structured and unstructured interviews

The semi-structured interview differs from the structured interview in that it is open-ended and thus provides much greater flexibility. In the semi-structured interview, the action researcher generally uses prepared guide questions or alternatively has some overall directions in mind. These guidelines are then used, in no fixed order, to provide the underlying focus for the interview. This type of interview has the advantage of enabling the interviewee's as well as the interviewer's perspective to inform the research agenda, and therefore gives rise to a more equal balance in the research relationship. In addition, it allows for the emergence of themes and topics which may not have been anticipated when the investigation began.

At the furthest end of the spectrum is the unstructured or informal interview where the interviewer and interviewee engage in a free-flowing conversational process based on the issues and topics of the research study. Unstructured interviews originate in ethnographic research conducted in anthropology, and a classic source of guidance on interviews of this type is Spradley (1980). The aim of the unstructured interview is to give as full a scope as possible to the informants' perceptions of themselves, the social situation and their experiences within it. While this is clearly the most open of the interview types, the researcher still exercises some slight degree of control, in order to ensure that the focus remains on the issues being investigated.

The following unstructured interview (unpublished data) is taken from situation (b) described above. It illustrates how this kind of conversational interview can be used in a group situation to uncover students' perceptions about their educational and learning experiences. The class was similar in profile to that described by Linda Ross in Chapter 1. It was composed of both ESL and non-ESL learners who were attending a 15-week literacy and numeracy class provided by the Australian government for unemployed people. Because there was a requirement by the Commonwealth Employment Service (CES) for class attendance, there was a strong atmosphere of resistance amongst most of the learners. The students had limited education as well as negative attitudes towards previous schooling experiences. These factors affected the classroom dynamics, and the teacher, Lenn de Leon, aimed through her research to find teaching strategies which would facilitate a more positive learning environment (see Chapter 8). Lenn had discussed her investigations with the students and invited the research coordinator with whom she was collaborating to help her explore the classroom issues further (RC = Research Coordinator; S = Student).

> RC: What about ... were you worried at all about coming to the class?
> S1: I was at first.
> RC: 'Cause of the idea of you just don't know what to expect. How did you feel about the CES sending you here?
> S1: There wasn't any choice.
> S3: They didn't send me.
> S2: I was sort of half and half. They just said to me ... I keep saying I'm just like back to school ...
> RC: So how long is the course for?
> S2: Too long?
> S1: That's the first words I said.
> RC: What would you rather be doing right now?
> S2: Right now? Put the car back. Get it done faster.
> RC: Do it as soon as you get out.
> S2: Yeah ... getting there.
> RC: So is there any possible ... given that they ... as you don't really want to be here, is there anything you can, that you can get out of it? Is there any sort of way you can kind of turn it so that you ... How can it help you?
> S1: Well you see I signed an agreement to do the course.

RC: Did you all do that?

S3: When I went, I didn't get asked to come here. I asked 'Could I come to this course?' And they said yeah and they fixed everything up and called me for an interview. And I started on the Wednesday, didn't I?

RC: OK. So you got … ahh … so this is just the start of the third week and there is [*sic*] twelve and a half weeks to go. So what do you really want to get out of it? For you I know it won't be the same. Is there something …

S3: Yeah, well at the moment I just want to learn to read a bit better. And then when I learn to read a bit better, when I come home with my work and that, I would like to work in a shop. You know on the cashier.

RC: Mmm. So you need reading and some numeracy. How about the rest? How about you?

S4: Yeah I wanted to do this as well.

RC: So you're aspiring. You're not fighting. So what do you want to get out of it, S4?

S4: I'd like to work with animals but you've got to have real good skills but …

RC: So that's a long term goal, but you still … take it step by step … or is it mainly reading, or writing and maths?

S4: Just all of them.

RC: What about you?

S1: You didn't come voluntarily, did you, S5?

S5: No, no. But I reckon it's good for me anyway.

Drawing on interview data such as this, Lenn was able to gain a greater understanding of the range of perceptions and attitudes underpinning individual student responses and approaches to the tasks they were being asked to undertake in class. She began to use explicit discussions about the students' feelings and opinions as a regular aspect of classroom interaction and these 'non-language' learning factors were increasingly integrated into the teaching strategies she developed, such as voluntary learning contracts and out-of-class excursions and activities which called on the students to make practical use of their newly developed literacy and numeracy skills. The teacher therefore used the interviews as a way of motivating and informing the planning of tasks undertaken both in and outside the classroom. At the end of the course she reported that:

> After that brief period of settling in, each student became actively involved in class tasks. Many struggled with their reading, the majority had difficulty with the writing tasks but most of them seemed to enjoy rediscovering the world of numeracy. They were even keen to take home work for the night. It was an exciting time; there was something new for each one to learn (or re-learn).

> (de Leon 1997: 110)

In a very different vein, reflecting situation (c) above, with a class of beginner learners with limited skills in English literacy enrolled in a competency-based course, Margaret Carew used unstructured interviews as part of the data she collected to track in more detail the progress of two learners, Ricarda and Abdullah. Margaret first profiled her two students using data from student records as well as information she gained in discussion with them. (Adapted from Carew 1995: 12.)

Name:	Ricarda
Country of origin:	Philippines
Age:	32
Arrival date:	September 1993
Occupation:	Assistant in a bakery shop
Years of education:	5
Script:	Roman

Previous English learning
None

Present and recent life experiences
'Mail-order bride' who lives with her husband, a naturalised Australian of British origin who is 25 years her senior. No members of her family live here and her husband does not speak her language. She has complained that her husband is abusive and has a 'girlfriend'.

Name:	Abdullah
Country of origin:	Afghanistan
Age:	55
Arrival date:	October 1992
Occupation:	Professional soldier – high ranking officer
Years of education:	17
Script:	Farsi

Previous English learning
Learned English at secondary school, two hours a week for a year. Maintains this entailed mainly learning the alphabet, which he said he had completely forgotten by the time he arrived here.

Present and recent life experiences
Has suffered severe recent trauma, both in his flight from Afghanistan to India with his family and in his life there as a refugee awaiting resettlement in Australia. He lives here with his wife and children and also has one sister and her family here.

At the end of the course, Margaret conducted interviews to investigate further the learners' experiences of their course and the roles they saw themselves playing in their learning. Margaret comments on the interviews:

> The questions I asked were very simple given their level of English. I wanted their feelings about the course as a whole, their perceptions of what competencies were difficult for them, and their responses to the assessment process.

> (Carew 1995: 115)

Margaret recorded and transcribed her interview with each of the students. This is the transcription of the interview with Ricarda:

M: Are you happy with this English course?

R: Yes, I'm happy for English because just you know I'm learning English.

M: Any particular reason ... is anything specially good or helpful?

R: Yeh ... it help for me ... help for me for speak and for writing. I'm very happy this one.

M: What competencies are hardest for you?

R: Um, for writing, for spelling, I can't ... and a little bit for reading because just er ... if you just read me and I read er too difficult and I can't. Must just I must do easy ... slowly. I can't just very fast like that ... yeh, that's my problem.

M: Is the reading in class sometimes too fast for you?

R: No easy ... and I'm really happy this ... class because you know before I just start I can't understand ... anything. I can't but now just um ... a little bit ... before I don't know for reading or for writing, for spelling. No, I don't know how before I'm start this one this year – and now I'm just a little bit for writing, for spelling a little bit only ... but before no, I don't know.

M: What is specially difficult about writing?

R: Um ... long words and spelling.

M: Anything else?

(At this point Ricarda talked a bit about her problems in writing in her own language. She said she can write a little bit in Warai, her mother tongue, but not in Tagalog. We discussed this and then I repeated my question about her problems in writing English.)

R: Just, um, writing for what the next ... next ... next ... like that – just my problem for me straightaway like that.

M: Putting your ideas in writing – is that a problem?

R: I can't – just a problem.

M: Do you like to do assessment tasks – tests – for the competencies?

R: Just um, if if just um I'm hurry – my teacher said that ...

example you just um hurry on like that ... just you only give me time how many minutes like that – I'm going quickly and then just I can't because I don't know ...

M: You don't like the tasks – tests – because there isn't enough time?

R: I like the tests – I like that but just, um, I don't like the ... quickly.

M: You need more time?

R: Yeh.

M: Do you like to know if you are having an assessment?

(Explained this further and gave her an example of a task they had done without knowing it was an assessment.)

R: Yeah, I like if I don't know.

M: Why?

R: Because just um, thinking ... I'm thinking ... slowly ... feel just um you tell me and just test like that – the day like that ... I'm very I'm thinking and then I'm just – no I just forgot it.

M: Do you get worried?

R: Yep.

M: So it's better if you don't know?

R: Yep.

(Carew 1995: 120)

The interview with Abdullah yielded less information as his English was more limited. Even though he had agreed to be recorded, he was also nervous about speaking on tape.

M: Are you happy with this English course?

A: Yes ... I'm er English course ... yeh, I'm go when I'm go ... very sad ... sad when I go.

M: How does it help you?

A: (inaudible)

M: What competencies are hardest for you?

A: Hardest is er spelling, very difficult. Writing, yes. Speaking is problem, difficult. Writing not bad, spelling ... reading not bad, good, spelling problem. Is, er, my age, 55, very problem the age.

M: Do you like to do assessment tasks – tests?

A: Yes – yes I like ...

M: Why do you like to do tests?

A: I think tests help me – tests – English ... reading, writing ... I like tests.

M: Do you like to know if you're having an assessment?

(He didn't understand the question and said so. I tried to explain, but he didn't really understand, merely repeating his assertion that he liked doing tests.)

> A: Good test for me good tests. Tests help my English, reading,
> writing, speaking.
> M: You like assessment?
> A: Yes, for me help my English.

(page 121)

Although Margaret felt that the students' limited knowledge of English prevented them from fully indicating their opinions on the competency-based nature of the course, she felt reasonably confident from their responses that the students understood what competencies were. At the beginning of the course, she had expected Ricarda to make much faster progress, as she had already achieved some of the competencies in a previous course and her spoken proficiency in English was greater. However, over the weeks before the interview, Margaret had observed that despite Abdullah's limited speaking ability, his reading and writing skills improved rapidly in contrast to Ricarda, who made very little progress. Of interest to Margaret from the interview data was the fact that the students' perceptions appeared to coincide with her own observations of their progress:

> Ricarda felt reading and writing were especially difficult for her,
> whereas Abdullah said that 'writing not bad ... reading not bad,
> good', though spelling he said was 'very difficult'.

(Carew 1995: 115)

The interview data added to Margaret's analysis of the learning strategies employed by these two students. Ricarda lacked formal learning skills and strategies and what strategies she did employ were related to the needs of her personal circumstances, to speak to and understand others quickly. Abdullah, on the other hand, could call on strategies he used for literacy in his first language and had employed them to make more effective progress in literacy development. Margaret felt that she had gained insights into the nature of the differences among learners' various skills, the areas of learning with which they had difficulty and what factors in their background and current circumstances influenced their achievement of the competencies in the course. She noted that:

> The conclusions I drew from my study of the two learners
> applied to the whole class. The requirements of the case studies
> meant that I had to understand the learners' problems thoroughly
> ... What I learned applied to most of the other learners ... There
> is perhaps a tendency for teachers to regard all students with
> literacy difficulties as being the same and likely to need the same
> remedies for their problems. I discovered that this need not be
> the case.

(page 117)

5.2.3 Classroom discussions

For many teachers, classroom discussions are a viable alternative to setting up more formal interview situations. I suggested previously that it is valuable whenever possible to integrate data collection into regular classroom activities. As the interview data I have just presented imply, the more unstructured forms of interviews lend themselves well to being adapted to many types of ongoing classroom discussions. Michael Carroll, the teacher involved in situation (h) from the examples above, describes how he and other teachers with whom he worked collaboratively were able to incorporate regular discussions into classroom activities as part of both their programme goals and their investigations:

> An important element of the course   was aimed at building independent learning strategies. In order to do this and collect part of the data for our research, the students were involved in regular discussions, both in and out of the classroom, about the usefulness of various activities and situations for language learning. Their responses to these discussions were then documented. In addition I carried out a feedback session with the students after each competency assessment which, although focusing mainly on the text used for the assessment, also included some discussion of the assessment task. Again I documented the students' responses.
>
> (Carroll 1995: 97)

Other teachers who have undertaken action research have reported that this kind of integrated interviewing technique not only provides systematic data as the basis for reflection, evaluation and further diagnosis of the research issues, but also contributes to a more open and positive classroom environment, where the factors which may be central to the success of the teaching–learning process can be discussed explicitly with learners.

Sue Whitham, a teacher of post-beginner learners in a 15 week literacy and numeracy class, found 'guided discussions' an appropriate and valuable way to investigate her learners' perceptions of their learning and their classroom participation. She was also concerned about improving the classroom dynamics within the learner group to encourage them to interact more. She discusses why she chose this method of collecting data:

> Written questionnaires were beyond the reading ability of the class members. Individual interviews would have been revealing, but since the students were interested in my involvement in the project, it seemed a good idea to include them in the class discussions and

> provide the sort of group dynamics needed to gain more interesting
> and useful information.

(Whitham 1997: 33)

While she was initially nervous about asking her students their
opinions, Sue discovered that they responded enthusiastically and therefore she extended this method to become a regular part of her teaching
programme. She continues:

> During the last half hour of some class sessions we discussed how
> the students felt about the class, their participation in it, their
> fellow students, and their feelings about having students of various
> levels and language and literacy needs in the same class ...
>
> The students participated readily in the discussions ... The students
> remarked that they liked being asked about their class. It helped
> them to think it was their class, not just the teacher's or the
> institution's.

(page 34)

The discussion ranged over key questions about learning that became
of increasing interest to both Sue and her learners:

> The students were asked what they thought about being in a
> class with people of varying levels. They were asked about their
> feelings at the beginning of the class compared to now, and
> their expectations of the class. They were asked how they
> felt:
>
> - when they got things wrong
> - when they finished their work quickly
> - when they couldn't understand
> - when something was really easy
> - when someone else asked them for help
> - when there was no-one to ask for help
> - about being in a diverse class.

(page 34)

There were several positive outcomes from these discussions. Sue
believed that they reduced the load on her as the teacher, because the
students shared in the discussions and became more prepared to use
themselves, as well as resources recommended by other students, such
as dictionaries and calculators, as learning aids. Having gained more
confidence that a 'hands-off' teaching approach could be positive, Sue
relaxed and allowed her students to take more charge of their learning.
She felt that she had gained insights into how she could introduce a
more cooperative model of interaction into her classroom. She
concludes:

To ask your students what they think of the class may be a risky thing to do. It can threaten the teacher's own self esteem ... The discussions actually helped to unify the group and to help the students to work cooperatively. Saying out loud, rather than leaving unspoken, that they liked to work together, made them want to work together more. When one of the students said that he liked to work things out slowly, everyone agreed. When one said that she had trouble with numeracy, another offered to help her.

(page 36)

5.3 Surveys and questionnaires

Surveys and questionnaires offer an alternative form of data collection to interviews. Unlike interviews, they involve predetermined questions presented in written form and thus they also assume adequate literacy skills on the part of those surveyed. This is a point which language teacher researchers will need to consider carefully when using questionnaires with second or foreign language learners, as some learners may not have sufficient reading skills in the second language.

Questionnaires have the advantage of being easier and less time-consuming to administer than interviews, and the responses of larger numbers of informants can be gathered. The informants can also usually respond more rapidly to the questions and, as the responses are supplied in written form, the researcher does not need to further record them with supplementary techniques such as recordings or notes. On the other hand, surveys and questionnaires require more preparation time than interviews as the researcher needs to be confident that the questions can be interpreted independently as well as easily and unambiguously. Also, questionnaires do not cater as well for the more in-depth or unexpected responses that may be obtainable from interviews.

When using surveys and questionnaires, an important consideration is the construction of the questions or response items. Care needs to be taken to make the questions clear and to ensure that the way they are constructed will lead to the kinds of information being sought. It is often beneficial to pilot the questions first by trialing them with colleagues or a small number of students, so that any ambiguities or misunderstandings can be identified beforehand. The main things to take into account in constructing questionnaires for second language learners are: the language level of the students, the brevity and clarity of the questions, and the extent to which learners have the knowledge required to answer the questions. It is also beneficial to keep questionnaires relatively short and uncluttered so that respondents are not overwhelmed with a large and daunting document. Many of these issues are covered by Munn and Drever (1990) in a useful and accessible guide to constructing and using questionnaires in small-scale research.

Three types of response items are generally used in questionnaires: closed items, scale items and open-ended items. Closed items are those where informants are asked to select from fixed alternatives. The most common require a *yes/no* or *agree/disagree* response, although in some cases a third alternative such as *don't know* or *undecided* is added.

The following example of a closed item survey is drawn from the research of Anne Fowler (1997), a teacher who wanted to investigate whether using learning plans helped her intermediate learners to develop more independent learning strategies. Anne described a learning plan as a 'contract with themselves' developed by the students to find ways of practising English outside the classroom. One of her approaches to promoting the learning plan was the preparation of self-study tapes which the students could use at home to practise the oral language they had learned in class. The questionnaire was administered at the end of the course to those students who had chosen to use the tape.

These statements are about the individual homework tapes. Put an X in the column that shows your response. If you didn't use a tape, just answer question 1.

		YES	NO
1	I chose to use an individual homework tape this term.		
2	I used the tape in a regular way (e.g. daily/weekly).		
3	I used the tape for listening practice.		
4	I used the tape for speaking practice.		
5	I think it was a helpful way of learning.		
6	I would use this way of learning again.		

The second kind of response items used in questionnaires and surveys are scale items. These are alternative responses placed on a cline representing degrees of agreement or disagreement. Informants are requested to select their responses from amongst a set of fixed alternatives. There is no restriction to the number of alternatives that researchers can include, but it is probably preferable in learner surveys to restrict the possibilities to no more than three or four in order to avoid confusion. A further example from Anne Fowler's research will serve to illustrate this category.

These statements are about your independent learning plans. Do you agree with these statements? Put an X in the column that shows your response.

	A LOT	A LITTLE	NOT AT ALL
1 I kept my 'contract' with myself.			
2 I think using my individual learning plan has helped me practise a new skill.			
3 I can find ways to continue learning outside the classroom.			
4 I have the commitment to continue learning outside the classroom.			
5 I liked setting my own goals.			

Other forms of scale item responses are ranked responses or checklist responses. Ranked responses ask informants to rank preferences from a number of fixed options. A rank order giving a picture of overall preferences can then be obtained by calculating the rank given to each response. An example of a ranked item question used in an action research project is shown below.

How do you prefer to learn? Please number the following in the order you prefer. (1 = the best; 5 = the worst)

- Alone _____
- In pairs _____
- In small groups of 3–4 people _____
- In large groups of 6–8 people _____
- As part of a whole class _____

Third, open-ended items can be utilised in questionnaires and surveys. These equate with the flexible and open questions that are used in unstructured interviewing and they are constructed so as to provide a minimal reference point for the informants' responses. The aim of these types of items is to explore the informants' own perceptions, beliefs or opinions and to provide opportunities for unforeseen responses or for those which are richer and more detailed than responses obtainable through closed questioning. A third example, again from Anne Fowler's research, illustrates this type of response item. Anne's questionnaire demonstrates how open-ended items can be combined with those that require a more fixed response, as in question 1.

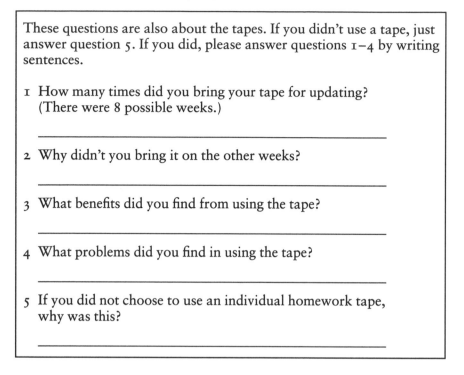

These questions are also about the tapes. If you didn't use a tape, just answer question 5. If you did, please answer questions 1–4 by writing sentences.

1 How many times did you bring your tape for updating? (There were 8 possible weeks.)

_____

2 Why didn't you bring it on the other weeks?

_____

3 What benefits did you find from using the tape?

_____

4 What problems did you find in using the tape?

_____

5 If you did not choose to use an individual homework tape, why was this?

_____

Learner surveys are frequently employed as tasks for communicative language teaching and form part of the repertoire of classroom activities used by many language teachers. Questionnaires are therefore a productive way to integrate the collection of action research data into regular classroom activities. Alison McPhail recounts how she used questionnaires as a way of not only getting systematic data for her own action research but also of involving her learners in processes of course evaluation:

> To gather data for my research, I decided to survey the students regularly over the course, as a way of getting systematic feedback from them. As the students were fairly advanced learners, I devised written questionnaires, which I administered for different purposes at different stages of the course ...
>
> Week Two
> ... A questionnaire was administered to find out the students' previous experience of different types of assessment and their preferences ...
>
> A second questionnaire was given out for evaluation of the week's work. The aim of this exercise was to encourage the students to monitor the usefulness of class activities, their own learning in and out of the classroom and the reasons for both of these. They were

therefore asked to comment on work done both with my co-teacher and myself.

(McPhail 1995: 89)

Survey and questionnaire techniques can be usefully combined with interviews in action research. The researcher can, for example, choose to follow up issues raised in interviews by surveying a larger number of informants or other types of informants to complement the interview data. Alternatively, action researchers may wish to conduct surveys as a way of focusing their preliminary ideas and then follow up the initial results of these enquiries with more in-depth interviews.

5.3.1 Student diaries and journals

An alternative, but related, form of gaining introspected written data is to use student journals or feedback responses. Journal writing has for many teachers become a popular task within communicative teaching approaches. When it is oriented towards issues the teacher wishes to investigate, it can provide valuable insights into classroom interactions and the students' responses to their learning experiences. It can also act in tandem with the teacher's own observations or journal-writing as an interesting way of making comparisons of perceptions on the topic. Student journals can usefully pinpoint areas of difficulty in learning, in both a general and an individual sense, as well as provide feedback on classroom tasks, learning processes and strategies, or preferences for classroom groupings.

When introducing this technique for research purposes, many teachers find that sharing information about their investigations with their students can increase student motivation to write a journal. In an action research investigation designed to address levels of anxiety in language learning, Mark Brophy (1995), a teacher working on a Small Business course in an Australian Technical College, decided to involve two of his second language learners, Helena and Mario, as research participants. He found that 'Not only did they agree, but they seemed flattered and eager to participate. It was my belief that Helena's participation might even have helped strengthen her self-concept. As Helena was the main focus of the research, she regarded her input as important and worthwhile' (pages 49–50). Mark's students used feedback response sheets on a regular basis, 'like a type of weekly short journal':

Week Two

Helena: The cours is excellent. I get a lot of information what open my mind. The thing that my english is not excellent so I need more time for analise a lot of things plus maby I am a slow thinker and shuy to ask a questions. The group discuss I find very useful for me.

Mario: The course is informative, educational and detailed. it provide confidence to a person who is planning to go to a small business. it is becoming clear to me that I belong to this group especially when the course let us fill some forms to know who we are ... I am still craving on business and reckoned I am on the right track ...

Week Three

Helena: The course is running excellent. In every day I feel more confident. All the information from this cours will be very, very useful in the future. Also I would like to tell fro Peter and Mark thank you very much for undertanding my English problem.

Mario: In my everyday attendance, I noticed that what I got from the class cannot be found elsewhere. There are books to read but the discussions are very relevant and actual. What an experience!

Week Four

Helena: This cours is realy excellent for me. I learn a lot of things every day. I started to thinking more logiclly, and an important I think – they will be very usefull for me in the future. I feel more confident to asked the questions.

Mario: Everything comes in order and clearer. Although for me and my business idea, I get confused. However, with the guidelines and forms to fill up I was able to erase all those confusion. In my everyday attendance, I notices that what I got from the class cannot be found elsewhere. There are books to read but the discussions are very relevant and actual. What an experience!!!

Week Five

Helena: No comments submitted.

Mario: It was all a mess for me before I took this course. Now it's getting in order and the vision becomes clearer and I would expect a bright future in business. This course is helpful. Although we need more time to apply the principles in actual scene. More time for research and time in the computer.

These responses were combined with other techniques, including interview data, to build up case studies which provided a picture of the factors affecting the students' anxiety levels. Student journal-writing in language classrooms will clearly need to take into account the students' second language literacy skills, and obtaining data in this way will be more difficult in classes where learners are at beginning stages. One way to assist beginning students is to provide a framework for journal-writing, as Vivienne Campbell (1995: 125–6) describes in her account of her investigation of her 'post-beginner' students' perceptions of their learning. Like Mark, Vivienne involved her learners as participants in the research:

> In the first week of the project, I discussed my research with the students, explained the purposes for it and asked them for their involvement. I also handed out simplified written summaries of the project for their information so that they could ask me for further explanations of it if they needed to ... The final activity of the first week was to introduce students to the concept of the journal which was to be written in about fifteen minutes, set aside at the end of each day to evaluate the day's lessons. In the journal, I asked them to express their feelings about learning, what they thought about it and what they had learned. I decided to use this method of data collection as a way of helping them to monitor their learning ... For example, Christian's entries provide some of his reflections on what he had learned and on his progress:
>
> 14/4/94
> I feel happy to look new teacher. I think English is more easy. I learn new verbs in the past tense. Example: teare – tore.
>
> 18/4/94
> I feel unhappy because Thuan didn't say, good morning Christian, How are you? I think she was a bad weekend. I learnt contraction.
>
> 19/4/94
> I feel happy because it was a day very interesting. I think I progress every day. I learnt to apply an accident form.
>
> 21/4/94
> I feel very well because I was encouraged. I think to teach soon if possible. I learnt to apply an accident form but it was a little bit difficult.
>
> 2/5/94
> I feel happy because I learnt some new words about money ... and it is important because you can apply for yourself. I learnt to answer for an interview.

Although these responses are limited and follow closely the structured framework supplied by Vivienne, the student produces a number of comments which provide feedback that the teacher can use – on his relationships with other students in class; on his view of his overall progress; on his awareness of the grammatical structures he has learned; on his beliefs about how his language skills can be applied outside the classroom; on his responses to classroom tasks and activities, and on the degree to which he has developed some metalinguistic knowledge.

5.4 Life and career histories

Second language teachers are often provided by their institutions with personal records or interview profiles of their students that include both subjective and objective information collected by previous teachers, student counsellors, year coordinators or directors of studies, or by interview and class placement staff. The life/career history extends and deepens this information by enabling us to study and interpret experiences told from the perspective of the individuals concerned. This is essentially a qualitative method that can be usefully employed in building up a more detailed picture of personal career or life experience factors that may be having an impact on learning. Histories may need to be developed gradually over a period of time as they rely on a high degree of cooperation, trust and sharing between the researcher and the subject of the research.

Learner histories can be built up through a number of conversational techniques, such as interviews, discussions and casual conversations with students, or through written accounts such as personal descriptions and recounts of personal life events. Histories can be documented through audio recordings and narrative accounts and added to over a period of time as new information comes to hand. McKernan (1996) points out that any other sources that illuminate the subject of the investigation, such as documents and records, can also be included The researcher's role is to record the subject's version of his or her own story as he or she defines it. The life history is a technique that relies on capturing learner stories in order to explain and understand in greater depth their actions and responses in the classroom. Yow (1994) and Connelly and Clandinin (1988, 1990) are useful resources on oral history and narrative techniques. Hitchcock and Hughes (1995) also discuss the use of the life history interview to develop biographies. Their discussion includes a useful checklist of 'do's and don'ts' (after Humphries 1984: 19–22) which contains good practical advice for successful life history interviewing, or indeed for conducting other kinds of interviews:

- Do make an interview checklist (containing essential biographical and career details).
- Do be friendly and reassuring.
- Do be clear.
- Do show interest.

- Do use questionnaires flexibly and imaginatively.
- Don't talk too much.
- Don't interrupt.
- Don't impose your views.
- Don't contradict or argue.
- Don't rush away as soon as the interview is over.

(Hitchcock and Hughes 1995: 221)

Marie Muldoon's research (Muldoon 1997) provides an example of how life/career histories can be used to illuminate the impact of affective and psychological factors on second language learning processes. Over the period of a 15-week course aimed at literacy and numeracy tuition for unemployed adults, Marie compiled data from biographical student records, as well as from casual conversations, interviews and observations of her students. Her intention was to gain a clearer picture of the 'very stressful physical and emotional problems' she believed were affecting most of her students' ability to learn and to interact positively in class. While gaining an overview of the whole class was important to her, she was particularly interested in the progress of five of her students, whom she felt mediated the interactions of the whole class. Three of the students, Mahoud, Hans and Sheena, she saw as 'linchpins' in the class structure, either because of the positive learning attitudes they inspired, their ability to motivate and work with others or because of their ability to model learning strategies for other students. Here is the profile of Mahoud summarised at the end of her observations. It contains narrative on Mahoud's history as well as Marie's responses to what she learned about this student:

> Mahoud from Lebanon was 44 and had been in Australia for 25 years ... He had worked for 22 years as the foreman of a carpet manufacturing firm. When the firm went bankrupt during the recession, Mahoud was retrenched [made unemployed] without redundancy payment. He was angry about what had happened and not optimistic about his future:
>
>> The class is helping me for sure but I don't believe if I come in here I'm going to find a job after because the way thing is going for me to get writing proper English I'm gonna be 50 before I finish this. If nobody wants me at 45, how are they gonna take me at 50?
>
> Mahoud had enjoyed his work and the status and responsibility of his position as a foreman, and despite his unfortunate position, he was very positive in his attitude to the course. He had four school-age children – three boys and a girl – and they kept him busy. As he said:
>
>> For me learning and keeping everything in my mind, I'd have

> to be single, I don't have a wife and kids, I don't have to have
> finance problems. I put everything in my mind here and then I
> go home. She wants something, he wants something, the other
> one wants something. That in trouble at school, that in trouble
> in the street. See, everything interrupts you.

> The class thought that the 'literacy-numeracy' label denigrated the
> skills with which they had survived some 20 years in Australia. I
> responded by focusing on my role as a teacher helping them to
> develop skills that would be useful to their future life. I always
> referred to the course as 'English Expression and Maths'. Mahoud
> seemed to respond to this approach and his frustrations in class
> were to do with his inability to make progress as quickly as he
> wished. He said, at the end of the course, that a part of his brain
> that had been frozen had thawed and he hoped that he wouldn't be
> left so long without a course that it would freeze up again.
> Mahoud was one of the strengths in my class, both emotionally
> and intellectually, and became one of the three linchpins in the
> group.

> (Muldoon 1997: 19–20)

Life/career histories can also be used by teacher researchers individually or with other colleagues to delve into the personal meanings they attach to their own classroom behaviours and actions. Such accounts can trace teachers' personal educational and career histories as well as the values and beliefs they attach to their teaching practices and can be used as a way of illuminating critically how personal theories of teaching and learning impact on the classroom. They can reveal how we bring our own educational experiences to the role models we follow as teachers. Dominice (1990) provides further information on the use of educational biographies.

Allan (1994) describes the experiences of a group of adult Basic Education teachers of mathematics with whom she worked in a cooperative discussion group over a period of eight sessions. During the sessions the group used a number of reflective techniques to research relationships between theory and practice in their teaching. These included 'educational biographies' to explore how their personal educational histories affected the meanings they constructed about mathematics teaching. Before the workshop, participants spent time recalling and writing down their educational experiences. They then took turns in telling their stories to the group and recorded them for future reference. Between workshops, each participant constructed a written account of his or her own story to share with other members of the group and to contribute to a composite picture of influences on their teaching. Samples included:

My maths learning in a city environment seemed generally a non-event. It was a subject that was taught in a specific way – Chalk and Talk – you followed the rules and got the right answers. I generally got the right answers and could remember the rules, so I succeeded. However, my understanding of maths is not very good with regards to the hows and whys. Consequently when I began teaching I was keen to develop understanding and to make maths as interesting as I could. I wanted to develop concepts and language. At times I wonder if it's enough, do I need a deeper understanding of maths? Is my lack of knowledge a problem?

(Allan 1994: 38)

I found my maths education an extremely frustrating experience because my enthusiasm, my questioning, were never addressed, never acknowledged. And these two qualities are what precisely – I realise – I am facing now; trying to draw out the enthusiasm and the inquisitiveness of my students – actually really demanding and expecting that they ought to be questioning and to be enthusiastic about the wonder of it all. Perhaps I am hoping to address these personal qualities of my own, through my students?

(page 38)

Based on their analysis of their biographies, the group affirmed that the way they were taught maths was a recurring theme in their discussions. This led to a hypothesis, *Our own maths learning influences our teaching*, which they used further to bring to consciousness the complexity of maths experiences that had an impact on their practice. These included their memories of strict or intimidating maths teachers, their experiences as beginner teachers and of mathematics outside the classroom and their reactions to their children's experiences of maths learning. In order to focus these analyses, the group used a series of probe questions:

- Do common themes emerge from the biographies?
- What were the factors in the positive educational experiences of the group?
- What were the factors in the negative educational experiences of the group?
- What factors are important to each of you for learning?
- How has your experience as a learner affected you as a teacher?
- What impact does the educational biography have on you as a teacher?
- What changes would you make to your role as a teacher?

(page 40)

The sessions rekindled the group's interest in learning more about maths, for example the history of mathematics. One participant, commenting on the experience of analysing educational histories, remarked:

It made me realise why I do things in the classroom. I knew I was doing these things. I didn't know why. Nothing has much meaning to me unless I know why.

(page 37)

5.5 Documents

Documents are a readily accessible source of data in action research as many already exist in the institutional system. Documents accumulated during the course of an enquiry can illuminate numerous aspects of practice. There is a wide range of documents that could be pertinent to the research focus, including student portfolios of written work, student records and profiles, lesson plans, classroom materials, letters, class memos and newsletters, and previous test or examination papers. Examining documents can help researchers to complement other observations by building a richer profile of the classroom or institutional context for the research. They can also give insights into how theoretical and practical values connect and the degree of 'fit' between organisational and curricular concerns. The 'raw data' from the primary sources of the documents available in the research context allow the researcher to create a 'secondary' level of interpretation of what these documents mean. Two examples are presented to illustrate how this technique can be used in action research. They are examples that can easily be encompassed within routine communicative classroom activities.

5.5.1 Student texts

A source of documents readily available to all language teachers is students' written texts. Student writing lends itself very easily to analyses which track development linked to deliberate interventions made through action research. Collecting samples of texts over a period of time enables teachers to assess the progress which students make as well as to diagnose areas for further action in classroom research. Portfolios of texts related to similar genres can be collected at regular intervals and strategies for changes in teaching approaches can be identified. Further collections of texts can then be made to analyse to what extent the changes that have been implemented are working. Researchers can design different ways to collect student texts, for example work can be collected from selected individuals or groups of learners, or samples can be gathered covering a particular set of topics, content or subject areas or text types.

An example of how analysing collections of student texts can proceed hand-in-hand with the deliberate use of a teaching intervention is provided by the research of Pieter Koster (1996). Pieter, a teacher of intermediate adult students, decided to monitor developments in students' written texts while at the same time pursuing an interest in functional grammar (Halliday 1985) which he had developed during his Master's studies. Pieter explains:

> I began to wonder if language teaching could benefit from an orientation to 'language as exchange', or what Halliday presents as the interpersonal dimension of grammar. Such an approach would focus on the clause as an 'interactive event, involving speaker or writer and audience' (Halliday 1985: 68) ...
>
> Looking at clauses from the perspective of language as exchange I wanted to focus attention on the next process in the communication cycle, that is how the message is received by the reader. I thought that focussing on the interpersonal role of the clause might equip the student with a more effective means of self-correcting their writing.
>
> (Koster 1996: 28)

Pieter's research involved working with a small group of five more advanced students, drawn from a larger class, to trial one aspect of functional grammar in the development of their writing.

> I looked through samples of the students' writing and selected five students for a withdrawal class. The basis of this selection was any evidence of confusion which might be addressed by focussing attention on Mood, that is the subject and finite of a clause.
>
> (page 29)

Having gained the students' agreement for the research, Pieter provided an hour's grammar instruction twice a week on the Mood component of sentences. At the end of the research he compared the texts produced with those collected at the beginning of the research. The first text for student C1 (segmented into clauses) and Pieter's comments on it follow.

> (1) *There are four seasons in a year in Shanghai.* (2) *While Australia in summer season Shanghai in winter.* (3a) *In summer, Shanghai is very hot and* (3b) *the temperature up to 38 degrees Centigrade.* (4) *In winter the temperature down to −7 degrees Centigrade.* (5a) *the pollution of the city has increased and even* (5b) *can not breath fresh air and* (5c) *drink fresh water because* (5d) *there are many factories there.*
>
> Comment: Messages (2) (3b) and (4) lack finites, while messages (5b) and (5c) lack subjects.
>
> (page 29)

Pieter introduced a teaching sequence designed to promote the development of the students' language structure in the area he had chosen. Exercises included:

1 Tag questions and contradictions (*he loves her, doesn't he – no, he doesn't*).
2 Message expansions (*he loves the woman in the blue dress*) and clause expansions (*he loves the woman in the blue dress, because she loves him*).

In response to these exercises, student C1 produced the following:

> You stole it; you stole it yesterday; you stole it in Burwood yesterday; you stole the book from Burwood library yesterday; you stole the books from Burwood library more than one time since 1995; you stole the book from Burwood library yesterday because you short money to buy it, didn't you?

3 Mood analysis of a simple graded reader. Students identified each clause and contradicted it.

The reader text (with clause boundaries marked with /) was:

> /Last weekend Jane had a good weekend./First, on Friday night, she stayed at home and watched TV./Then, on Saturday morning, she went shopping/ and bought a wedding present./ After that, in the afternoon, she went to a wedding/ and came home very late./ On Sunday morning she cleaned the house/ and then in the afternoon she visited her family./Finally in the evening she did a jigsaw puzzle with her sister./ Jane had a good weekend/but she was very tired.

4 Analysis of three more texts, an excerpt from a graded reader, a short newspaper item and an informal radio news item transcript.
5 Analysis by students of their own texts.
6 Analysis of a Monty Python video, *The Argument Room*, which contained many contradicted propositions. The students watched the video and analysed a transcript.

At the end of the eight-week research period, Pieter asked his students to do a writing exercise.

> They had about twenty minutes to write four brief texts: a. recount; b. description; c. request; d. thank you letter. The texts were written in response to the following tasks:
>
> (a) How did you get to school today?
> (b) Describe the street you live in.
> (c) Order a new grammar book from the bookshop.
> (d) Write to a friend thanking them for a birthday present.

(page 32)

Student C1's responses to these tasks follow:

(a) *After lunch I took my bag to go to school. The school is located in Burwood area and is not very far from my home. Usually I drive the car to school. Today the traffic is very bad. So I spend a lot of time on the road. I have to wait the traffic light. Fortunately I was easy to find a car space to park my car.*

(b) *I live in F-street, Ashfield. This street is a small street but everyday pass a lot of cars. So it would be very hard if you want to cross the street. It is a very noise at night because so many cars passing the street. The most houses in this street are old style.*

(c) *I would like to buy an English grammar book in you shop. I need grammar book that is a lower level and learn it by myself. I'd like the exercise in the grammar book with the answer.*

(d) *I've received you birthday present already. I like the present very much. It's very interesting and very useful. I believe this present will give me a deep impression. Thank you so much for my present.*

(page 32)

Although some Mood errors (*I was easy to find a car space* and *I need a grammar book that is a lower level and learn it by myself*) still existed in the writing of student C1 and the others, Pieter concluded that a general improvement in the readability of the students' text was evident. He also observed that students were using their awareness of subject and finite structure to self-correct their work. C1 in particular was seen to insert finite verbs into the texts during the checking process. Although the research had been brief, student enthusiasm was high and this also motivated Pieter to continue to use a functional grammar approach in his teaching practice and to extend it to other aspects of written text analysis.

5.5.2 Letters

An interesting variation on the use of documents for data collection is to ask students to write letters, which can function similarly to questionnaire or journal data, but are a less formal or regular alternative. Like writing diaries or journals, writing letters invites introspection on the part of the respondent, but letters may be more manageable for many learners who may be more familiar with letter-writing than journal entry formats. Learners can be invited to write their opinions, views and responses on a variety of topics, depending on the focus of the research, and to a variety of audiences, including parents or other relatives, other students, their own or other teachers, programme administrators and course book or curriculum writers. Teacher researchers can also opt to respond to such letters, thus setting up more extended dialogues.

An interesting example of the use of letter-writing both as a data collection technique and an enjoyable communicative classroom activity is provided by Sue Shaw (1997). Working with her group of 23 newly arrived adult immigrant learners in Western Australia, Sue was concerned about how she could improve student interaction and group dynamics. Consulting the professional literature led her to *Classroom Dynamics* by Hadfield (1992), in which the author proposes the concept of focusing on 'whole groupness' as a basis for introducing affective and cognitive activities into the classroom. Making group processes more explicit to her learners became the central issue in Sue's research, through a dual focus on both language development and effective group dynamics. A number of methods were employed to gather data:

> As I proceeded to select activities, to plan their incorporation into my programme and to put them into practice in the classroom, I systematically monitored and documented the process and the consequences. In monitoring classroom interactions, I employed techniques of observing and making field notes, diary keeping and collecting students' work. The diary notes were reflections made immediately after the lesson. At times, I also had the support of colleagues to assist me in observing classroom interactions and to get feedback from students on their attitudes to particular activities.
>
> (Shaw 1997: 55)

In addition to collecting regular student feedback on her teaching approach and the activities she was using, Sue collected a summative evaluation of her course through the technique of 'the old lag's letter' (Hadfield 1992). As 'expert' learners, students were asked to write to 'novices' about to begin their learning in the following term's course. One student wrote:

> 27 June 1995
>
> I hope that you still feel well in this class. I attended this class last term and maybe I can help you with some advice.
>
> I first think what I can tell you. I found surprising a method of learning English. It's an outstanding method with many different and interesting activities. It's seems you play with language and not study hard. So you can learn English easy, step by step without an exertion.
>
> I enjoyed learning in this method, because when I started to be

tired of one activity we already started another. For this reason you will always be fresh and ready to learn.

Sometimes, I thought that it was too difficult for me. But this was for psychological reasons. Sometimes I lost my self confidence. I lost my patience. And it's one of the most important thing when you would like to learn a language.

Finally, I think you should have much patience. Learning language like learning to walk, You should walk step by step and you will sure succeed. Don't hurry! Don't lose your self confidence.

Good Luck!

All but one of Sue's students presented positive images of their learning experiences. Sue believed that the activity provided her and her students with a sense of learning progression, of 'handing over and moving on'. It enabled her to evaluate language progress as well as become more aware of what learning strategies her students had found effective. She was able to identify the affective areas that were important to her students and to share these perspectives with new students in her next course.

A further example of the use of letters as a tool in action research is provided by Patricia Bradley (1995). Her action research was conducted with a collaborative group of student peers and their lecturer in a tertiary level TESOL professional development course. Patricia saw her learners, also, as co-researchers. Her research was directed primarily at comprehending the needs of her advanced students as they participated in a further education certificate course, the Certificate of Cosmetology, a preparatory programme for the Associate Diploma of Health Sciences (Beauty Therapy). Her 22 students were mainly second language learners with a small number of native English speakers. The 'Open Letter' technique used to investigate her students' feelings towards their programme and towards her teaching is outlined by Patricia:

> The *Open Letter* strategy consists of asking students to write an anonymous response to a number of questions regarding a particular issue – in this case to do with their participation in the Cosmetology course. Initially I had planned to use just the one *Open Letter* but after implementing some changes and following through with modified teaching strategies, I decided that the changes and the students' reactions to both the changes and the planned teaching, would be more effectively monitored by the completion and analysis of the second *Open Letter*.

> (Bradley 1995: 61)

Having explained to her students the purpose of the letter as part of the research, Patricia provided on the whiteboard a schema for their response:

Open Letter – Communication Skills
Date: 24th October 1994   'no name'

- What did you expect?
- What could be different?
- What could be better?
- What worries (concerns) you?

I then checked that students understood each question by re-phrasing them in the form of concept questions without giving them examples related to the course (to try to minimise any influence on their own ideas). I explained that the letter could be anonymous, that they were only to focus on the Communications part of the course, that they were to keep their comments brief, to write as they felt, and not to discuss their letter with fellow students as they wrote ... each [student] was given a sheet of paper with the college letterhead, which I felt would reinforce the idea of writing a real letter to me.

(page 63)

The students' letters provided Patricia with the basis for analysing: changes that could be made immediately; changes that could be implemented during the course; changes that were outside the current curriculum and could not be implemented and changes that could be negotiated to provide useful materials for the students. These categories were discussed with the students, and changes in content, teaching strategies, classroom management, timetabling of subjects and assessment were trialed by Patricia in the next phase of her research. In order to monitor the effects of these changes, Patricia administered a second 'open letter' a month after the first, where students were asked the question, 'Were your expectations met?' Fourteen of the 19 students who wrote letters felt that their expectations had now been met. However, the more interesting outcome of the two letter-writing exercises was that Patricia felt she had uncovered some 'hidden agendas' issuing from mismatches between the *felt* needs of the students and the *perceived* needs of the course offered by the institution (see Berwick 1989). For her students, these agendas were related specifically to how the course could eventually enable them to gain professional recognition and employment and to establish and manage a successful business. Their participation in the course was also shaped by their concerns about earning money through part-time jobs while they completed the course. Patricia was able to recommend a number of strategies to her institution that could go some way towards addressing these concerns. She saw the 'open letter' technique as a fruitful and professionally informative way to probe students' needs more effectively, and her own perceptions were confirmed by her students' recommendations of the use of this technique by other course teachers.

5.6 Metaphor development

Metaphor development is less a data collection method than an introspective and reflective tool. I have included it here as a somewhat more innovative and less established technique for generating qualitative data, but one that may have potential in tapping the kinds of meanings practitioners create about their own professional actions, practices and personal theories. Block (1992: 52) describes metaphor development as:

> an approach which posits underlying metaphors and then combines them to construct cultural models construing and critiquing meanings which make up our professional community.

The reasoning behind this approach is that:

> if members of a community ... can make sense of the comments made by an individual, then the folk and cultural models underlying and motivating these comments must in some way be held across the culture.

(page 46)

Block suggests that the notion of metaphor can be usefully built into reflective self-monitoring or explorations of practical decision-making patterns.

A fundamental concept in the use of metaphor in action research is that people think and act according to certain commonly held and underlying metaphors, but that those that surface may not be the ones that are preferred. Allan (1994) proposes that the conscious use of metaphors can lead teachers to describe themselves and their teaching in unusual and imaginative ways. Metaphors can bring into play new sets of beliefs and attitudes that can be accompanied by changes in behaviour. The following steps, that can be undertaken by a collaborative group in developing metaphors, are adapted from Allan (based on Tobin 1990):

1 Before the group workshop, consider the following questions.
  (a) What do you do when you teach? (Choose a specific teaching context and answer: *I listen, negotiate, ask for feedback ...*)
  (b) What roles do you use when you teach? (Continuing from above: *Organiser, mediator, observer ...*)
  (c) What metaphors do you associate with these roles? (Continuing from above: *I see myself as a ...*)
2 At the workshop, discuss the metaphors until participants are satisfied with those they have constructed.
3 Discuss and reflect on responses and explore the following questions for the next workshop:

(d) Do these roles and metaphors represent what you do, what you want to do, or a mix of both?

(e) Do these roles and metaphors change when the context changes?

(f) What roles and metaphors do your students see in your teaching?

4 Report your reflections/findings from the above questions. Work in pairs or small groups to discuss the next set of questions:

(g) Are the beliefs associated with each of your roles and metaphors consistent with each other?

(h) Are you comfortable with your roles and metaphors or would you like to make changes? How would you like to change?

(i) How do your roles and metaphors link with the theoretical approaches in your teaching field? What are the consistencies/inconsistencies? What do you feel/think about this?

5 Use your metaphors as a guide to evaluate your teaching. Reflect on your metaphor as you teach. If there are inconsistencies you can make choices about changing your teaching or your metaphor. Share your experiences in future workshops.

In Allan's collaborative workshop group for Adult Basic Education teachers, metaphors enabled individuals to name aspects of their teaching in increasing detail and depth. Some metaphors revealed aspects of teaching that were acceptable representations of a teacher's personal theories of teaching that, having been named, could be extended further:

> The metaphor of a crossword-puzzle maker took a while to come up with. This was how I saw myself at the time. I didn't want to give students the answers. I could give them clues about how to get the solution, but I wanted them to come up with the answers ... The crossword-puzzle maker metaphor also recognised the fact that I as the teacher still had a responsibility to know my subject area. Then I looked at what I would like to be. This didn't require a total change of my metaphor but rather an extension. I wanted to make the puzzle more cryptic, so that students could take more responsibility and extend themselves into areas they may not have ventured. Eventually I would like to make them the puzzles.
>
> (Allan 1994: 29)

Other metaphors uncovered personas that the individual found displeasing, but could rationalise as a necessary, but temporary, state of affairs in a process of personal change.

> My metaphor for one particular class is being a parent. This does not reflect what I would like to do in my teaching, but meets the needs for a temporary time. As a parent I lead, I give direction, help to reassure them in personal situations and give advice if

asked. The role fits easily for me, already being a parent, but it has become a burden.

By naming this as a metaphor, I force myself to change tack so I won't continue in it. I see this as an awareness (a naming) of something that I may have just ignored. Because I don't want this metaphor, I have had to force a change in how I, or the students, perceive my teaching.

(page 30)

Yet other metaphors produced thought-provoking portrayals of differences between learner and teacher perceptions, which challenged the researcher's ideals and acted as a catalyst for rethinking.

Talked about my metaphor with my students. A lighthouse was mentioned. I'm there guiding, steady, shining, warning about the rocks and channels but only guiding. I think maybe that's a bit unflattering so I am not quite happy with it. I thought I had more interaction with them than that. It seems a bit stand-offish.

I feel like a staple gun in the trades [classes] – like a bandaid only quicker and more violent – okay, formula – bang, staple, okay, ratio – bang, okay, trig – bang. Rosie the Riveter – bang, bang, bang. But in other classes it's not that at all – there's time, there's enjoyment. But the lighthouse is interesting – a problem. Blink, blink, blink, remember this, what do you already know, what's the question saying, question, prompt, blink, blink.

(page 30)

Metaphors such as these focused the group's analyses of their teaching philosophies. Individuals could explore consistencies and discrepancies between theory and practice in ways that provided new directions for personal theory-building and practical teaching approaches. Developing metaphors also enabled the group to go on to identify institutional barriers that had an impact upon their classroom practices, such as syllabus constraints and timetabling arrangements.

A further use of metaphors is illustrated by Chris Pearson (1997), a teacher of intermediate adult ESL students in Victoria who had been, unwillingly, enrolled in a literacy class in line with government and institutional funding arrangements. A metaphor helped Chris to express his initial dilemmas about motivating and unifying his student group.

It was apparent from the outset that working with this group was going to pose problems that I had not encountered before. I often felt that I was driving a big bus down a particularly bumpy road with a group of passengers that did not seem to know what stop they wanted or why they had gotten on in the first place. As a consequence, passengers continually got off at the wrong stop or attempted to jump off while the bus was still moving. This meant

> we were constantly stopping to check for missing people and to
> encourage stragglers to get back on.
>
> (page 138)

Through a process of trial and error, Chris and the group eventually
evolved a 'stop, think, write, stop and think again' formula for writing
tasks. Although to Chris's mind this appeared 'very mechanical', it
produced writing outcomes for his students that provided them with an
effective learning structure and allowed them to gain results both
through group processes and individually. Chris extended his metaphor
as a way of evaluating what he believed had been achieved through the
research process.

> While the bus has become in part more oriented towards a
> common goal than it was at the onset of this particular journey,
> there will no doubt be more flat tyres and blown head gaskets to
> come.
>
> (page 141)

5.7 Summary

In this chapter and the last, I have presented a range of methods for
conducting action research. Aiming to provide a broad overview, I am
aware that these techniques have not been discussed in great detail; nor
do they include all available action research tools. However, each of
these methods presents starting points for practitioner research which, I
believe, can be feasibly incorporated into classroom practice, as illustrated by the accounts of teachers who have utilised them as part of
their own collaborative action research. My firm belief is that as far as
possible action research data collection techniques should be extensions
of, rather than burdensome additions to, teaching. I am in accord with
Anderson *et al.* (1994: 107) when they state that:

> Research techniques and approaches must always be tempered by
> practice and seen through a filter of one's own environment and
> needs. How you can improve your practice, what you can
> contribute to the field of knowledge about learning, curriculum,
> teaching, and running a school necessitates an adaptable research
> methodology. It is important for practitioner researchers to
> remember that, despite traditional qualitative techniques, 'The
> "sedentary wisdom" of long-established traditions offers
> legitimation rather than liberation; the biggest breakthroughs in
> scientific thinking have often required a break with investigative
> traditions rather than blind allegiance to them.' (Wolcott 1992: 17)

Action research has the potential to redesign traditional paradigms for data collection, as it becomes mediated by practitioner needs. If educational research is ever to move towards uniting research and practice, the exigencies of the educational context rather than the demands of technical prescriptivism will need to be the driving force in the selection of appropriate methodologies.

Group discussion tasks

1 Section 5.2 suggests a number of combinations for conducting interviews and provides examples of how these can be used for different purposes. With your colleagues, develop a list of possible interview combinations and purposes which could be proposed in your situation.

2 Share ideas on how learner to learner interviews could be used and recorded in your teaching situation. How could they be integrated with the regular activities in your classrooms?

3 What are the relative advantages and disadvantages of structured, semi-structured and open interviews?

4 Select some of the 'guided discussion' questions described by Sue Whitham in Section 5.2.3 and try them out with your class. Compare your findings with those of others in your research group.

5 With others in your group develop a short questionnaire on a topic of mutual interest that includes closed, scale and open-ended items. Compare your findings and discuss the relative advantages and disadvantages of each item type.

6 Can you see a role for learner journals in your research? What guidelines for writing journals could be developed with your students? Discuss these in your group.

7 Share your 'life history' as a learner and/or teacher with others in your group. How has your own life history shaped your beliefs and teaching practices?

8 What key documents in your institutional context could be collected by your group to provide a background to your research? What kinds of teaching and learning approaches are suggested by these documents? How do they influence teaching practices in your situation?

9 Brainstorm a series of questions relating to your group's research topic that could be used in an Open Letter activity. Compare your students' responses to this activity. What aspects of their responses relate to institutional factors and what aspects relate to the classroom itself?

6　Analysing action research data

> There is a certain degree of vulnerability in sharing classroom
> practices, but I think it is one of the most important aspects of
> professional development. By allowing others to observe our
> activities and discussing what we are doing with our colleagues, we
> are better able to evaluate our courses and lessons ourselves.
>
> (Margaret Clarkson, New South Wales)

6.1 Introduction

In many ways this is the most difficult chapter in this book to write, as it
deals with an area of action research which is the least well defined and
still the most open to development. Because action research is a
relatively new research approach, particularly in the field of second
language education, the issue of how action research data should be
analysed is a challenging one for teacher research. This situation has
been highlighted by Winter (1982, cited in Cohen and Manion 1994:
197–8):

> The action research/case study tradition does have a methodology
> for the creation of data, but not (as yet) for the interpretation of
> data. We are shown how the descriptive journal, the observer's field
> notes and the open ended interview are utilized to create accounts
> of events which will confront the practitioner's current pragmatic
> assumptions and definitions; we are shown the potential value of
> this process (in terms of increasing teachers' sensitivity) and the
> problem it poses for individual and collective professional
> equilibrium. What we are not shown is how the teacher should
> handle the data thus collected.

The aim of this chapter is to present some perspectives on analysing
data for teachers who may not have had extensive training in research
methods, as well as to suggest some practical strategies. Again, these
strategies come as far as possible from the experiences of the collaborative groups I have worked with. As a result they reflect some of the
struggles we have experienced when analysing data, which could
perhaps best be epitomised by Argyris and Schon's (1991: 85) comment
that 'from the action researcher's perspective the challenge is to define

and meet standards of appropriate rigour without sacrificing relevance'.

The chapter does not claim to present an in-depth treatment of qualitative data analysis. This can be found elsewhere (for example, Agar 1980; Bogdan and Biklen 1998; Goetz and LeCompte 1984; Maykut and Morehouse 1994; Miles and Huberman 1994). My intention is to offer a very basic guide to some possible techniques for teacher researchers who need starting points for thinking through the data analysis process. The motivation and the emphasis in the chapter is the notion of relevance for teacher researchers of different forms of analysis in relation to the particular research context, circumstances and practices being investigated, underpinned by the idea of the systematic approach to which Argyris and Schon refer.

The questions addressed in this chapter are:

1 What is meant by data analysis?
2 At what point in the research cycle should data be analysed?
3 What are key considerations in ensuring that data are analysed systematically?
4 What techniques are available to analyse data?

6.2 What is data analysis?

Data analysis in action research involves moving away from the 'action' components of the cycle, where the main focus is on planning and acting, to the 'research' aspects, where the focus changes to more systematic observing and reflecting. Data analysis is the point where statements or assertions about what the research shows are produced. These statements are based on broad patterns or themes which emerge from the data (Erickson 1986; Davis 1995). Data analysis involves describing (the 'what' of the research) and explaining (the 'why' of the research). Through the 'what' aspects we aim to set out what the data show, while the 'why' aspects lead us to find explanations for what emerges from the descriptions of the data. Through this process, we hope to bring more informed applications of classroom practice into play. We may also wish to evaluate particular sets of actions in the light of broader organisational policies or practices. The process of explaining the data also involves developing more explicit theories and concepts about practice, as Carr and Kemmis (1986: 162) emphasise in the following statement:

> Action research is simply a form of self-reflective enquiry
> undertaken by participants in social situations in order to improve
> the rationality and justice of their own practices, their

understanding of these practices, and the situations in which these practices are carried out.

The notions of self-reflection, rationality and understanding highlight the aspirations of action research conducted in critical collaborative groups to generate not just 'technical' and practical improvements in practice, but also self-critical awareness and theoretical ideas about the nature of teaching and the personal values or beliefs we bring to it. These theoretical ideas are developed through the process of collecting and analysing data. Carr and Kemmis (1986: 189) go on to express this idea in the following way:

> While practical experience can be gained through unsystematic reflection on action, a rational understanding of practice can only be gained through systematic reflection on action by the actor involved. The knowledge developed by action researchers about their own practices is of this kind; it includes what Michael Polanyi calls 'personal knowledge'.

6.3 When should data be analysed?

In practice it is difficult – as well as unnecessary – to separate the processes of data collection and analysis in action research. They are 'dynamic' in the sense that they inevitably overlap, interrelate and recur. It is certainly not the case that analysis begins only when all the data are collected. An essential feature of action research is the 'reflexivity' which results from cycling backwards and forwards from data collection to analysis to further data collection and so on as the need arises. This is an integral part of the whole process and it is fluid and dynamic. Somekh (1993: 33) points out that reflexivity is 'a belief that interpretations, theories and meanings must be subjected to a continual process of questioning and scrutiny, in which the researcher's attention shifts back and forth between interpretation and evidence – exploring, hypothesising, checking and reformulating'. As data are collected, explanations, ideas and hypotheses about the data inevitably emerge and the 'fit' between the data and explanation of the data is further tried out as the research proceeds.

The framework shown in Figure 6.1 (adapted from Hopkins 1993) attempts to capture the recursive nature of the collaborative action research cycle. Reflexivity is the central concept in this process, the idea that data collection, action and analysis are interrelated and recycle into each other. Collecting data enables us to generate hypotheses, by noting events and finding explanations for them. In turn this gives rise to further action, in the light of our own personal observations, theories and what the data seem to be telling us. Well before the investigation is

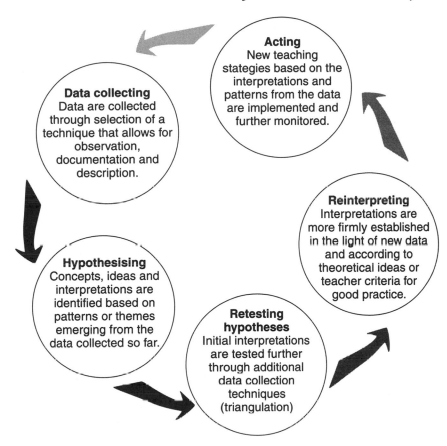

Figure 6.1   *Data collection and analysis cycle*

finished, we will have already developed numerous predictions, noticed emerging patterns or trends and trialed different strategies to test out what seems to be happening in the classroom.

Analysis, then, involves us in making some kind of sense of the data by identifying broad trends, characteristics or features across an event or a series of events. We can then begin to draw out theories and explanations and attempt to interpret the meanings of these trends or features. In action research, however, activity does not stop at analysis, description and interpretation. The whole point of action research is that analysing the data, interpreting it and developing theories about what it means are constantly fed back into practice.

This discussion raises the questions of how many research cycles should be completed and how the researcher knows when he or she has enough data to end the research. The answers to these questions are not clear cut. They depend to a large extent on personal and group time and resources and the nature and purpose of the research. An initial question or focus may well be satisfied through a single research spiral. This may be sufficient to gain some understanding of the actions and behaviours which are the main research issues. Alternatively, the original issue may lead to other questions or to the need to look at underlying factors, so that the research spirals off in new directions or becomes multi-dimensional (McNiff 1988). As the following observation by Meg Quinn illustrates, the scope of the research and the time-span available for completing it often depend on organisational matters such as whether teachers change classes or new ways of placing students are introduced or whether classes or courses are structured differently:

> The time period for data collection was quite short, constrained by both the schedule of the research project and the fact that the students were in a ten-week course, after which it was unlikely that I would continue to be their teacher. In fact only seven weeks were available to set up the research and collect data ... Students usually change classes after those ten weeks so it would be very difficult to follow a larger study through.

(Quinn 1997a: 44)

However, at some point in the process, whether this is after a short investigation over a school term or throughout a whole year, groups will wish to complete their research. The data are then likely to be scanned again more comprehensively to draw out overall interpretations, to evaluate the implications of the research for further action and to make the outcomes of the research public through written reports or presentations (see Chapter 7). There are various techniques developed from qualitative research approaches which can be used for data analysis, such as identifying patterns, categories or themes that are repeated across the data and making connections between these categories. Quantitative techniques, such as calculating percentages or making tallies of repeated behaviours, also have a place in action research, as do 'good guesses', personal hunches and speculations which are part of reflexive thinking and can be tested out against the data.

6.4 Processes of analysis

I have stressed that the reflexive nature of action research means that analysis occurs over the entire investigation. It is useful to have a framework such as the following (adapted from McKernan 1996) to shape the overall processes of analysis, particularly when the end point is the presentation of the research to a wider audience. Throughout this process, constant checks must be made to ensure that it is the data, rather than one's intuitions or assumptions, that are leading the analysis. The data provide the evidence for the statements or assertions that are made about the research insights or outcomes.

STAGE 1: ASSEMBLING THE DATA

The first step is to assemble the data that you have collected over the period of the research: field notes, journal entries, questionnaires and so on. The initial questions that began the research provide a starting point for rereading the data, which can be scanned first of all in a general way. It is useful to note down thoughts, ideas or impressions as they occur to you during this initial examination. At this stage, broad patterns should begin to show up which can be compared and contrasted to see what fits together. By scanning the data in this way, you begin the process of more detailed analysis by bringing up possible patterns which you can adapt or add to as you proceed.

For example, in a study of intermediate learners' use of first language in the classroom, by rereading your own field notes and the learners' responses to a survey, and replaying a recording of classroom interactions you may begin to observe patterns such as the following:

L1 is used to
- check with friends what the task involves
- ask the teacher questions about grammar usage
- check or discuss meanings of new vocabulary
- compare responses to exercises or tasks.

STAGE 2: CODING THE DATA

Once there has been some overall examination of the data, categories or codes can be developed to identify patterns more specifically. Various coding techniques, discussed later in this chapter, are available. Coding is a process of attempting to reduce the large amount of data that may be collected to more manageable categories of concepts, themes or types. With closed or ranked questions, in a questionnaire for example, responses or behaviours may be assigned to a code relatively easily. Data analysis becomes much more messy and coding becomes less clear cut when you are dealing with diary entries, classroom recordings or open-ended survey questions.

In a study using closed-choice questions, learner responses are easily assigned, as the following example shows:

Question 6
How would you prefer to be assessed?

(Tick one)
(a) short assessment tasks at regular intervals

    (b) longer assessments mid-way through the course and at the end
        of the course
    (c) several assessments during the last week of the course
    (d) one major assessment at the end of the course

In open-ended questions, researchers must scan through the responses and develop categories that seem to be repeated in the data, as in the following example:

> Question 6
> What do you do to try to learn English outside class?
>
> Response categories:
>   'Listen to English programmes on the radio'
>   'Watch English movies with subtitles on television'
>   'Read English comics/magazines'
>   'Talk to tourists or English visitors'
>   'Listen to English pop songs'
>   'Speak to neighbours'

STAGE 3: COMPARING THE DATA

Once the data have been categorised in some way, comparisons can be made to see whether themes or patterns are repeated or developed across different data gathering techniques. You may notice hierarchies or sequences of data or identify relationships and connections between different sources of data. At this stage you may also be able to map frequencies of occurrences, behaviours or responses. Tables may be created using simple descriptive techniques to note frequency counts or percentages. The main aim at this stage is to describe and display the data rather than to interpret or explain them.

For example, in her study of two of her learners' attitudes towards writing, Meg Quinn (1997a) collected informal recorded comments about their readiness for writing and their perceptions before and after writing tasks, her own journal notes to compare her expectations with what the learners did or produced, structured interviews with each learner and samples of the learners' written work. After six weeks she realised that one student was progressing much more rapidly than the other. Scanning the data, Meg noted that the learner who was making progress, Student A, consistently attached positive attitudes, not only to writing, but to learning in general (e.g. 'Sometimes it is difficult but they will understand me'). These attitudes were displayed in the way the student was able to articulate behaviours and strategies for a 'good language learner' (e.g. taking risks, learning independently, maintaining interest in learning, observing learning strategies used by others, interacting outside the classroom). This student also displayed metalinguistic awareness, or understandings about how language works, in the strategies she brought to writing tasks (e.g. sound–symbol relationships, differences in structure between spoken and written language).

Student B, on the other hand, generally displayed negative attitudes about learning and her ability to learn (e.g. 'I don't know English too much'). She tended to focus on the immediate task in hand, recounting actual activities she had to do, rather than referring to learning strategies or to strategies for completing tasks. Student B also made continual references to barriers to learning (e.g. 'I hope my English is very well, but too much problem') and saw herself as dependent on others to help her (e.g. 'If I don't know some words I ask my husband or daughter'). Unlike Student A, Student B was unable to articulate any metalinguistic awareness related to written structures or texts, or metacognitive awareness related to strategies for undertaking writing. These findings were repeated quite consistently across all the sources of data that Meg had collected.

STAGE 4: BUILDING INTERPRETATIONS

This is the point where you move beyond describing, categorising, coding and comparing to make some sense of the meaning of the data. This stage demands a certain amount of creative thinking as it is concerned with articulating underlying concepts and developing theories about why particular patterns of behaviours, interactions or attitudes have emerged. You may need to come back to the data several times to pose questions, rethink the connections and develop explanations of the bigger picture underpinning the research. Discussing the data patterns and themes with other members of your research group can be a catalyst for new discoveries or interpretations, as can noting down thoughts or insights as they occur and questioning what lies behind surface descriptions.

In Pam McPherson's study (McPherson 1997b), where she experimented with the management of a mixed-ability adult learner group, her data collection and analysis revealed that, despite attempts to group her students in different ways and to devise material suitable for different levels of language skill and proficiency, hostility and resistance to learning grew. The learners would not cooperate in joint activities or interact generally and the whole classroom atmosphere was tense. An explanation for this behaviour was eventually found in the cultural and social differences within the group, which was composed of refugees from a war-torn country where deep religious, ethnic and political differences existed. The classroom activities directed towards cooperative group work had created major anxieties about causing offence, as the learners were often required to expose and discuss different views and opinions.

Pam's understanding of the 'bigger picture' of sociocultural factors led her to reflect on theoretical ideas, particularly about teaching as a decision-making process which is influenced by a wide range of very specific and local organisational and classroom factors. Part of her theory-building was 'to bring into question all the teaching values I held and ... to justify to myself and my students, the theoretical principles underlying my teaching practice' (page 30). It also led to changes in her teaching approach in terms of tasks, materials and classroom interactions that she would normally have discarded, but which ultimately proved very effective with this group of learners.

STAGE 5: REPORTING THE OUTCOMES

The final stage involves presenting an account of the research for others. There are various ways to report the research, which are discussed in more detail in the next chapter. A major consideration is to ensure that the report sets out the major processes of the research, and that the findings and outcomes are well supported with examples from the data. What makes action research different from other reflective processes associated with teaching is that data have been systematically collected and analysed. This systematic aspect needs to be shown in a report. This means at the very least setting out and discussing the original issue or questions that prompted the study, describing the context of the research, outlining the findings and providing data samples to support them, interpreting how the findings relate to the context and suggesting how the project has been fed back into practice or could lead to other areas for research.

6.5 Validity and action research

In quantitative educational research, validity is an essential criterion for evaluating the quality and acceptability of research. Although action research involves a different set of assumptions and research activities from quantitative research, action researchers are still faced with the challenge of responding to questions about the rigour and credibility of their investigations. Internal validity asks the question: How trustworthy are the claims that the outcomes are related to the experimental treatment? In other words, do the interventions researchers make in the research context result in the outcomes that can be inferred from the data? On the other hand, external validity asks: How generalisable to other contexts or subjects is our research?

The notion of validity in the sense that is applied in experimental research is problematic in action research. First, action research is a form of investigation which aims to describe and explain events and activities in a specific context. We are not aiming to establish relationships between variables or to isolate causes and their effects. Second, because of its highly local nature, action research is interested in specific participants and phenomena. Selecting subject samples from which generalisations can be made to larger populations is inherently in opposition to the purpose and aim of action research. Action research is concerned with gaining insights in one specific situation that may be useful or relevant in illuminating issues for other teachers. Having said that, in collaborative action research where teachers may be working from different perspectives but on a common theme or focus, a different kind of generalisability may be built up through the greater depth and coverage of the research area and the composite picture of the issues that can be portrayed.

As qualitative approaches have gradually become more common in educational research, new concepts of validity have emerged. Erickson (1986), for example, argues that a basic validity criterion is the immediate and local meanings of action as they are defined from the participants' point of view. This implies that qualitative research approaches are less concerned with uncovering truth values (internal validity) than with representing the 'credibility' of the researchers' interpretations (Davis 1995). In other words, is what the researcher is claiming on the basis of the data believable and trustworthy and does it 'ring true' to those who provided the data (Anderson *et al.* 1994)?

As practitioner action research evolves to meet different purposes and contexts, there is likely to be less dependence on criteria for validity which are normally sought in experimental educational research. Anderson *et al.* (1994: 30–3) argue that criteria for validity in practitioner research will probably differ from academic concepts of validity in qualitative research more generally, as they will need to respond to the rather different purposes and conditions of practitioner research. These purposes are more to do with using the knowledge gained from the research in specific practical contexts than with creating knowledge or generating theories in order to disseminate them to the wider academic research community. These authors set out a list of five validity criteria that they see as applying best to action research that is 'transformative' in nature, in the sense that they are linked to changes in educational and/or institutional practices. These five criteria are glossed below:

1 **Democratic validity** This criterion relates to the extent to which the research is truly collaborative and allows for the inclusion of multiple voices. Key questions include: Are all parties who have a stake in the research (teachers, administrators, students, parents) able to offer perspectives? Do solutions benefit all stakeholders? Are solutions locally valid, in that they have relevance or applicability to the context?

2 **Outcome validity** This criterion relates to the notion of actions leading to outcomes that are 'successful' within the research context. Anderson *et al.* argue that the most effective outcomes would involve not only a resolution of the problem but also the reframing of the problem in such a way that it would lead to new questions. Outcome validity also depends on the validity of the process of conducting the research, which is the next criterion considered.

3 **Process validity** This criterion raises questions about the 'dependability' and 'competency' of the research. Key questions here are: Is it possible to determine how adequate the process of conducting the research is? For example, are the research participants able to go on learning from the process? Are events or behaviours viewed from different perspectives and through different data sources in order to guard against simplistic or biased interpretations?

4 **Catalytic validity** This criterion relates to the extent to which the research allows participants to deepen their understanding of the social realities of the context and how they can make changes within it. This may be addressed by recounting changes in teacher and learners' understanding of their role and the actions taken as a result of these changes, or by monitoring other participants' perceptions of problems in the research setting.

5 **Dialogic validity** This criterion parallels the processes of peer review which are commonly used in academic research. Typically, the value or 'goodness' of the research is monitored by peer review for publication in academic journals. Similarly, peer review in action research would mean dialogue with practitioner peers, either through collaborative enquiry or reflective dialogue with 'critical friends' or other practitioner researchers, who can act as 'devil's advocates'.

Anderson *et al.* stress that these criteria are suggestive. They are 'in flux' and reflect the emerging status of action research. Nevertheless, they offer alternative concepts of validity for action researchers which may eventually prove to be more effective in terms of the research issues, methods and findings that are considered important to the teaching community.

6.6 Enhancing trustworthiness in action research

How can we know whether the assertions we are making about our data are trustworthy? In this section, I discuss techniques drawn from qualitative approaches for providing validity checks on action research data. The purpose of using these techniques is to test out the trustworthiness of our data and to encourage ongoing reflections on them as part of the process of data analysis.

6.6.1 Triangulation

Triangulation is one of the most commonly used and best known ways of checking for validity. The aim of triangulation is to gather multiple perspectives on the situation being studied. It is a term which is used in different senses by qualitative researchers. R. B. Burns (1994: 272) states that triangulation is a way of arguing that 'if different methods of investigation produce the same result then the data are likely to be valid'. Silverman (1993: 156) defines triangulation as:

> Comparing different kinds of data (e.g. quantitative and qualitative) and different methods (e.g. observation and interviews) to see whether they corroborate one another... This form of comparison, called triangulation, derives from navigation, where different bearings give the correct position of an object.

These interpretations differ from the way triangulation has been described by some contemporary writers on action research. Elliott and Adelman (1976: 74), for example, define triangulation in action research as follows:

> Triangulation involves gathering accounts of a teaching situation from three quite different points of view; namely those of the teacher, his [sic] pupils, and a participant observer.

Action researchers use multiple methods and the perspectives of different participants in order to gain a richer and less subjective picture than they obtain by relying on a single data gathering technique. Cohen and Manion (1994) point out that using a single method gives us only a partial view of a complex social situation, such as a classroom, where people interact. Any one data gathering technique is not in itself neutral, but a filter through which experiences are sampled. We can be more confident that our analyses are not simply the result of using a particular method when similar outcomes are obtained or supported by other techniques.

For example, let us say a teacher, John, wants to examine his student questioning techniques. He makes a recording of his lesson and asks a colleague, Alison, to observe the same lesson and make notes on his questioning. He then listens to the recording and notices that he directs more questions to male students than to female students and allows very little time for student responses. He gets together with Alison and asks for her observations. Alison corroborates John's analysis and also points out that he often answers his own questions. By using multiple methods, John can be more confident about these findings and can develop intervention strategies in classroom interaction based on this analysis.

Helen Mulvaney, a teacher from Victoria, investigated strategies to increase her adult learners' literacy skills through the use of computers, drawing on the support of a bilingual teacher aide. She describes how she triangulated her methods of data collection (1997: 92):

> My data collection techniques included field notes of what I did in class. These were valuable in the earlier phase of the project in helping me decide on a specific focus for the research. I also kept other documents relevant to the course, such as lesson plans and checklists of the skills acquired by individual students. These helped me keep track of the needs and accomplishments of the group ... Data were also gathered from other sources to evaluate the effectiveness of the program. I gave all the students a questionnaire at the end of the course to ask them how they had felt about the class. And finally I interviewed the bilingual teacher aide to get some insights into her perceptions of the course and suggestions of how it might be improved.

Besides using multiple methods, there are other forms of triangulation (after Denzin 1978) which could be particularly valuable in collaborative action research focusing on similar focus areas:

1 Time triangulation: data are collected at one point in time (cross-sectionally) or over a period of time (longitudinally) to get a sense of what factors are involved in change processes.

For example, a teacher group agreed to collect data on their strategies for teaching pronunciation over two lessons. They compared their data and used this information to develop research questions and classroom intervention strategies. The changes in approaches to teaching pronunciation were then monitored by the group over a term.

2 Space triangulation: data are collected across different subgroups of people, to avoid the limitations of studies conducted within one group.

For example, data were collected by teacher research teams across different language proficiency levels and nationality groups to test out whether different or similar language learning strategies were used.

3 Investigator triangulation: more than one observer is used in the same research setting. This helps avoid observer bias and provides checks on the reliability of the observations.

For example, a teacher in one research group noticed that certain students in her class were reluctant to participate in group tasks. She asked another teacher to assist her as she observed students interacting in a discussion task and they then compared notes.

4 Theoretical triangulation: data are analysed from more than one perspective.

For example, a team of three teacher researchers analysed from three perspectives an audio recording that one of them had made of a small group of his students: the extent to which the students used a grammatical structure they had recently learned; which students produced the most language; and what errors were made.

Triangulation is valuable in enhancing validity, but it can pose problems for teachers initially. Students may not be used to being asked their views by teachers, and colleagues may have had little previous experience of observing each other's classrooms. Considered more positively, however, triangulation, with its emphasis on gathering accounts from the various participants in the classroom situation, is also a very valuable way of promoting dialogue and developing student enquiry into their own learning.

6.6.2 Other processes for validation

In addition to triangulation, there are other processes for increasing internal validity in qualitative research which can be used for collaborative action research. I will outline a few of these processes briefly.

MEMBER CHECKS

Member checks, or 'respondent validation' (McCormick and James 1983; Lincoln and Guba 1985), involve taking your data analysis and interpretations back to the actual participants involved in the research, such as teaching colleagues, students or parents. If these participants from the research setting recognise and support the findings, you can be more confident of their validity.

PEER EXAMINATIONS

Peer examinations (Hitchcock and Hughes 1995) are similar to member checks, except that peers may not have been present in the research setting. Peer examinations involve asking those who know the research situation well, such as curriculum or teaching staff within the organisa tion, teaching colleagues with similar class profiles, or other members of the collaborative group, to comment on the data. Debriefing by peers can also be an integral part of the research process. You may wish to talk through your research experiences, findings and decisions with 'non-involved' professional peers. Again, the validity is increased if the findings and interpretations are acknowledged by others to be plausible.

RIVAL EXPLANATIONS AND NEGATIVE CASES

Here the researcher scans the data searching for alternative or 'rival' interpretations or explanations to those already produced. This involves looking for any evidence that other explanations of the data could be made. Patton (1980: 327–8, cited in Hopkins 1993) offers this description:

> When considering rival hypotheses and competing explanations the strategy to be employed is not one of attempting to disprove the alternative; rather the analyst looks for data that *support* alternative explanations. Failure to find strong supporting evidence for alternative explanations helps to increase confidence in the original, principal explanation.
>
> Closely related to the testing of alternative explanations is the search for negative cases. Where patterns and trends have become identified, our understanding of those patterns and trends is increased by considering the instances and cases that do not fit within the pattern.

MONITORING RESEARCHER BIAS

As we analyse the data, we examine as explicitly and critically as possible, our own beliefs and values about the situation and subjects being researched. This is done in order to raise our awareness of 'taken-for-granted' biases and assumptions. It means attempting to clarify either individually or with other members of our research group our own 'assumptions, worldview and theoretical orientation at the outset of the study' (Merriam 1988: 169–70). Reflexive diaries or journals are a valuable way of displaying personal thinking processes, philosophical positions and the bases of one's decisions about the data, as are discussions conducted with other members of the research group. The role of personal theory in action research was discussed in Chapter 3.

6.7 Techniques for analysing data

In this section, a number of techniques for analysing data are discussed briefly. Different questions and data collection techniques give rise to different ways of coding and tabulating data. Qualitative techniques that are commonly used in educational research can be considered by action research groups in the overall data analysis process. These are outlined in more detail by LeCompte and Preissle (1993) and Lincoln and Guba (1985).

6.7.1 Analysing content and developing coding categories

Content analysis is concerned with analysing the meanings of the structures and expressions contained in a message or communication. Messages or communications can be included in written documents, video recordings, films or observations of behaviour. Content analysis is commonly used with written forms of data to uncover incidences of certain words, phrases or key themes. However, it has also been used in observations to focus on such things as gestures, touching, dominating behaviours and so on. Once working categories are set up, the researcher observes, notes and often counts instances of the category.

The most challenging aspect of content analysis is setting up relevant coding categories. The more specific you can be about defining the category so that it is unambiguous and does not overlap with other categories, the easier it is to code the data. The main advantage of using content analysis is that others can check the way you have classified the data, thereby increasing the reliability of the analysis. Butler-Wall (1979: 13, cited in Bailey 1990: 225) provides some insightful comments on the processes of conducting a content analysis in a diary study:

> One of the uses of diary studies is to clarify issues ... These issues emerge when one looks at the data again and again – to see what is included, what is left out, what kind of language is used, what kind of perspective is taken, what kind of reactions are noted, what kind of tone is adopted, what kinds of connections are made, what the cumulative weights are, what the parts add up to, what projections can be posited, what the cycles can reveal.

Procedures such as the following are commonly used in content analysis:

1 Define the 'universe' of the content – the text, message, communication, etc. For example, let us say that action researchers are interested in critically examining textbooks used for intermediate students in their organisation. They collect a number of books and consult other members of their group to estimate the level of agreement.
2 Write clear definitions of the key categories. The researchers decide on the type of analysis, for example topics, characters, grammatical items, themes, pictures.
3 Analyse the data and code the categories.
4 Quantify the data and carry out counts.

In the process of completing your action research, you are quite likely to find that you have generated quite large amounts of qualitative data. This is particularly the case if free-form or open-ended responses have been assembled. The challenge is to reduce this data in some way so that meaningful interpretations can be made. One way of handling the descriptive data collected through techniques such as discussion responses, diary entries, field notes and interviews is to develop codes using specific categories. Some of these categories may have already suggested themselves as certain words or phrases, patterns of behaviour or events stand out as you conduct the research. There are numerous ways of arriving at coding categories, some of which are to do with the nature of the research question or the particular theoretical approach that a researcher has adopted. It is beyond the scope of this book to discuss these in detail. For the more practical purposes of action research, it is helpful to be aware of a range of coding possibilities. For this purpose I will draw on Bogdan and Biklen's 'family of codes' (1982) to set out the kinds of ways that coding can be accomplished. These categories are not meant to be prescriptive but to illustrate how codes can be arrived at. This discussion is concerned with codings that emerge from the data, rather than those that are ordered according to a pre-existing scheme.

SETTING/CONTEXT CODES

This category includes information about the setting, topic or subjects. Such information helps to place the study in its larger context and may be obtained from institutional descriptions of the class, brochures, pamphlets, yearbooks, as well as general statements – made by the teachers, students or parents involved – about classes and how they fit into the educational community. The description may also include quantitative data related to numbers of students or achievement scores.

Following are two examples of the kind of data that would fit into this category:

> The learners were enrolled in an Introductory Vocational Education Certificate for Learners of English as a Second Language (IVEC). The IVEC course includes modules in English, Maths, Science, Basic Computing, Career Planning, Occupational Health and Safety and Adult Learning. The course was an experimental program run from February to July 1994 at the Centre for Applied Linguistics, University of South Australia (CALUSA), Adelaide. It was aimed at assisting immigrants intending to study at colleges of Technical and Further Education (TAFE) but who had insufficient formal qualifications for entry. The students were at Stage 3 of the Certificate in Spoken and Written English (intermediate level English) and were enrolled in three classes of approximately 12–16 students.
>
> (Carroll 1995: 96)

> The class I monitored for this research was a low intermediate class … There was a spread of ages from 20 to 40. There were 7 men and 13 women. Most had arrived in Australia in the previous three years. All the students had more than 10 years of education in their country. While over half the class had attended two previous English courses, 3 students were experiencing their first English

class. They had worked in a wide range of industries and
occupations before coming to Australia. The class included
speakers of many different languages ...

(Grayson 1997: 40)

DEFINITION OF THE SITUATION CODES

Data that indicate people's broad definitions or views of the setting are
identified in this category. This is where participants' world views, their
goals, and how they see themselves in relation to the setting or topic in
which you are interested are placed. You may also wish to distinguish
between data from different categories of participants – co-teachers,
students, parents or teacher's aides. What do participants hope to
achieve? How do they view what they do in this setting? What is
important to them? Do they have a particular belief or viewpoint that
frames their participation? These are all questions that are pertinent to
this category.

An example of this category, which could be coded as 'students' views
on their placement in a language class', is found in the following
excerpt. The teacher's aim in this class was to examine methodological
approaches to working with a group of learners who had relatively high
oral skills and low proficiency in literacy. The learners were required to
attend English class in order to increase employment opportunities.

> The learners made it known from the outset that reading and
> writing were areas that they did not see the need to emphasise.
> Regardless of reading and writing skills, they saw the reality of
> their employment prospects as factory work or work of a similar
> type. As one student said:
>
> > Reading and writing, bloody hell, what I'm needing reading
> > and writing for working in a factory? I'm reading and writing
> > well enough already.
>
> (Pierson 1997: 139)

PERSPECTIVES HELD BY SUBJECTS

This category is related to the previous category in that it includes
participants' ways of thinking about the setting or topic. Here, however,
it is more specific and particular aspects of the setting or topic that are
identified, rather than the overall shared definition. What are the shared
rules or norms? What are participants' points of view about the
situation? Responses to these kinds of questions are often captured in
specific phrases or expressions that participants use. For example, in a
study of intermediate students' use of English outside the classroom
(Kohn 1997: 100–1), 'lack of vocabulary' was repeatedly mentioned as
a barrier to greater participation:

> I had most difficulties because I do not understand words and I find it difficult to express myself.

> I have difficulties because I don't have a big vocabulary.

> Some words I can't explain and I don't know.

In another study (de Leon 1997: 113), 'embarrassment' emerged as a common factor affecting students' perceptions about their placement in a literacy class:

> on the fast week of class I felt in inboris a felt like a five yars old ked I didnot no want to exspack I like going to class Because I got out of the house

> On the FIRST day of class. I flet like I did not want to be here. Because I was embesst about my Reding and writeing also I flet I was to old to be here

SUBJECTS' WAYS OF THINKING ABOUT PEOPLE AND OBJECTS

This category includes participants' ways of thinking about each other, of outsiders or of the phenomena in their setting. Typical examples would be students' views of the teacher's role, teachers' definitions of the students they teach or the way teachers classify or define the types of classroom materials they use. For example, teachers may classify and refer to students according to their language proficiency levels, their language or nationality backgrounds, their special needs or learning requirements or their personalities. Learners may have sets of concepts about the role of the teacher or preferred types of teacher behaviour.

The following extract illustrates material that could be coded under this category:

> The perspective she [the bilingual aide] offered was most interesting and valuable and contrasted in some important ways with my own perceptions. While I thought I was focusing on the impact of bilingual support, the aide, who, from my point of view was the key resource in offering that support did not perceive her role in those terms at all. Although she acknowledged that the students had benefited from her ability to translate for them, she was adamant that her primary role in the class was as an aide in computer skills, not as a bilingual aide. This she felt was an incidental adjunct. In her words:

>> I see myself first as a teacher's aide not just as a bilingual aide. I was there to help all the students. The bilingual aspect was an added extra.

> (Mulvaney 1997: 93)

PROCESS CODES

Process codes identify words and phrases that categorise sequences of events, changes over time or shifts from one type of status to another. Changes in people, events, organisations or activities must be perceived over a sequence of at least two phases. Time periods, stages, phases, passages, steps, careers and chronologies are categorised as process codes, as are turning points or transitions. Process codes are frequently used in ordering life or career histories where various periods are separated by the informant into important segments. It is the subject's classification that is used to suggest the codes. In studies of organisational or classroom changes, the transition points in these changes is the focus of interest, for example changes across different phases in teacher–student relations, or distinct transition points in a student's progress.

The following example recounts material which could be coded under a process code of 'early experiences of immigration' and 'working experiences':

> The time when I first came I was not learn English. I had my first baby. My husband had to have operation ... no child care. We didn't know about social security or nothing. I left my daughter. I gave her to some organisation. She was only three months old ... I went started in the morning at 5 o'clock and sometimes when I got home, it was going after 5 o'clock.
>
> (Muldoon 1997: 21)

ACTIVITY CODES

Activity codes are directed towards regularly occurring behaviours or activities within the research context. They can include relatively informal behaviours such as 'student games' or 'coffee break activities', or activities that are a more formal part of the setting, such as regular 'student writing conferences', 'class excursions', or 'student placement interviews'. An example of data that would fit into this category follows:

> The final activity of the week was to introduce students to the concept of the journal which was to be written in about fifteen minutes, set aside at the end of each day to evaluate the day's lessons. In the journal I asked them to express their feelings about learning, what they thought about it and what they had learned. I decided to use this method of data collection as a way of helping them to monitor their learning. At first we used the journals daily and then weekly. Although after a short time, I realised that it was becoming repetitive for the students and perhaps had limited usefulness, it proved helpful as it served the purpose of stimulating them to think critically about their learning experiences.
>
> (Campbell 1995: 126)

EVENT CODES

These kinds of codes relate to specific activities or happenings that occur infrequently or once in the setting or in participants' lives. These events usually attract some kind of attention or discussion as they may mark an occasion of significance or interest. An example of data which could be coded under the event code 'using first language' is given below. It is an event related about a 63 year old Bosnian student who was found to be very withdrawn in class. The event marked a transition point in the student's participation in class:

> The first instance of this was in naming the parts of the body, when the learner was asked to give the word in Bosnian. Her response was remarkable. Her posture changed markedly. She made eye contact, her back straightened and the volume of her voice increased. When new language was being introduced, this learner was encouraged to vocalise the translation into her L1. While the oral use of the target language by this learner did not increase dramatically, her participation and involvement in the class did.

> (Hatcher-Friel 1997: 83)

STRATEGY CODES

These codes refer to the conscious strategies, methods, techniques or tactics that people use to accomplish various activities. Teachers, for example, define specific ways that they use to teach writing, to group students, to plan their lessons or to encourage greater learner interaction. Learners refer to strategies for learning English grammar at home, improving their spelling or completing tasks. Strategies must be identified from explicit statements made by participants, rather than inferred from the way they behave. In the following extract, a student identifies a number of strategies that might be classified as 'techniques for improving pronunciation':

> I think the best way to improve my pronunciation outside the classroom is to listen to Australians speaking, especially listen to the radio, watch TV, and I feel confidence is important for learning pronunciation. I enjoy trying to be clear. I like to try my English when shopping so I don't always use an interpreter. I want to sound more Australian. I feel confidence starting conversations with strangers and speaking on the telephone. My main problem with pronunciation is making particular sounds, for example, 'thing', 'straw', 'rain'.

> (Phillips 1996: Appendix 7)

RELATIONSHIP AND SOCIAL STRUCTURE CODES

These codes note regular patterns of behaviour that make up the relationships within the group. Data that direct attention to friendships, cliques, rivals, competitors or mentors are included in this category. More formally defined relationships, such as the 'official' roles played by different people within the social structure of the classroom, can also be included. A description of the overall social structure of the classroom can be developed from coding data in this category. An example of this type of data, which could be described as 'student friendships', follows:

> Tina likes to sit next to Len as he helps her with her writing. She has gained confidence from this friendship.

> (Goodman 1997: 66)

6.7.2 Analysing classroom talk

In qualitative classroom-based action research, the use of spoken language in classrooms is a major focus for analysis. Classroom discourse analysis focuses on the way talk is structured, often using units of analysis such as turns or topic initiations. Data are analysed quantitatively by counting instances of things that are of interest (number of teacher questions, number of student questions, number of utterances by individual students) or qualitatively by analysing the texts closely and noting patterns of interaction (who initiates topics, how the teacher gives task instructions, how first language is used, how errors are corrected, how feedback is provided).

In my own work with teachers, these have been some of the observations made on the patterns that have emerged from audio- and video-recorded classroom interaction. This kind of pattern analysis often provides a basis for undertaking further classroom investigation:

> Well ... I didn't realise ... I use 'OK' and 'Right' so much. But I've noticed that I do that quite a lot, um ... when I want to begin a new task or phase of the lesson.

> I gave the students very little time to answer questions ... I either answered the question myself or, er ... moved on to ask another student.

> It took a long time giving the instructions for the group task ... I realised that all the instructions, I gave ... verbally ... um, I should ... probably have modelled the activity using a small number of students.

> I didn't realise my pacing was so ... sort of slow and stilted.

> I mean, just listening ... it's very much teacher–student, teacher–student the whole time.

> It's interesting. I didn't think I was working as much on pronunciation.

> This was a vocabulary activity. I notice that each time a student

supplies a word ... I try to place it in a context, sort of by
elaborating on it with a complete sentence.

An analysis of the language of classroom data can be shaped in the
following way to provide either quantitative or qualitative information:

1 Do a 'global' reading of the transcript and note any features of the
   interaction that immediately strike you (for example, questioning,
   student involvement, strategies used to correct errors).
2 Decide which patterns are the most significant for the issues or
   questions you wish to investigate.
3 Count the instances of this pattern (for example, number of questions
   asked by teacher, number of questions answered by different students,
   number of open/closed question types, number of errors made/
   corrected, time spent on different tasks). Draw up tables or bar charts
   of numbers or percentages for aspects that have been counted.
4 Identify excerpts from the data that can be used to illustrate the
   patterns you have identified (for example, what problems can be
   noted in questioning techniques, how is first language used, what
   kinds of clarification strategies do students and teachers use).
5 Use this information to plan further teaching strategies or techniques
   or to include as examples in reports of action research.

Tania, a teacher who took part in a collaborative action research in-
service group, used pattern analysis to gain insights into her own
interactions with her students during a listening task. Her class was
composed of a small number of mainly elderly beginner learners who
had lived for less than three years in Australia. The students had very
limited education in their own countries of origin, they were all from a
non-Roman script background and had few literacy skills in their first
language. Tania had been teaching the class for about five weeks when
the recording was made and had been experimenting with various tasks
to help students improve their speaking abilities. Progress in the group
was slow but Tania believed that intensive listening was an important
way to help her students to learn. The lesson started with a listening
dialogue which was then written up sentence by sentence on the board
and copied by the students:

Transcript 6.1: I can't find my glasses
T: Glasses. OK, he says, 'I can't find my glasses'. 'I can't find my
     glasses.
Ss: I can't find my glass.
S1: I can't.
Ss: I can't find glasses. Glass. Yeah.
T: I can't.
Ss: I can't.
T: Find.

Ss: Find.
T: My glasses.
Ss: My glasses.
S2: I can't find.
Ss: Glasses. Classes. Find.
T: (writing up the next sentence in the dialogue) 'Where are they?'
S2: Where are they?
T: Where are they?
Ss: Where are they?
S3: They? They?
T: They? Glasses.
Ss: Glasses.
(students copy sentences from the board and practise reading individually)
Ss: Where are they?
S4: (reading aloud to teacher) I ... can't find   my   glasses.
T: Glasses.
S4: Where ... are ... they?
T: Good.
(Tania circulates around room listening to individual students read)
T: OK. (points to sentences on board while students read them
    aloud together)
Ss: I can't ... find ... my ... class ... classes.
T: G ... L ... ass ... es.
Ss: Glass. Glass.
S4: I can't find my classes.
S3: (responding to pointing) Where are they?
T: Where ARE they?
Ss: Where ARE they?
T: Where ARE they?
Ss: Where ARE they?
T: OK.
Ss: Where are they? Where are they?
(Tania points to individual words in the sentences)
Ss: My. I. My. I. Can't. Can't. (pronounced kent)
T: Can't.
Ss: Can't. Can't. Find. Are. Are. They. They. Class. Classes.
T: Be careful with that.
Ss: Classes. Classes. Classes. Can't. Can't.
T: Can't.
Ss: Can't.
T: My.
Ss: My.
T: I.
Ss: I.
T: (indicating S4) Can you read it for me?

(A. Burns 1991: 55–6)

The transcript revealed to Tania how she interacted with the students during the reading task. She noted that she had provided plentiful opportunities for the students to repeat words to themselves and that she had modelled the pronunciation of individual words both for the class as a whole and for individual students. She also noted that some students, such as S3, were prepared to initiate more than the others. Unexpected patterns also emerged such as the way that a dialogue reading task had shifted into a drill in pronunciation, which had not been Tania's original intention. She felt that the focus of each task had become blurred and that there had been too many tasks overall in the lesson. The transcript was used as a basis for brainstorming with her research group strategies that could be used to plan classroom tasks. They came up with the following list:

1 Reflect on aims for specific tasks within the lesson as well as on aims for the whole lesson.
2 Break the activities down more clearly into those that focus on speaking/listening and those that focus on reading/writing.
3 Model speaking tasks first and then introduce pronunciation or reading tasks that recycle the topic or material.
4 Allow students to do some silent reading and then introduce speaking activities that draw out their comprehension of what they have read.
5 Model reading in a more holistic way by reading whole sentences rather than individual words.

Transcripts are also valuable in studies of the language used by learners or to focus on their patterns of classroom participation. In action research that she carried out as part of a collaborative project on classroom spoken discourse, Catherine Kebir saw an opportunity to identify strategies her learners used to cope with communication problems. Having recorded and transcribed the language used by groups of four learners in a communicative task, she analysed her data by identifying instances of different types of communication strategies. She describes how she undertook her analysis:

> To analyze the data, I underlined instances of communication strategies in the transcript, putting a number in the margin to signify which type. To help with classification, I used different colored pens to indicate for example, word coinage or circumlocution. This left me with a detailed list of strategies in their differing contexts.

(Kebir 1994: 30)

Table 6.1 shows samples from her analyses.

Michael Harmey, Paulette Sansey and Desi Sinclair, the team of high school ESL teachers whose research was referred to in Chapter 2, also

Table 6.1. *Samples of transcript analysis (adapted from Kebir 1994: 30)*

Communication strategies	Partial transcript
1 Clarification requests *What means river?* *boat?*	S1: more down..more down (S2 yes) eh..eh (one boat between..between line inside..line beside..all right..line between line inside..river is river S3: yes
2 Interlocutor's confirmation of comprehension *ah yes* *ah*	S1: river S2: what means river? S1: river (ri: va)..river..river..is river..is very nice..no here. All right. All river it is river..Line inside is river..is river..is river
3 Confirmation checks by interlocutor *boat?*	S2: river (ri: va)? What means? S3: boat..ocean (river, river) All: river
4 Comprehension checks by speaker *all right?*	S1: in american..'river' (ri: va) S4: is here..rather nice..the river..Torrens boat inside
5 Use of approximations *boat, ocean* (for river)	S2: ah yes, yes S1: inside river..boat S2: boat?
6 Use of repetition for clarification *tree, river, boat*	S3: boat S4: boat, yes S1: All right? S2: yes

analysed short transcripts to identify the nature of the interactions of four of their newly arrived immigrant students, who were of Chinese, Vietnamese, Serbian and Portuguese background. Concerned that these students were very withdrawn and reluctant to participate in classroom activities, they introduced games and other communicative activities into their lessons with the aim of lightening the classroom environment and increasing the students' involvement. In the following extract (Harmey *et al.* 1996), they are playing a game of Monopoly:

D: I has no more money
C: Yes (C and B argue about whose turn it is)
B: No
C: Yes
B: No
C: Yes ... Miss
B: No
D: Is me?
B: No
C: No ... no, no, no, me
B: Me

C: Miss, Miss, here
Tr: How many did you take to get there?
    Where are the dice? When you rolled the dice, how many...
C: Seven (checking) ... six
D: Six, not seven
Tr: Six times four ... how much?
C: Twenty four
B: Twenty four dollars
D: Oh! (turning suddenly to C) Um ... wa.. is you name? Listen
    you, you, what's your name?
C: Phu
D: What?
C: Phu, my name Phu
D: What?
C: Phu
D: (pointing) ... Is not your money. Me ... eight
B: Nine
D: Nine
C: You
D: 1..2 ... 3 (etc.) ... 9
C: (looks at cost of property) Three hundred twenty
B: (points to A's card, gives $25)
A: (points to $50 on card)
B: No ... one ... one (points to correct amount on card)
A: (nods)

This transcript was first analysed quantitatively to give the group an overall sense of the relative amount and type of participation by each student. They used a series of simple categories to clarify how many turns each student had taken and which students in the group asked questions, responded to questions or volunteered information. This information was then set out as in Table 6.2.

The research team also analysed the transcript qualitatively. There were three areas of the transcript that proved of interest. First, that Student A, a student who was making the least progress and who generally did not participate in classroom activities, had made two appropriate non-verbal contributions to the interaction. Second, Student B, who had been very distressed and withdrawn during her first few weeks in class, had participated enthusiastically and had argued for her turn in the game. Third, that Student D had challenged and corrected Student C and in doing so had used a number of extended linguistic forms that she had never used before. The research team continued to use this data to monitor the students' subsequent developments, as the following comments suggest:

> The transcript gave us some baseline data with which to compare subsequent oral performances. The participation of students and

Table 6.2. *Number and type of student turns*

Student	Turns	Questions asked	Responses given	Information offered
Student A	0	0	0	0
Student B	8	0	2	1
Student C	12	0	6	0
Student D	9	5	0	2

[their] perceived enjoyment of learning increased markedly over the next couple of months. The mood of the class changed from being quiet and nervous to one of laughter and enjoyment. Participation increased markedly. Student A who at first had not spoken or responded at all began to initiate conversations with teachers and other students ... We believed strongly that our strategy of maximising participation through games and interactive activities had been successful.

(Harmey *et al.* 1996: 2)

Analysing classroom talk provides research groups with a powerful way of capturing the details of classroom interaction patterns in relation to the research questions or issues. Because they provide relatively objective records of the actual language used in the classroom by teachers and learners, they can provide insights into research areas for further investigation or evidence of the nature of changes that have occurred over time.

6.8 Summary

Data analysis is an important aspect of the reflexivity of action research. Analysis and interpretation of data are the basis from which decisions about further action and intervention in the practical context will be determined and such decisions need to be made from a solid basis. It would be unfortunate if readers gained an impression from the chapter that data analysis occurs in a linear sequence and only after the data have all been collected. In fact, it is a dynamic process that is interrelated with the whole process of action research. Raw data collected at the beginning of the cycle are synthesised and summarised in order to suggest further episodes of data collection and analysis. In turn, these data add to the assembly of information that permits ideas to be formulated and further action to be taken. Further action means that the initial data analysis can be verified and conclusions can be drawn. Miles and Huberman (1984: 21–2) capture the dynamism of this process in the term 'analysis episodes'. They suggest that data analysis is a continuous, iterative process where patterns, regularities, explanations and propositions emerge gradually for the researcher, 'inchoate and vague at first, then increasingly explicit and grounded' (page 22).

This chapter has provided pointers for action research groups analysing different types of data within the action research cycle. Given that much of the data collected in action research is likely to be text-based and descriptive, it has attempted to provide a broad overview of ways of reducing data of this type through simple quantification and pattern analysis and to exemplify these processes with examples of analyses conducted by teacher researchers. In the chapter that follows, we trace a further phase of the collaborative research process. This phase raises the questions of how the outcomes of collaborative research can be disseminated to the wider teaching community and how a research orientation can be encouraged and sustained within educational organisations.

Group discussion tasks

1 What does your group understand about data analysis within an action research cycle?
2 If you have already conducted some action research in your group, outline to other group members how and at what point in the research you began your own process of data analysis.
3 Use the comments by Helen Mulvaney in Section 6.6.1 as a starting point for a group discussion on triangulation. Consider how you could achieve triangulation both within individual studies by group members as well as across the group as a whole.
4 Given the time constraints on doing research that may exist for your group, how feasible is it to use the codes outlined in Section 6.7.1? Which of these codes could be applied to your own analyses?
5 Examine the transcript from Tania's class provided in section 6.7.2. Develop (a) a quantitative and (b) a qualitative analysis of the transcript using the suggestions in this chapter.
6 What further suggestions for classroom teaching strategies would your group make to Tania based on the data provided in section 6.7.2?
7 Record a brief segment from your teaching situation (e.g. whole-class interaction, students doing group work, an interview with a student or fellow teacher). If you have time, transcribe some of the data to present to the group. On a first listening or reading, what patterns or themes seem to emerge from the data? How could these be analysed in greater detail?

7 Disseminating the research and sustaining the action

> At the end, the teachers who research could present their efforts to all the staff so that they don't just 'get lost' in the printed form.
>
> (Carmen Hannon, Western Australia)

> I found it particularly useful to be forced to put thoughts on paper so they could be examined objectively . . . this made looking at process/practice easier.
>
> (Meg Quinn, Queensland)

7.1 Introduction

A central aim of collaborative action research is to strengthen professional action. While actual research periods may reach completion, it is important that the climate of enquiry about practice set in place by the research should continue. Maintaining interest in supporting and debating curriculum problems and issues means that an environment is created where new research spirals can begin and new players can form and enter research groups.

The issues of disseminating and sustaining action research are beginning to be more widely discussed in the TESOL profession (for example, Allwright *et al.* 1997). However, in terms of actual practice, there are relatively few descriptions of how to disseminate action research and sustain a practitioner research atmosphere. This chapter considers practical ways of disseminating the work of collaborative action research groups and fostering organisational and professional structures that help to create a situation where action research can flourish.

7.2 Disseminating the research

Outlining effective ways to disseminate information about action research, or indeed other forms of applied research, as opposed to describing techniques for data collection, is an area that is generally under-developed in educational contexts (Walker 1985). Traditionally, academic research in applied linguistics is reported through journal publication. However, as we have seen, collaborative action research is essentially a localised and communal activity within the classroom or school. True to its collaborative and practical nature, we should therefore expect that reporting action research and disseminating its outcomes should involve people-oriented strategies. They are more likely to occur through networks in the teaching community than through academic journals (cf. Crookes 1993; Koenig and Zuengler 1994). Walker (1985: 187–8) words this idea cogently:

> The classic device of publication through journals is perhaps inappropriate when the emphasis of the work is on groups and networks actively collaborating in the research. In this context the main outcomes for the research are likely to be discussion documents, discussion itself and a plethora of multi-media, multi-channel, mostly locally disseminated materials. The parallel is perhaps of cable television as compared to state-owned national networks, or of community presses as compared to national daily newspapers.

McDonald *et al.* (1993) argue that 'people-centred', combined with 'people-assisting' activities, are more effective ways of communicating about research than 'information-centred' activities that simply distribute material. People-centred activities involve getting people together to exchange and interpret information, while people-assisting activities aim at helping them to obtain information and make choices. Like Walker, McDonald *et al.* recommend the use of 'multiple simultaneous strategies' that involve a range of processes for making research available, cater for different levels of awareness and interest, and offer different forms of reporting for different audiences (see also Burgess 1993). The essential concept underpinning the idea of multiple strategies is that 'the focus of dissemination initiatives and strategies is the need to change people, not to deliver information' (McDonald *et al.* 1993: 69). In ways that parallel the ethos of action research, the dissemination approach advocated by these writers places emphasis on social and participatory modes of communication. Transformation and change rather than transmission are at the centre of people-oriented approaches.

Applied to teacher research, this view implies 'a two-way street' where teachers, by reporting on their research, become both critical consumers and disseminators of research. Walker (1985: 184) points out that action research might be small scale, and even 'amateur', but it involves teachers in the methods and processes of research. What is disseminated is not so much 'findings' as a research orientation towards teaching. This approach helps to build a community of practitioners aligned towards teacher research and a professional climate that is open to public scrutiny and constructive critique. This section suggests strategies for disseminating action research through both written, oral and visual formats. Such strategies should be seen as starting points to be used flexibly to explore any number of other creative ways of involving others in the research.

7.2.1 Written formats

Creating a written account of a collaborative action research process is a step to be highly recommended. Certainly, writing about one's research has important benefits, as many teachers themselves have pointed out. Amongst these benefits are that writing:

- provides a record of the research for the teacher researcher and other teachers
- becomes a reflective tool in the research process
- offers a starting point for collaborative discussion
- expands the collaborative base of action research by offering models and ideas to other teachers wishing to do research
- disseminates the research to a wider audience in the school and beyond
- opens up the research to feedback from others
- provides a medium for developing personal theories of teaching
- creates a sense of challenge and achievement
- provides a closure to the research.

Most importantly, writing opens up the research to public commentary and evaluation by others, which is a significant part of the peer review process in research.

7.2.1.1 *Reports*

Some commentators argue that without a written report, the actions that have been investigated cannot really be considered to be research (Ebbutt 1985; Stenhouse 1981), while others suggest that the report has a 'crucial' role in the research process (Hustler, *et al.* 1986). The specific ways in which the research is reported will, of course, vary depending on the purpose for undertaking it. They will also vary depending on the audience for the research and the expectations of that audience. Teachers enrolled in formal courses in which action research is a component are likely to work within the requirements of academic genres. This may mean following the genre of thesis or dissertation-writing with its conventional sequence of rationale, literature review, methodology, findings and conclusions. Other teachers, like the majority of teachers whose research is illustrated in this book, will conduct action research outside formal courses as part of a professional development programme or an informal collaborative network. They are, therefore, more at liberty to experiment with less orthodox genres. It has been recognised for some time that, in general, teachers dislike the typical structures and styles of reporting academic research (for example, Cane and Schroeder 1970). Alternatives such as narrative, anecdotal or even semi-fictional formats, where the processes of the research and the personal voice of the researcher are to the fore, may be more acceptable to an audience of peers.

The choice of format for a report may also be determined by resources. Crookes (1993: 136) states:

> Since action research starts with the immediate needs of a group of teachers, and is carried out by these individuals with their limited time and resources, their reports ... should reflect such realities and limitations.

A basic report outline developed collectively by one group of Australian teachers was designed to take such limitations into account. It was developed partly because the teachers expressed some anxiety about writing reports and wanted an agreed framework. Aware of limitations of time, the teachers also came to an agreement on the length of the report and the period of time to be spent on writing it. The outline was not intended to be prescriptive but to provide an overall coherence and a sense of the collaborative context of the research. It is glossed below with questions that a writer might need to ask during the writing process.

Suggestions for report writing

1 Title and author's name
   To give an idea of the purpose, thrust or content of the report.
   - How can I encapsulate the contents of the report through the title?
   - How can I interest or intrigue potential readers?
2 Research setting
   To explain details of the educational context, class context and type, and specifics about learners or teachers relevant to the context.
   - What essential information do I need to give readers not familiar with my organisation or school?
   - What information is needed about the class as a whole?
   - What information is needed about individual learners?
   - What details should I include that puts the research into perspective?
3 Purpose of the research

To clarify the reasons for the research and the research question or focus.
- Why was this area of interest or concern to me?
- Why was it of concern to others in my research group?
- What did I decide to focus my concerns on?
- How did this fit in with any others in my group or with my learners?

4 Steps taken
To describe the actions taken and strategies developed and to outline methods of collecting the data.
- What happened as the research proceeded?
- What strategies or actions did I put in place?
- What techniques did I use to collect the data?
- Were any changes in direction or techniques necessary?
- How were others involved in these processes?

5 Discoveries made
To discuss findings, insights and interpretations and to give examples of data.
- How did I analyse the data?
- What patterns or insights emerged?
- What did these patterns or insights mean in the contexts of my class or organisation?
- How did these insights compare with what others were finding?

6 Responses to research process
To highlight personal and professional reactions.
- How did I feel about this research?
- What were the pros and cons?
- What would I suggest to other teachers?
- What would I change next time?

7 References, acknowledgements, or appendices of materials or data techniques
To present any further details considered of interest to readers.
- What sources of literature need to be supplied for other readers?
- What materials might be useful to others?
- What examples of techniques developed by me or my group should I include?
- Who else was involved who influenced and supported the research?

(author's data from workshop discussions)

This framework reflects teachers' views of a possible structure for reporting. Other frameworks have been offered by writers outside the second language teaching field who have considerable experience in facilitating teacher research. Elliott (1991: 88) recommends that a case study report of action research should adopt a historical format which narrates the research as it has unfolded over the research cycle. The report should include – though not necessarily as separate sections – accounts of:

- How one's 'general idea' evolved over time.
- How one's understanding of the problem situation evolved over time.
- What action steps were undertaken in the light of one's changing understanding.
- The extent to which proposed actions were implemented, and how one coped with the implementation problem.
- The intended and unintended effects of one's actions and explanations for why they occurred. The techniques one selected to gather information about (a) the problem situation and its causes and (b) the actions one undertook and their effects.
- The problems one encountered in using certain techniques and how one resolved them.
- Any ethical problems which arose in negotiating access to, and release of, information, and how one tried to resolve them.
- Any problems which arose in negotiating action steps with others, or in negotiating the time, resources and co-operation one wanted during the main course of the action research.

Winter (1989: 74) endorses the narrative format. He suggests that reports might:

- recognise the *sequence* of practice and reflection
- consist of *plural texts* that express collaborative relationships and the open-endedness of action research
- be written from a *first person*, rather than a third person perspective
- emphasise *concrete detail* rather than abstract ideas.

Hopkins (1993: 166) insists that researchers should 'not be constrained by the traditional research report format when sharing the products of their research' and that 'imagination is the only limit on possibilities of presentation'. Amongst the alternative formats he suggests for presenting reports are cartoons (to get key findings across in a powerful and accessible way); fiction (to tell a story in which real data or events are embedded in order to encourage reflection) and data reductions and displays (to reduce data to a manageable quantity and to draw out key issues through accompanying questions or commentary).

7.2.1.2 Portrayals

A further possibility for written reporting is through 'portrayals' or synopses (Stake and Gjerde 1974, cited in Walker 1985). Portrayals are drawn from larger written reports to provide brief maps of the terrain of the research without attempting to go into the details of analysis. They can be provided by individuals to show variations in how the research focus is taken up across the group. The two examples that follow are variations on Stake and Gjerde's format.

Title: Functional grammar in the classroom

The teacher:
Annabelle Lukin is now a curriculum officer in the Program Support and Development Services of the Adult Migrant English Service in New South Wales. At the time of her participation in the project, she was a teacher at the Liverpool Region in Sydney.

The background:
10-week course at Certificate in Spoken and Written English (CSWE) Stage 3 (intermediate level) with a focus on English for Study. Learners included professionals, students, and people with experience in semi-skilled or unskilled work. Most were interested in articulating into advanced ESL courses at a College of Technical and Further Education or into a vocational training course.

The issue:
I was concerned about the practicalities of implementing the CSWE. There were theoretical implications, since the document was based on a theory of language which I was only beginning to understand. Politically, I was concerned about the implications of connecting language learning to the wider context of competency-based training. I was also concerned about the impact on learners of my choices of course content and methodology.

Reflection:
What emerged for me was a much clearer sense of the bases of my planning decisions. In many respects my practice remained unchanged. In some respects, especially in my approach to teaching grammar, there were some very important changes that occurred.

Key quote:
The outcome for me has been a huge increase in my job satisfaction. The process of learning about a very rich theory of how we make meaning in language has been engaging in its own right.

(based on Lukin 1995)

Title: Topics, text types and grammar: Making the links

The teacher:
Susie Llewelyn has been a teacher with NSW AMES since 1981. Susie teaches at the Liverpool/Campbelltown Region. During the research, she was co-teaching with a colleague, Rachel Katz.

The background:
During my initial research in 1993, I was co-teaching a Certificate in CSWE Stage 2 (post-beginner level) course. The students were almost all newly arrived migrants just beginning their entitlement to English language provision. Most had over 10 years education in their first language. I also drew data from a later course I was teaching in mid 1994. It was also a Stage 2 course of 150 hours and was the first of two courses the students would participate in towards a Statement of Competency.

The issue:
A particular concern was to avoid a narrow interpretation of competencies as 'things' that should be taught in a block and ticked off. I wanted to look at the elements or grammatical features that could be threaded across topics and across competencies throughout the course. I also wanted to explore applications of functional grammar and genre theory to my teaching.

Reflection:
I attempted to situate my participation in the research in a context of ongoing reflection and change in my teaching. I noticed a number of key influences on my teaching practice, but focused particularly on the impact of the CSWE and my own developing understanding of functional grammar.

Key quote:
My reflection on my course design, as it related to the implementation of the new curriculum framework, led me to learn more about the theory of language that underpinned the curriculum.

(based on Llewelyn 1995)

Clearly such accounts provide only the briefest outline and are likely to be one of a series of ways of reporting. They are particularly useful for collaborative groups that want to get across a broad composite overview of their research. But they are obviously limited in providing depth concerning data procedures, action strategies and interpretations

and may need to be supplemented by fuller accounts that can be
followed up by interested readers.

7.2.1.3 Writing for journals

Teacher researcher groups should not discard the possibility of journal
publication, which is an excellent means of both professional development and widespread dissemination of the research. An increasing
number of journals are directed at teacher rather than academic
audiences. Well-known examples are *TESOL Journal* and *English
Teaching Forum* in the US, *The Language Teacher* in Japan, *Prospect*
and the *ELICOS Association Journal* (*EA Journal*) in Australia,
Modern English Teacher and *English Language Teaching Journal* in the
UK, *RELC Journal* in Singapore and *TESL Canada Journal*. Journals
depend on submissions and it is not the case that all are well subscribed.
While reviewed or refereed journals with an international circulation
tend to receive large numbers of submissions, there are numerous
others, particularly those whose submissions are not refereed, that do
not. They welcome approaches from teacher researchers and would be
able to provide advice on writing. The chances of acceptance are
increased by taking some practical steps:

1 Target the journal carefully to identify its aims and audience.
2 Find out about editorial policies, either by contacting the editor or
  perusing the editorial statements in the journal.
3 Obtain previous copies of the journal and examine the types of
  articles included and the style.
4 Obtain the style sheet or notes for contributors for the journal.
5 Follow the requirements of the in-house style carefully.
6 Write the article in an accessible and clear style that conforms with
  the genres represented in the journal.

Many journal articles, especially those written in the empirical style,
have tended to follow a format involving: a statement of the rationale
and nature of the enquiry; a literature review citing the major references
that have a bearing on the research; a description of the setting,
objectives/questions and subjects in the study; an outline of the research
methods employed; a statement of the major findings of the study; a
discussion of conclusions or implications; and a complete list of the
references cited. However, more recently these conventions have
become blurred, particularly in the reporting of qualitative studies,
where writers are becoming more interested in constructing the conceptual frameworks that guide the research than literature reviews, and
where accounts of the research methods used may be very brief or even
non-existent with much greater focus being given to setting out,

describing and interpreting examples from the data. The best advice for action researchers wishing to submit accounts of their research to a particular journal is to study the types of articles that appear in that journal and the style in which they are written.

Not all submissions to journals need to be full-blown articles. Many accept opinion pieces and commentaries, short reports of research in progress, letters and reader responses, book reviews and calendar or activity updates. These all provide opportunities for experimenting with different genres for publicising action research. While, to date, there is no TESOL journal specifically dedicated to action or teacher research, *Educational Action Research* is a relatively new journal targeting practitioner research in general educational contexts. Possibilities for electronic publishing are also becoming available through new teacher research journals, such as *Networks: An Electronic Journal of Teacher Research*, launched in 1998.

An excellent and accessible source of general information on writing for journal publication is Day (1996). Benson (1994) and McKay (1997) provide valuable ideas for publishing in the ELT field, while the annual Journal Editors' Session, Getting Published: Demystifying the Process, at the TESOL International Convention provides an opportunity to meet language journal editors face-to-face and to raise questions about publishing. Contact details for the journals mentioned in this section are to be found in the section on further reading at the end of the book.

7.2.1.4 *Written updates*

Other options for teacher researchers who do not wish to go as far as journal publication are in-house newsletters, broadsheets, or staff bulletins in which short synopses, updates on the research, examples of data collection tools or reflections on research can be shared. Collaborative groups may be able to produce their own news sheet of short, regular updates on research. Preparing regular updates is also excellent preparation for the writing of the final report and makes the final task of producing it easier. Alternatively, existing circulars, or even noticeboards, can be used if appropriate. The following extract, drawn from a slightly longer piece on a completed research project, provides an example of the kind of short account that can be produced when the research is finished:

> I decided to look at how I taught writing, and the impact that developing a metalanguage would have on developing writing skills. The research consisted of two parts. As part of classroom practice, I collected data on students' writing and the methodology I was using to teach writing. This involved talking to students about writing tasks and determining how ready they felt to attempt

the task. I also collected student texts and kept observational records based on the development and use of a metalanguage.

I then focused on two students, one who appeared to be making progress and one who did not. The students were both from non-Roman script background and at the beginning of the course were at a similar level in terms of writing skills. I interviewed these two students to determine their approach to the learning situation and their feelings about writing. From these interviews I was able to determine the learning strategies they employed and the restrictions they felt were affecting their learning. From this data I made some tentative generalisations about the use of genre to develop writing skills and the use of a metalanguage. I also became aware of the need to observe how students approach learning tasks and the learning strategies that they employ.

(Quinn 1997b)

Some of the written forms suggested here challenge the 'received wisdom' of the research academy on the reporting of research. Nevertheless, they open up avenues whereby relevant forms of research can be accessed by teacher audiences who have not traditionally been considered to be part of the research community. Such avenues are to be encouraged. They should serve to bridge the gap between theory, research and practice, without losing sight of the systematic nature of research.

Readers may have remarked that throughout this book I have had little to say about teachers using the second language literature. A major reason for this is that, for collaborative groups researching in their school contexts, arranging and maintaining meetings and data collection is in itself a major challenge. Many teachers with whom I have worked have reported that unless they are enrolled in a course of further study requiring such reading, they simply do not have sufficient time. Some have felt daunted by incorporating 'formal' readings into their research process as this smacks of 'going back to studying', while others have enjoyed reading extracts that are supplied or mentioned by members within the group, especially when they are relatively short and written in an accessible manner. Yet others have remarked that collaborative discussions with peers, unhindered by pressures to refer to the literature, as in formal courses, enables them to develop their own new understandings about practice particularly relevant to their specific teaching contexts (cf. Naidu *et al.* 1992). Others would agree with the sentiments of Bassey:

> Action researchers use the literature only to the extent that there is something significant and germane to the issue under study; they do not genuflect to Pavlov and Piaget in order to impress their readers.

(Bassey 1986: 24)

None of this is to suggest that searching out relevant sources from the second language research and other literature will not be part of a collaborative research process (see Bell 1993; Wallace 1998 for useful and accessible guides). However, my overall viewpoint, based on the experiences outlined above, is that referring to the literature should be a matter of choice rather than necessity, such as when individuals or groups wish to complement their thinking, find resources for new classroom strategies (see Susan Shaw's work, Section 5.5.2, for an example), gain further insights into research findings or look for suggestions for data collection or analysis.

7.2.2 Oral presentations

While written reports are extremely valuable in concluding the research process and offer a valuable means of dissemination, oral presentations, with their 'people-oriented' characteristics, may speak more directly to other teachers. Oral presentations made by teacher researchers range in scope and intended audience from conference and forum papers, colloquia or workshops to short updates included in the agendas of staff meetings. However, like the written report, an oral presentation is a significant aspect of the research process and opportunities to present verbal accounts of the research are in themselves a formative professional development experience.

7.2.2.1 *Individual presentations*

Many collaborative groups plan oral presentations into their research timetables as a way of acknowledging the completion of the research cycle. Where action research is undertaken as part of a school-wide curriculum reform process, this enables participants to share their insights with each other and to identify areas for further improvement or decision-making. Similarly, cross-school or cross-institution presentations within the same organisation can signal larger system-wide issues, highlighted by individual research. If necessary and appropriate, the audiences for organisational presentations can be targeted to include a range of representatives, such as teachers, teacher trainers, school principals, administrators and ministry representatives. An example of one organisational issue highlighted by collaborative action research in the AMEP context was the need to develop more effective learning programmes, activities and support for adult learners who were victims of war torture or trauma. This issue was taken up as a priority for further research and professional development at a national level (McPherson, 1997c).

Within the time allocated to the presentation, collaborative groups may wish to timetable individual presentations to reflect logical connections between aspects of their research. This arrangement is illustrated in the following programme: shown below.

NSW AMES Collaborative Action Research Group

Investigating the teaching of disparate learner groups

Collaborating in the teaching of literacy and numeracy

1   Linda Ross: Strategies for classroom and materials management
2   Lenn de Leon: Strategies for non-language outcomes

Learner profiles and perceptions

3   Marie Muldoon: A profile of group diversity
4   Pam McPherson: Social and cultural difference in the classroom
5   Sue Whitham: Learners' perceptions about being in a disparate class

Teaching language skills

6   Margaret Clarkson: Teaching writing in a disparate learner group

---

7.2.2.2 *Group presentations*

Alternatively, a research team may wish to present their findings jointly. For example, one group of Australian high school ESL teachers, who presented their research at a staff development day, first highlighted the key aspects of their combined research through the series of overhead presentations reproduced below. They then extended the discussion of the joint findings through individual presentations which fleshed out the specifics of the research.

Overhead 1

Team 3:

Ron Cole
John Blackhawk
Elaine Camm
Glenda Jones

Research question: Constructive oral interaction

Will the inclusion in every lesson of strategies to elicit oral responses improve the constructive oral interaction of students?

Participants:
Classes 2B, 2C, 3C

Overhead 2

Observations: Perceived problems/needs

- current emphasis on reading/writing
- insufficient oral interaction
- instruction inclined to be teacher-focused
- ethnic groups sitting together in same gender groups
- little interaction between different ethnic groups
- lack of confidence
- students unable to use language of mathematical conversion
- students unable to talk about art works

Overhead 3

Strategies agreed by team

- introduce more oral interaction into programming
- introduce pairwork, group work, whole-class participation, modelling and acting out [role play]
- facilitate student initiated instruction
- divide class into male/female pairs of different language backgrounds so that English becomes the common language

---

Overhead 4

Benefits of research

(a) Team members
- cohesive teamwork discussion
- satisfaction in observing success of the project
- skills gained in carrying out research
- increased knowledge in lesson programming
- less isolation from colleagues and greater awareness of their talents and strengths
- satisfaction in seeing increased confidence and ability of students

(b) Students
- increased confidence to participate in interaction across all groups
- more competence in communicating in all skill areas
- increased performance in all macro-skills

Overhead 5

Problems encountered
- baseline data collection affected by faulty video and audio equipment
- colleague support outside team not always available because of time constraints, timetabling, other commitments
- students removed from class for meetings and other reasons
- time constraints
- timing of research at end of year not good

Clearly the time allowed for presentation will affect its organisation and the amount that can be said. Longer presentations with time set aside for discussion facilitate deeper exploration of the issues and can open up the research to quite extensive and constructive feedback from the audience and further opportunities for reflection. Short presentations of, say, ten minutes, have the advantage of focusing one's thinking by obliging the presenter to crystallise the central aspects of the research and pare them down to their essential elements.

7.2.2.3 Interactive presentations

Another way of making presentations is to depart from a passive lecture format into a more interactive structure. Workshops, where participants are presented with a description of the research context and the focus area and asked to brainstorm their own solutions, or are given data samples and invited to analyse them, allow for comparisons and more extensive interpretations. Debates or presenter panels where different perspectives on the collaboration are taken can also stimulate discussion. A variation on a debate is the use of 'advocacy/adversary statements' sometimes used in evaluation studies (Stake and Gjerde 1974; Wolf 1975; Popham and Carlson 1977, cited in Walker 1985) where two participants take different slants on the same issue. Here is one example of this procedure based on the evaluations of two teacher educators of their positive and negative experiences of initiating teacher research groups.

> Advocacy statement
>
> Action research fits in well with our own organisational principles for professional development, which are learning in the workplace and collaborative processes. Teachers in our organisation have done action research over a number of years and it is generally seen as very positive. Also it seems to us that teachers learn most in the classroom and with other teachers, so that doing research actually in the workplace can close the gap between theory and practice and this is where ongoing professional development begins.

The teachers in our group had never been involved in action research before. What particularly attracted them to volunteer was the fact that this was part of a national project. We chose the issue of teacher mentoring and action research and this topic fitted well together. We took the approach that action research involves active collaboration and participation by the whole group. The teachers chose their own focus for the research, but there was a common theme and so they could come together to discuss things in which they all had an interest.

The teachers all commented favourably on the process. They said they gained research skills and recognition as teachers. They found discussion with other colleagues stimulating and challenging. Other staff who became involved incidentally in the research also felt that their skills and expertise had been recognised.

Adversary statement

Teachers in our organisation have had bad experiences of action research. A few years ago, it was the main form of professional development and they were told they now had to do research without additional time or resources. Some of them only worked casually, didn't want to be researchers and after that experience didn't ever want to do research again. As one of them said to me, 'I don't mind the action but I don't like the research'.

The other issue is that some teachers don't see the point of action research. They say, 'It's not really research. It's only a piddling little exercise and what difference does it make what's done in one classroom'. Many teachers also don't have the time to do research; they've already got too many things to do in class. They've got to assess students much more now and also do so much paperwork.

So although we were meant to be part of the research network, the research group never got off the ground in our programme. We called for volunteers but no-one came forward. When we asked people we thought would be interested why they hadn't volunteered, they said things like, they didn't have time, they hadn't enjoyed it much last time, it was too much work, it wasn't proper research, or they didn't feel confident enough to do research.

(author's data from Collaborative Action Research, Presentation at the ATESOL Summer School, Sydney, January 1997)

Statements such as these offer different perspectives emerging from experience. They also incorporate data from the research process itself. Because they highlight perceptions and evaluations that are likely to be common to other research contexts, they can be productive starting points for further discussion. The advantage of this kind of presentation is that it deliberately offers a critique with diverse perspectives on the topic. As a result, it sets up relatively open-ended conditions for presentation and invites participation by others.

Walker (1985) makes the point that experimentation with forms of presentation for reporting research has been limited. Amongst the ideas he outlines for interactive presentations are interviews between members of the research group, and dialogues which highlight aspects of the research that may be contentious. Panels of presenters where each panellist provides a brief account, followed by questions from the audience to individual panellists, and colloquia where issues arising from individual presentations are summarised by a discussant and the discussion is then thrown open to the audience are other possibilities. With the advent of internet facilities, more extensive informal interactive dialogue is now also possible through email lists. One such list is ARLIST which encourages discussion of the theory and practice of action research and the relationships between them (details for subscribing are provided in the section on further reading).

7.2.3 Visual displays

Visual displays offer an alternative to written or spoken presentations or can be incorporated into them to provide the audience with a sense of direct access to the research context. Displays are based on selections from video or photographic data. Care needs to be taken that visual displays represent the research situation as fully as possible and do not give only a skewed version of the issues. Visual displays may be a particularly relevant way to highlight areas such as face-to-face interactional patterns or classroom organisation and behaviour.

7.2.3.1 *Video displays*

Video recordings made as part of the data collection process are an invaluable means of homing in on classroom phenomena revealed by the research. Teacher researcher audiences are usually particularly amenable to recordings that highlight issues common across classrooms. Video excerpts can be used to illustrate different aspects of the action research, including the physical context and the main players (with their permission), samples of the problematic issues that were the starting points for research, patterns of behaviour between different combinations of participants, changes in behaviour and interactions over periods of time.

Elaine Camm was part of the high school ESL research team whose joint session was described in Section 7.2.2.2 above. Elaine's individual presentation was based on video recordings focusing on the oral presentation skills of her students. As part of her research, Elaine introduced project work on environmental issues which involved her students in visiting and researching a local nature reserve. Her intention was to integrate oral and written tasks and skills, and to prepare her students for the kinds of projects they would be required to complete for high school subjects, such as geography or social studies. As a conclusion to the project, Elaine and her students planned oral presentations where each student discussed his or her written project. They decided to give these presentations at the school's parent–teacher evening. During their rehearsals for this event, Elaine videoed the students' presentations and discussed them with her class. What was highlighted was the need to structure the presentations more effectively and to develop language to signal what each section of the written project report was about. Elaine and her students worked intensively on the oral presentations and the students were again videoed in the final rehearsals before the parent–teacher evening. The pre- and post-instruction videos were shown to Elaine's colleagues as part of her description of her research.

Erickson and Wilson (1982) offer guidelines for incorporating video recordings into presentations. Their advice is particularly useful where unedited footage selected from research data is to be used.

1 Choosing a place to start and stop
   - Decide in advance where to begin and end and select segments carefully to represent the situation fairly.
   - Select a complete, connected series of events.
   - Limit the amount that is shown (on the principle that 'less is more').
2 Describing contexts outside the tape
   - Before or after screening, describe aspects of the setting pertinent to the events.
   - If necessary, describe what happens immediately before or after the recording.
   - If necessary, compare or contrast the events shown with others in the classroom or school community.
3 Orienting to important features in the segment
   - Point out in advance significant physical or spatial arrangements or key players (for example, desk arrangements).
   - If relevant, outline the sequence of actions and if necessary, the key relationships amongst them (for example, teacher questioning and student answering patterns).
   - Alternatively, allow the audience to induce the relationships or key aspects and offer some framing for observations (for example, 'What do you notice about the way the students respond to my questions?').

4 Showing the complete segment

(a) Playing the segment of interest all the way through without stopping

- Orient the audience to the sequence by screening the recording at least 10 seconds in advance.
- Continue 10 seconds beyond the sequence to give a sense of the contrast in events.
- If necessary point to the monitor during screening as a way of foregrounding key events.

(b) Replaying the segment of interest

- Replay the segment completely or show a key excerpt, as many times as necessary.
- If necessary, stop a segment and intersperse comments.
- When replaying, begin slightly ahead of the segment or excerpt.
- When appropriate, alert the audience to significant elements in advance or use 'talk overs' with or without sound.

5 Moving on to the next segment

- Recycle steps 1–4 above.

6 Discussing after showing

- Invite responses from the audience before pointing out details or giving analyses yourself.
- Encourage the audience to provide evidence for their assertions from the recording.
- Promote discussion on events and their meaning.
- If necessary, replay the tape to back up discussion points.
- Focus the discussion on active interpretation, which problematises the interpretations implicit in the footage

(adapted from Erickson and Wilson 1982: 51–52)

7.2.3.2 *Photographic displays*

Introducing photographs of the research context also adds interest to a presentation. Photographs represent the cultural site of the school or classroom and convey something of the nature of the interaction and setting. Photo 'exhibitions' can summarise the research effectively, by capturing the key messages and presenting an immediate and accessible portrayal of the significant points in the process. As with video recordings, the choice of photographs will necessarily be selective, but the selectivity can itself become the basis for discussion if the audience is invited to participate. Questions relating to the research, or the researchers' own interpretations can be placed next to each photograph to stimulate discussion. Alternatively, photographs can be distributed without captions for group discussion where participants analyse the messages conveyed and present their interpretations in a plenary session.

7.2.3.3 Poster displays

An interesting form of visual display, which is becoming increasingly a part of conference and summer school programmes, is the poster session. Poster sessions, as the name implies, are exhibitions where individuals present multiple sources of information on their research within the confines of a poster. The poster may include data samples such as photographs, student texts or drawings, teacher diary extracts, short synopses or summaries of the outcomes. The posters are left on permanent display throughout the conference, or, alternatively, presenters are allocated times when they can exhibit their poster and be present to discuss the research personally with others. Mazillo (1994), a Brasilian teacher, conducted an investigation on the use of first language in the classroom, based on her observations with a colleague. As research tools, they used classroom activities such as pairwork, group work, debates, discussions, peer communication and teacher–student communication that were all a part of normal classroom activities. Mazillo presented her findings in a poster session, as shown in Figure 7.1.

The point of a poster session is to provide a stimulating basis for discussion. Mazillo's is an excellent example of a well-designed poster that lays out the material clearly and does not include densely packed discursive information.

Reporting on and disseminating the outcomes of research is a vital part of the research process. Forms of presenting teacher research are not yet well established and new genres of presentation are potentially available to collaborative groups, which could include relatively untried and exploratory modes such as narrative/personal 'story telling', poetry, performance, group interactions or graphic displays. Whatever the choices, presentations involving collaborative groups become a question of how a particular group from a particular teaching context perceives their audience in an interpersonal and social sense. Ultimately this involves decisions about what is said, to whom and for what purpose. However, presenting and disseminating the outcomes of collaborative action research is only one dimension in generating and promoting an enquiry-based orientation to language teaching. In the next section, we turn to the question of how environments may be fostered in which collaborative action research approaches can grow and be sustained.

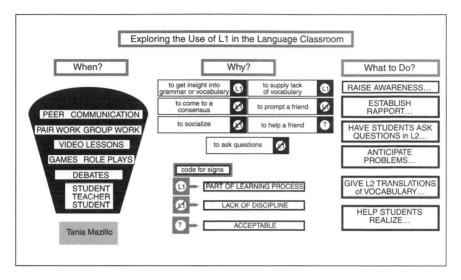

Figure 7.1   *Example of poster display (Mazillo 1994)*

7.3 Sustaining the action

As I discussed in Chapter 2, impediments to conducting action research are very real for most teachers and should not be underestimated. Stenhouse's remark that 'the critical problems involved in an effective system of support for schools are those of power and authority' (1975: 181) apply equally well to individuals or groups of teachers wishing to work innovatively through action research. However, without the enquiring and exploratory approaches to practice generated by a research perspective on practice, teachers lay themselves open to being categorised as 'technicists', whose job it is merely to translate the curriculum decisions of others into practice. In contemporary political climates, where education is becoming increasingly accountable to external agencies as well as subject to curriculum intervention from those agencies, this puts the professional judgement, skills and knowledge of teachers in jeopardy (see Section 3.2).

Even in organisations that are generally in favour of the idea of action research, criticisms are sometimes levelled that it may be worthwhile for the few teachers immediately involved for a short term, but that the research effort is impossible to sustain. A further criticism is that it is difficult to provide action research opportunities for large groups of teachers and that action research 'hothouses' a few teachers who are then given preferential treatment. This seems to overlook the central role of teachers in curriculum renewal within any organisation, and the capacity of action research to be used in a flexible way to generate a climate of research that facilitates renewal. If action research is interpreted collaboratively rather than individually, it provides a space for teachers to break down the isolation of individual classrooms and to talk more openly about problematic teaching and learning issues. This means that they are given greater freedom for curricular experimentation. McKernan (1996: 230) elaborates this point:

> One way in which it is possible for teachers and others to experiment with promising approaches is for them to test their action ideas against the sounding board of others in the profession. Curriculum innovation and educational practice tend to isolate individuals rather than expedite the flow of information. Such constraints are no longer acceptable. This professional discussion is a prerequisite for action research to feed the development of curriculum knowledge.

The key idea motivating the discussion in the sections that follow is that it is the underlying philosophy of collaborative action research that needs to be facilitated and sustained. This means that teachers do not have to be continually engaged in research, but that the potential for enquiry through research should be permanently available within their educational contexts. Mechanisms for establishing and sustaining an organisational climate for action research are now briefly considered.

7.3.1 Integrating a research base into professional development

Opportunities for professional development available to second and foreign language teachers vary enormously. In many contexts, the dominant mode of in-service is the 'one shot' workshop or, alternatively, a 'smorgasbord' of loosely related activities. Typically, these sessions involve presentations and discussions of information and strategies, rather than shared reflections on experiences of practice (van Manen 1991). At best, short professional development in-service programmes are decided in consultation with teaching staff; at worst, they are decided by bureaucrats or administrators in order to implement agendas which teachers may not consider relevant to their immediate concerns. The limitations of these approaches in promoting critical changes in practice are well known (Rudduck 1981; Hopkins 1993). Lomax (1990: 9) argues that a research-based approach to staff development stands in contrast to:

- a political approach – where staff development is defined in the political arena and consequently influenced by non-educational concerns: an example of this is the notion that teachers can be trained in technical competencies that are divorced from practical ethics

- a managerial or administrative approach – where staff development is defined by organisational pressures that exclude individual initiative: an example of this is the way in which the need to manage directed time has led to a blanket approach to staff development where everyone does the same thing
- a restricted professional approach – where staff development is defined in terms of a parochial focus on the child in the classroom to the exclusion of organisational and political issues.

An effective way of preparing the ground for a research base in staff development is through in-service programmes which adopt an integrated and collaborative approach. In an integrated system, in-service workshops and courses arise directly from curriculum issues or concerns which are generally agreed to be priority areas by different groups or stakeholders within the whole organisation. An integrated series of activities is then developed around these priority areas. Activities may include workshops, short courses, curriculum representative meetings, course or syllabus planning groups, action research groups, reading circles or general staff meetings. The activities may also take place at different levels, local, school-based, organisational or departmental, and may be facilitated by different types of leaders, including guest speakers, curriculum consultants, directors of studies or teachers. Using different modes and types of in-service to address an agreed curriculum area provides an interface between the various activities. The key concept in an integrated approach is that there is a dynamic relationship between these multiple forms of professional development which enables participants to reflect in different ways on the curriculum issues that are professional priorities.

A project-related programme evolved in the Adult Migrant English Service, Victoria, is an example of an integrated approach which promoted a research orientation (Corbel 1992). In 1993, the organisation was faced with a major change in the form of the introduction of the new competency-based curriculum, *The Certificate in Spoken and Written English*. The project-related in-service approach adopted had two major aims. First, to recognise the private and personal as well as the professional development needs of teachers during a change process. Second, to acknowledge that individual responsibility as well as organisational responsibility are required for effective curriculum practice and change. The two main characteristics of this integrated approach were collaboration and networking.

> Rather than adopting a controlled, staged approach to implementation based on a few selected sites, it was decided that all teachers would teach the CSWE in 1993 and that a substantial amount of professional development funds and activities would go

towards supporting the implementation. Responsibility for overseeing the implementation fell to the two person Curriculum Support Unit (CSU). The basis of the CSU's approach can be further summarised as:

- focusing on attitude as much as knowledge and skills;
- ensuring local commitment to the innovation by involving a local staff member as a central link;
- ensuring everyone takes it on – not trialled in 'hothouse' locations;
- setting up and supporting networks;
- providing guidance rather than control;
- providing resources.

To ensure understanding of and local commitment to the innovation, a staff member was appointed by each teaching venue to assist with the implementation of the Certificate in Spoken and Written English. Known as the certificate representative (or 'rep') this person was to provide the main link between the teaching venue and the centrally based CSU.

The certificate rep was also responsible for disseminating information to the venue and providing support for staff in the implementation of the certificate. The aim was to put teachers in touch with each other and the new resources across teaching venues and regions. This allowed for a sharing of ideas and concerns and sense of cohesion or connectedness.

(Dalton and Bottomley 1994: 70–1)

This integrated model provided informal research opportunities for teachers, who were regularly encouraged to reflect on, discuss and report classroom practices that were being trialed as part of the curriculum implementation process. A further example of integrating action research into professional development programmes is provided by Jane Hamilton's research described in Chapter 8 (see Section 8.2).

7.3.2 Teacher networks

Closely related to integrated professional development approaches are teacher networks. The central concept of a teacher network is the formation of a linked community of practitioners who exchange skills and expertise and develop shared professional discourses. Networking takes many different forms, from informal discussions between colleagues at the same teaching centre, to groups promoted by local, national and international professional associations, to formal or semi-formal system level networks 'whereby geographically and intrinsically dispersed teachers can draw on collective strengths to support their own institution-based professional development' (Candlin 1996: 1). Depending on their scope and purpose, networks can promote a research orientation by offering support in terms of human resources, knowledge, or finance. Setting up ongoing networks demands time, energy and commitment but a networking system is extremely worthwhile professionally, both for individuals and for institutions. Candlin (1995: 2) suggests that effective professional networks can be characterised as:

- functional and purpose-oriented
- non-hierarchical
- open and collaborative
- non-competitive
- being based on personal links
- having an autonomous membership
- allowing different kinds and degrees of participation by individual members
- not belonging to any one member
- being based on trust, open-mindedness and a sense of purposeful cooperation.

The features of networking as outlined by Candlin are closely related to many of the processes that characterise collaboration in action research, such as collectivism, reciprocity, equality and social structures (Burns and Hood 1997). Existing or emerging networks are therefore important support systems for action research. However, to maintain themselves, networks must also rely on creating systems for their operation. Candlin raises some key questions in relation to this issue:

- What is the minimal system required to ensure the effective working of the network?
- How can this system be resourced?
- How can the participants participate?
- How can the system continue to regenerate itself?
- How can its products and achievements be monitored and evaluated?

These questions highlight the complexities of establishing and maintaining strong networks. They also highlight the importance that should be placed by educational organisations on facilitating teacher networks as part of professional development at the system level. Effective organisational networks would aim at enabling practitioners to shift away from transmissive processes of professional development and towards more interactive, open and practitioner-based forms. The value of networking is slowly being recognised in the field of TESOL and is likely to be enhanced by the possibilities provided by electronic media for international collaboration.

7.3.3 Research partnerships

There is a growing interest in the concept of research partnerships between teachers and academic researchers (Whitford *et al.* 1987; Oja and Smulyan 1989; Hudelson and Lindfors 1993). There are considerable advantages to be gained from academic facilitators and teachers working together in areas of curriculum development and teacher education. First, academic researchers, unlike teachers, are given time for research and have therefore been able to develop research expertise that can be shared with practitioners, through research 'apprenticeships', 'coaching' relationships or training courses. Second, working with teachers brings academic researchers more closely in touch with classroom realities, so that academic research can be contextualised educationally. Third, research partnerships can short-circuit the problems and difficulties teachers may encounter during the research process by providing an accessible human resource and source of research information. Fourth, the dialectic between research and practice can be strengthened through collaborations that focus on understanding the relationships between them.

In many Master's and Diploma courses in TESOL, new forms of partnership are beginning to develop through moves towards enquiry- and task-based approaches where teachers have opportunities either individually or collectively to complete small-scale action research projects as a component of their course. Other forms of partnership are where external consultants with experience in facilitating action research and curriculum enquiry processes are brought into an organisation to initiate and support the research. The involvement of the facilitator may vary in terms of time, direct contact with teachers and learners and ongoing support. Examples of these kinds of partnerships are to be found in Allwright 1991, Burton and Mickan 1993; Nunan 1993; Burns and Hood 1995, 1997 and Murphy 1996.

McKernan (1996: 235) provides a vision of the kind of outreach role that could be taken by an academic action research facilitator based at a university or applied education research centre:

> The role of the educational facilitator would be to move between schools and the centre studying problems, organising teacher-researcher working parties and training teachers in the use of research techniques for data collection, analysis, etc. There is little reason why a new appointment of teacher/action research officer could not be developed which could be funded partly by the local school district or local education authority, with the proviso that the appointee teach certain specified hours in schools, and be partly funded by the centre for applied research in education or local

university education school, where the appointee might give a
graduate course in action research procedures.

An alternative form of partnership may be possible with those who
are a more integral part of the existing structures of the educational
system. Central office school staff, curriculum officers and teacher
trainers who are currently hired by institutions as curriculum specialists
could have a redefined role that includes the facilitation of collaborative
groups that focus on curriculum development, practical experience and
action research (McKernan 1996).

Brindley (1992) offers an innovative model for collaborative research
in TESOL within which notions of research partnerships are embedded
in various ways. His model goes beyond the more localised research
facilitator and practitioner relationship by suggesting how collaborative
research could permeate an educational system or organisation. The
principles he offers for effective organisational research focus on three
stages of the process – initiation, execution and dissemination:

Principles of collaborative research

1 Initiation
  - As far as practicable, the research agenda should be derived from
    the expressed needs, concerns and requirements of all parties
    involved in the educational context concerned.
  - Research should capitalise on teachers' skills, interests and involve-
    ment.
  - Research should be problem-centred, i.e. it should have its origins
    in the problems encountered in the daily reality of the participants.
    This does not mean, however, that all research should be of the
    'applied' kind: the resolution of practical problems involves equally
    the search for theoretical insights.
  - Research methodologies should be determined in the light of the
    issues under investigation, the resources available and the target
    audience for the research.
  - Research should be collaboratively planned, executed and evalu-
    ated. Aims, methods, implementation and evaluation strategies
    should be negotiated by the principal stakeholders in the research.
  - Research should be interdisciplinary, drawing on the insights and
    experiences of those outside the TESOL field where these are
    relevant to the research issues under investigation.
2 Execution
  - Practitioners who wish to undertake research should have the
    opportunity of acquiring the skills and knowledge necessary to do
    so. They should also be provided with ongoing support and
    assistance in the execution, dissemination and follow-up stages of
    their research.

- As far as possible, research undertaken by teachers should be conducted within their own workplace.
- Research should support and be supported by teacher development and materials development.
- As far as possible, an evaluation component should be built into research projects.

3 Dissemination
- The form in which research results are reported should be determined by the target audience.
- The networks and mechanisms available within the educational institution where the research is undertaken should be used to disseminate research.

Collaborative teacher–researcher partnerships offer considerable promise. But there are also potential drawbacks. Taking teacher research out of the hands of teachers works against the grassroots and democratic philosophies of action research and places it in danger of becoming a 'new orthodoxy' of academic research. Outside researchers may influence the research agenda, changing in subtle ways the questions that are asked, the way that data are collected or the interpretations of the research. There is a risk that it is academic careers that will ultimately benefit most from involvement in teacher research and that action research could become a new form of research power and hegemony. Similarly, introducing action research into system level curriculum processes could reduce teacher researchers to the role of 'carriers' rather than 'challengers' of organisational agendas. When action research is taken up as an administrative tool for change, it is not a foregone conclusion that the directions for change are neutral or to the benefit of the teacher (Griffiths 1990). Miller (1990: 114, cited in Anderson *et al.* 1994: 25) raises a question posed by one teacher researcher in her research study group which focuses directly on this issue:

> Do you think that we could just turn into another form, an acceptable form of empowerment? Well, what I mean is that nothing would please some administrators I know more than to think that we were doing 'research' in their terms. That's what scares me about the phrase 'teacher-as-researcher' these days – too packaged. People buy back into the very system that shuts them down. That immediately eliminates the critical perspectives that we're working on, I'm afraid. But I'm still convinced that if enough people do this, we could get to a point of seeing at least a bigger clearing for us.

Research partnerships and system level support have great potential to generate favourable conditions for action research, but the extent of this potential is relatively untried in the field of TESOL. Second and foreign language teachers will need to draw on action research critically and develop their own criteria for operating and evaluating it within the contexts of their organisational systems.

7.3.4 Integrating action research into school renewal

At the present time, curriculum change is something that second language teaching organisations are experiencing at an unprecedented rate. Collaborative action research that is integrated into school or organisational change becomes a powerful way of facilitating school curriculum renewal and ensuring that language teachers retain greater ownership of curriculum implementation. It sets up a problem-solving orientation within the school which is potentially available to all staff, within which solutions and changes are negotiated internally so that they benefit students. Like change implementation itself, school-wide action research is complex and requires considerable time, energy and commitment. However, it has the advantages of providing a route for building collegiality as people work on common problems, of offering a process that breaks down teacher isolation, and of giving teachers specific opportunities, that may not otherwise be available, to reflect on practice. Glickman (1993: 54–55), a major supporter of school-wide action research for curriculum renewal, argues cogently that:

> It is irresponsible for a school to mobilize, initiate, and act without any conscious way of determining whether such expenditure of time and energy is having a desirable effect.

Collaborative action research offers a much-needed local mechanism for evaluating school-based change. The focus on systematic data collection, combined with group consultation and interpretation, means that school faculties have a more reliable basis from which to monitor change processes and to develop new action points.

Based on her experiences of implementing school-wide action research, Calhoun (1994) provides advice on the conditions and structures needed to sustain the effort. Each of Calhoun's conditions is presented and then glossed with comments.

Tangible conditions that support school-wide action research

1 A faculty where a majority of teachers wish to change the status quo of education in their school.

This will vary considerably according to the school's climate for accepting change. It may require introducing people to the idea of action research as a way of implementing school change and giving them time to reach agreement to go ahead. If the majority of staff are unwilling, more productive efforts are likely with a small collaborative group.

2 A common public agreement about how collective decisions will be made and implemented.

This is best facilitated in schools where administrators and teacher share curriculum decisions. This leads to a situation where administrators are already involved and more likely to support collective actions leading to improvements in practice. It may be possible to use existing school committee or meeting structures to implement this condition.

3 A facilitation team willing to lead the action research process.

Facilitation teams should meet regularly and include representatives from different levels of the school structure, who are keen to enhance processes of change. The first task of the team is to diagnose members' perceptions of how the staff works together as a community. This question helps to identify current practices and to formulate an action plan and timeline for the enquiry process. These discussions are then shared with the school or faculty staff for more detailed development. The facilitation team is essential to help staff establish routines for work, to keep things moving, to focus on collective goals, and to inform collective decision-making and action.

4 Small study groups that meet regularly.

Small collaborative groups are critical for large-scale implementation. Groups provide technical and social support, expand conceptual understanding through discussion and provide a forum for sharing outcomes. Key operational arrangements for effective groups include: scheduling and managing regular meeting time; keeping groups small and self-selecting; operating cross-grade-level and cross-department teams; maintaining team agendas and logs.

5 A basic knowledge of the action research cycle and the rationale for its use.

Knowing the basic processes and activities in action research supports groups in the doing of it. Even though fuller understanding of the benefits may only be achieved when participants have experienced action research, knowing what it involves helps to sustain their efforts. In particular, facilitation teams should be aware of the action research cycle in order to support their colleagues.

6 Someone to provide technical assistance and support.

An objective and knowledgeable outsider provides valuable support, especially at the crucial setting-up stage. This person should understand school change, know how to collect and organise multiple data sources, and provide advice to the facilitation team on sharing the data for study by the faculty.

(adapted from Calhoun 1994: 25–35)

While tangible conditions for sustaining action research can be structured into school life, it is less easy to ensure the attitudes and beliefs that are likely to promote implementation. Calhoun (1994) points to three major beliefs that sustain action research, which are discussed below. The extent to which these beliefs are already present personally or organisationally across school staffs will vary enormously. Beliefs are more likely to be at different points of development along a continuum of change, rather than fixed entities. If beliefs are viewed as developmental, facilitation teams can discuss to what extent each of these beliefs is demonstrated in their school as a way of gauging teachers' receptiveness to change. Teams will also need to tend actively to these beliefs if they are to sustain action research efforts within school change processes.

Intangible beliefs that support school-wide action research

1 To believe that a collective problem-solving approach to school renewal leads to individual professional enhancement and to better education for our students.

For many teachers, moving to collective models of interaction disturbs established workplace norms. New patterns of interpersonal behaviour and action may create anxiety and resistance. Appeals to professional efficacy and benefits to students, as well as to opportunities for professional development and 'learning by doing', go towards encouraging positive attitudes to evolve.

2 To value information that keeps us regularly informed about the health of our school community.

The isolation of most teachers means that information on successful teaching and learning remains unshared. If practice remains private, it is not possible to build a professional learning community. Changing from a fear of sharing to an eagerness to share enhances the chances that common professional goals can be reached.

3 To accept the developmental nature of implementation, both the technical and concerns-based aspects of using school-wide action research.

Working together collaboratively to reflect on instruction and its outcomes is a major innovation in most schools. Most efforts will require an acceptance that action research evolves gradually and that personal concerns over the innovation, the tasks, the information and the impact of action research will inevitably emerge. Support, continuity and patience are required.

(adapted from Calhoun 1994: 36–9)

Calhoun recommends that these conditions and beliefs are made explicit to faculty staff and discussed before a final decision to implement school-wide action research is taken.

7.4 Summary

This chapter has raised some key themes related to disseminating action research outcomes and sustaining an organisational climate of research. The discussion has focused on the notion of using 'multiple strategies' in relation to each of these areas. It was argued that 'people-oriented' approaches that focus on disseminating information in ways that are likely to be relevant to other teachers are appropriate to collaborative practitioner research. Various dissemination formats were presented, covering different forms of written reporting, oral presentation and visual display. Practical examples were included to illustrate ways that teacher researchers have already utilised these formats. The second half of the chapter focused on the challenging issue of how action research can be sustained in educational organisations. While there are no simplistic answers here, a number of possible processes and strategies were discussed. These strategies were intended to suggest how a practitioner research 'climate' could be developed and maintained within an English language teaching educational context.

Group discussion tasks

1 With your research group, brainstorm ways of disseminating your research that would be appropriate in your institutional situation. Consider:
   - the type and range of audience you will be attempting to reach
   - the audience's knowledge and receptiveness to the idea of collaborative action research
   - the audience's familiarity with the research issues and contexts.
2 What variations can you suggest for presenting written formats other than those suggested in this chapter?
3 How useful for your group are the teacher-developed guidelines for report-writing outlined above? Use them to guide your own report-writing. What modifications would/did you make?

4 In your group, arrange for each individual to provide a sample of one ELT journal. Categorise these journals according to:
   • target readership
   • editorial policy
   • purpose and aims of the journal
   • types of submissions included
   • format of submissions
   • style and readability of submissions.
   Which of these journals seems most appropriate for a submission on action research from your group?
5 With your colleagues, collect examples of posters or advertisements that seem to you to present information clearly. Alternatively, reflect on your collective experiences of attending conference, summer school or workshop poster sessions. Use these sources as a basis for developing group guidelines for effective action research posters.
6 Develop a list of ways of incorporating visual displays into your group's presentation. Use Hopkins' suggestions in Section 7.2.1.1 as a starting point for brainstorming more unusual formats.
7 Brainstorm a range of ways of representing the outcomes of action research that are not yet well established. In your situation, what is the feasibility of offering, for example, narratives, performances or interactive presentations?
8 To what extent do you draw on the second language literature in your own group's work, for example research articles, teacher resource books of ideas for teaching, teacher journal articles or newsletters? Do you agree with what Bassey says in Section 7.2.1.4 about teacher researchers' use of the literature?
9 Use the conditions presented by Calhoun in Section 7.3.4 as a framework to pose the following questions:
   • Where is our school as an organisation in relation to these conditions?
   • How do we feel personally about these conditions?
   • How would our work life change if these conditions were operating in our school?

8 Collaborative action research in practice

> The collaborative workshops were great as sharing ideas is always an eye-opener. One also always discovers that problems of the same nature are shared by many across the board: 'I am not alone!'
>
> (Lucy Valeri, Queensland)
>
> Interaction with colleagues, even though they were doing different individual projects sharpened up my ideas on their topics too.
>
> (Janette Kohn, Queensland)

8.1 Introduction

A teacher with whom I worked recently commented: 'Action research helps to formalise and structure what teachers describe as intuitive'. This remark seems to me to encapsulate the natural affiliations between action research and the kind of practical reflection and enquiry that teachers inevitably do on a daily basis. As the processes of second language teaching become more substantially researched and theorised, it is increasingly recognised that teaching is a dynamic problem-solving enterprise (see Woods 1996; Freeman and Richards 1996; Roberts 1998). It demands contemplating numerous complex and interrelated processes where evaluations are constantly made about students, events, activities and interactions, and where planning involves an intricate interplay between preparation, moment-to-moment decision-making and subsequent planning in the light of what occurs.

Collaborative research offers opportunities for informal individual thinking to be transposed into more systematic and collective problem-solving. It has the added advantage of involving teachers in actively constructing workable theories of teaching in relation to their specific teaching contexts. It can also mean disseminating ideas about teaching that usually remain personal and private to a wider audience. But what is collaborative action research like in actual practice? Published examples of action research undertaken by teachers in the language teaching field are still relatively limited in number (but see, for example, Edge and Richards 1993; Field *et al.* 1997; Richards 1998; Freeman

1998) and so currently language teachers have few examples on which to draw. Fortunately, the number of accounts in the general educational literature is growing rapidly and these resources provide a fruitful source for teachers in the second language field (see the list of further reading suggested at the end of this book).

The purpose of this chapter is to present examples that illustrate applications of collaborative action research in English language teaching contexts. These examples are not exhaustive; neither should they be judged as 'model' action research studies. All the examples are drawn from Australian sources. My justification for relying on Australian examples is that while they may be located in a particular context, the kinds of researchable issues illustrated are likely to be recognisable to many language practitioners and can be relatively easily adapted to other teaching environments. The following samples, then, are intended to provide 'snapshots' of action research in use.

8.2 Action research as professional development

Jane Hamilton, Victoria

Jane Hamilton's account has as its starting point an exploration of her dual role as a facilitator of collaborative research processes and a researcher of what this role entailed. Her account exemplifies how one individual's analysis of a team approach in her own educational context can broaden out to consider larger issues in the facilitation of teachers' professional development through action research. Jane's account traces factors which emerged for her during the course of the research as essential 'for action research to work'. A teacher educator at a Technical and Further Education college, the Northern Melbourne Institute of TAFE in Victoria, Jane describes the situation that motivated her to be part of a national AMEP teacher network exploring the teaching of diverse learner groups.

> A small centre can feel isolated from the bigger AMEP picture and our involvement was partly a way of linking with other providers and having the opportunity to discuss common issues with other AMEP teachers. Two teachers, Vicki Hambling and Lorraine Hatcher-Friel, expressed interest in being involved and I was interested in participating in action research as well as coordinating [my institution's] part of the project.
>
> As I am the Coordinator of the Curriculum and Staff Development Unit in the Language Studies Department, I decided to document the process and use the project as a case study to reflect on the possibility of incorporating action research into the staff development plan for teachers' professional development. None of

us had had any experience of action research and we went along to
the first workshop not knowing quite what to expect.

(Hamilton 1997: 146)

Based on her experiences of organising professional development,
consisting of 'up to five days of in-service training per year', for teachers
in her institute, Jane recognised the limitations of large-scale, 'one-off'
in-service events. She contextualises her interest in the potential of
collaborative action research in the light of her criticisms of more
conventional forms of teacher education, and her growing conviction
that professional growth means enabling teachers to generate their own
ideas about classroom practice.

> It has become clear that it is not possible to satisfy everyone's needs
> at such events, both in terms of focus areas and the varying levels
> of teacher experience. While there is an advantage in all teachers
> having the opportunity to come together to discuss common issues,
> it is questionable what lasting educational impact a one-day event
> has and how much can be translated into classroom practice. In
> addition, the focus has necessarily been on the bigger picture of the
> enormous changes in the vocational education and training field in
> TAFE, many of which impact directly on ESL teaching. Such
> information-based professional development does not always value
> what teachers have to offer.
>
> To have longer term effects, it seems to me that professional
> development needs to involve teachers in generating their ideas
> about classroom practice and being involved in the process rather
> than to have externally imposed professional development
> activities. Action research provides the potential for teachers'
> involvement at varying levels.

(page 147)

As part of her collaboration in the research, Jane paired herself with
the two teacher participants from her teaching institution for ongoing
dialogue on the nature of the process they were all engaged in.
However, her initial experience of doing action research involved what
she came to see as a 'logical and necessary' time-lag in beginning the
research process. She found she needed to allow the teachers to immerse
themselves in their own research activities and then to spend time
observing, monitoring and reflecting with them on the implications. She
describes how the process unfolded:

> Between workshops Vicki, Lorraine and I planned to meet weekly,
> which often proved difficult as other commitments took
> precedence. During the course of the project, the focus changed
> several times as we discussed what was happening in the classroom
> and explored what action research really meant. Although Vicki

came back to her original idea ... the 'digressions' proved to be a
useful and integral part of the project in terms of focusing and
clarifying the real issues.

(page 146)

In the process of cooperating with Vicki and Lorraine and observing
their research unfold, as well as being part of a larger collaborative
group of teachers in her state, Jane came to a realisation of the 'fluidity'
of action research. By this she meant the continual adaptation of the
action research process, the methods of data collection and the focus of
the research within the constraints and logistical problems of her
organisation. She also developed a stronger sense of the conditions that
promoted setting up action research within her institution. She identified five factors that framed her team's experiences. First, *self-selection*:
'in any action research project, it is critical that the teachers choose to
be involved'. A *realistic timeline* was the second factor: 'teachers need
enough time to collect data and go through the action research cycle of
planning, acting, observing, reflecting and replanning, but at the same
time it is important that the project does not continue for so long that
the momentum is lost'. A third factor was *ongoing support*: 'on-going
support is critical so that those involved have access to work-in-progress
discussion on a regular and frequent basis, as well as coordination
support where necessary ... other people are important for bouncing off
ideas'. *Tangible and recognised outcomes* formed the fourth factor:
formal presentation of the research was 'an important way of validating
the work and also of sharing some of the findings with other teachers'.
Finally, *'pay-offs'* in the form of workshop release time and receiving
published accounts of one's own and other teachers' research was an
added acknowledgement of teacher commitment.

In analysing these experiences, Jane's reflections ranged beyond her
immediate teaching context. The discussions she had participated in led
her to think more widely about the nature of professional development
in further education institutions. Part of this reflection centred on her
own conclusions about the research and the continued thinking of the
research team about how new models of professional development
could be created.

> I believe that action research has a valuable contribution to make
> by breaking down the relative isolation of most teachers' work. It
> allows them to reflect on and critique their practice in a supportive
> environment and to work together to improve their teaching.
> Experienced teachers need ways to keep their interest alive and to
> challenge themselves. Action research offers an opportunity for
> teachers to look at what they do in different ways. It can also
> document evidence to argue for more resources or to provide data
> on the impact of policy decisions which can then be fed back to

> policy-makers and funding bodies. While it involves a considerable
> rethinking of professional development, I believe that the rewards
> and the long-term benefits are worth the effort.

(page 150)

In pursuit of her continuing interest in exploring new avenues for professional development, Jane decided to involve herself and other teachers at her institution in a further phase of research. She explains:

> I continued to monitor the process, this time by setting up a new
> action research group within the Language Studies Department and
> trying to extend the culture of action research throughout the
> department. The Language Studies Department has a staff of
> approximately 70 ESL teachers working across three campuses in
> five different teaching units. A range of programs is taught
> including ESL and ESL literacy: AMEP settlement programs for
> new arrivals; retraining programs for retrenched [redundant]
> workers; vocational skills programs for specific groups such as
> women; and programs for migrant youth with disrupted schooling.

(page 1)

Several questions stimulated this new phase of her research. What models can be developed for integrating action research into a system level professional development programme? What organisational programmes and procedures need to be developed to support action research participants? What are the outcomes of adopting action research approaches in terms of individual professional development and for the quality of service provision? Jane hypothesised that her previous positive experiences of facilitating action research would be readily duplicated and she planned to execute the new arrangements over a period of nine months. Seeking to replicate the process she had initiated in the first project, Jane immediately encountered unanticipated difficulties. She describes a frustrating, and surprisingly prolonged, period during which, although she was receiving enthusiastic feedback about her professional development initiatives, several attempts were required to establish the research process.

> The timing of the project proved problematic. During first term, I
> sent out a memo to all teachers asking for expressions of interest:
> sixteen teachers responded. Due to a variety of circumstances, the
> project was put on hold before the initial meeting could be held. A
> second memo was sent out in Term 2 and a meeting organised. Ten
> teachers came to the meeting, only a few of whom had originally
> expressed interest. However, no proposals for research were
> received from these teachers and it later emerged that the timing
> was once again not appropriate. Teachers had not started their new
> classes and there were no pressing issues that they wanted to

explore. The project finally started in the middle of the third term which was not ideal timing [with three teachers].

(pages 2–3)

Coupled with the staff's reactions to organisational constraints, which determined their opportunities or inclinations to participate in the research, was their diversity and the differences in their individual research interests.

> The diversity in the department proved to be the first challenge in terms of finding a common theme that would encourage participation from across the department. I initially put forward the theme of 'dealing with difficult student behaviours' as this was a major professional development focus for the year. However, this was interpreted quite narrowly and proved to be a disincentive for participation. One teacher commented:
>
>> I lost some of my enthusiasm when I thought that the area of research was to be confined to a topic that was at that time not a major issue in my class . . . I regained enthusiasm when the area of research was broadened, enabling me to focus on issues that I was interested in.
>
> I decided to abandon the common theme and go with the individual issues of the three teachers, which were quite diverse. The collaboration was still an important part of the project in terms of teachers coming together to discuss their research. Also, all three teachers were based in the same staffroom so there were many opportunities for informal discussion and for teachers to sit in on each other's classrooms and provide feedback. All the teachers commented on the value of this shared dialogue and support.

(page 2)

Despite the various hitches that prevented the research from starting at a time Jane considered appropriate, her overall evaluation of the outcomes was that action research offered positive experiences both for individuals and for her department and institute. She reports on the different modes of collaborative professional discussion that eventuated. The teacher researchers, who met regularly with Jane, commented on the shared learning, interpretation and processing of ideas that motivated them to try out new teaching methods and critically appraise their teaching practices. Vicki Hambling, one of the teachers involved in the first phase of Jane's initiatives, became a mentor for the group, joining them to talk about her own experiences and relating these experiences to issues the teachers were currently exploring. Later, at a staff meeting, Vicki reported the personal 'spin-offs' from her involvement in action research, such as her recent mentoring of the new research group, presentations made at conferences in Melbourne and interstate, the impetus to re-enrol in her Master's degree, the development of new skills in public speaking and increased confidence in giving presentations about her teaching. Finally, more interest was generated and further discussion and feedback evolved when the three teachers spoke about their research at a staff professional development day.

Jane's account explores themes that reflect the constraints surrounding practitioner research and outlines the kinds of interventions that could be made in her organisational environment. She ponders on how to convince managers of the value of teacher research, so that further professional development funding allocations can be made. 'The instability of funding and employment is a major factor in contributing to the difficulty of maintaining an action research culture at the local level.' She asks how she can portray action research as an avenue for implementing and evaluating new policies and programmes. 'For example if a department is moving into a new area such as flexible delivery, then this could be signalled at the beginning of the year with teachers having time to identify issues within this theme that they would like to explore.' And she reflects on how she can continue to integrate action research opportunities into her professional development plan in a climate of policy change, programme funding insecurity and increasing casualisation of teacher employment. 'With an increased focus on outcomes and accountability and the consequent pressure on time and resources, the danger is that action research may start to be seen as a luxury that can no longer be afforded ... if we can continue to use the expertise of previous participants then this may not be a major problem'.

Reflecting on her experiences of facilitating collaborative action research initiatives over a period of two years, Jane comments finally on the nature of the change processes she had come to believe were required organisationally and personally:

> The challenge is to build and maintain a culture of research within the workplace. By building on a group of people who know the value of action research, know it can be done and can then encourage others to take it on, it becomes possible, through dissemination of the findings, to influence policy and for teachers' voices to be heard. For this to happen there is a need for flexibility, perseverance and responsiveness by program managers and curriculum and staff development coordinators to the interests, energies and passions of teachers. Action research involves incremental change and it may take several years of perseverance before the idea takes root and an action research culture becomes an integral part of the workplace. It is important to focus on the

reality of what is possible to achieve while always keeping in mind the ideal.

(page 9)

8.3 Using English outside the classroom

Janette Kohn, Queensland

Action research in ESL or EFL teaching contexts may build on questions that are 'perennial' ones for many teachers. It can be used as a way of systematising teaching and learning issues that have become ongoing quandaries and subjecting them to a more conscious level of observation and problem-solving so that new teaching strategies can be generated. It then becomes a way of documenting 'what works', a way of affirming or disconfirming the match between intentions and practices. Potentially, these discoveries can be discussed with other teachers who may also perceive the issue as a common problem.

Janette Kohn is a Queensland adult ESL teacher from Yeronga Institute of TAFE who, in her 20 years of ESL teaching, has taught students from beginner to advanced levels of proficiency. Her teacher research group had come together to investigate strategies for teaching diverse learner groups. A long-standing concern throughout Janette's TESOL career had been how to encourage students to use English outside the classroom. She describes how this ongoing concern came to motivate her research, as she observed her most recent group of post-beginner students in the early sessions of her course.

> Language learners differ in a number of ways which affect their second language acquisition, their rate of development and in particular, their ultimate level of achievement. I wanted to look at my learners' confidence, willingness and ability to use English outside the classroom. Three weeks into a ten week course, it became obvious that those learners who had opportunities or who made opportunities to use English were more confident, more fluent and appeared to be making faster progress. The class that started as being relatively homogeneous suddenly became quite disparate.

(Kohn 1997: 98)

Her class was composed of an extremely diverse group of 18 students from Vietnam, Taiwan, Bosnia, Iran and Thailand who were attending for three hours a day each week. A significant aspect of Janette's research planning was to involve her learners as co-researchers in a participatory approach that she saw as 'hands-on and practical'. Rather than simply discussing the importance of using English outside class,

Janette decided on a process that would address the research question: To what extent do the learners currently use English outside class? She believed that the data she collected would raise both her own and her learners' awareness of their actual current practices.

To collect data in this phase of the research, Janette used a survey that involved the learners in mapping their English using practices outside the classroom every day for a week. On the basis of the first week's use, the survey was modified and the learners continued with it for one more week. Brief discussions involving verbal feedback were carried out with the whole class on completion of these surveys and Janette also discussed the research with other teachers at her teaching centre, asking for their interpretations and input into what she was finding. The results of the survey were striking:

> From the students' survey sheets, it was obvious that many learners used little English outside the classroom. Learners in this class used English most at their children's schools or kindergartens (52%) ... and next at coffee-break time during English lessons, talking to other students, teachers or volunteer tutors (48%). The variety and number of different language groups in this small centre would have ensured this ...
>
> (page 99)

Collecting this information enabled Janette and her students to identify environments where English was and was not being used. For example, very few students were using English to read newspapers (1%), while none of them used English over the phone. Much more frequent was the use of English with neighbours (32%) or at Employment and Social Security offices (28%). For the learners, the collation and discussion of this information was a telling demonstration of their own exploitation of opportunities for learning:

> By the second week of the research, learners were beginning to see the importance of practising English in situations outside the classroom. By listening to the brief comments of fellow learners' experiences when the survey sheets were collected, they also saw the variety of opportunities there were to do so. The research seemed to supplement the lessons and was not seen as an interruption to the course.
>
> The learners certainly became aware of the need for them to become active language users. For some learners, three in particular, it came as a shock to see blank or almost blank survey sheets week after week, indicating that they never or rarely used English outside class time ...
>
> A communal class chart of situations for using English outside the classroom was drawn up and displayed. This made learners aware

of the possibilities and opportunities they could take for further English language use. It 'belonged to the learners' as they added their experiences each week and discussed them.

(page 102)

The results of the survey were extremely revealing to Janette as she had never systematically mapped her learners' out-of-class English language practices before. While she had suspected that use of English was relatively limited and had often discussed this issue anecdotally with other teachers, the survey gave her a more objective basis for considering what strategic interventions could be built into classroom tasks. She had created a closer partnership with her students by building up an informative picture of actual contexts where English was being used. She decided to maximise this through a new course of action promoting more active out-of-class English use and, in the process, cultivating good language learning strategies. This plan elicited a new research question: What kinds of tasks can be devised to ensure that learners have opportunities to extend their use of English outside the classroom? To capitalise on the awareness-raising and cooperation that had eventuated so far, Janette worked with the students to devise tasks that would enable them to gain information about community services or events in which they were interested, which could then be reported back to others in the class.

> These were based on learners' needs. Some I collected from
> colleagues and learners' suggestions and others I devised myself.
> About two tasks per week were set and accomplished over the
> following seven weeks. In order for the learners to be prepared for
> the tasks, each task and its purposes were explained and specific
> language features, vocabulary and possible scenarios were
> discussed and the learners were given a task format.

(page 99)

Examples of tasks included finding out about special local or national events, discovering how to join a sports club or enrol in a further education course or seeking information about holiday activities for children. On completion of the tasks, Janette instituted 'de-briefing' sessions where the learners evaluated how successful they felt they had been linguistically and shared their psychological and emotional responses to the tasks.

> Learners completed the tasks with varying degrees of success. One
> of the benefits was that learners gained confidence by actually
> doing them. Questions like 'How did you go?' and How was it?'
> became quite common amongst learners. Perhaps one of the
> greatest benefits came from the reporting back sessions which
> provided learners with opportunities to discuss the tasks and their

223

success or otherwise with the class and for fellow learners, as well
as the teacher, to offer suggestions for how to be more successful
next time. Lots of sharing, discussing and learning went on.

(page 101)

Janette ends her study with an increased appreciation of the
challenges her learners faced in using English outside the classroom and
how 'nerve-racking' that could be. She also examines her own role in
facilitating learners' use of English outside the classroom, her reflections
moving her away from a commonly held view of limited use as a deficit
in the students.

> I was reminded of the importance of including in each course,
> specific, guided tasks that take learners outside the classroom and
> provide them with opportunities to interact in English in a variety
> of situations. Discussions of these shared experiences were very
> beneficial for all learners. They provided important and interesting
> language learning opportunities in themselves. It was essential to
> provide the learners with this back-up support instead of simply
> throwing them into the deep end and saying 'Speak English!' As
> one learner said, 'I was successful when I had time to prepare
> myself. I could say what I wanted to say'.

(page 102)

Janette felt that the outcomes of her research had been constructive.
The research had enabled her to probe more deeply an aspect of
language learning she had been interested in exploring for some time. It
had also created a forum for stimulating professional discussions with
other colleagues in her teaching centre and with her collaborative
research group, who supported the focus of her research and were
interested in the results of her project. Similarly, her learners had been
given a participatory role in the research and this had inspired them to
practise their English within a structure that gave them support and
feedback. Compared with other classes she had taught, they had
become much more aware of the need and benefits of practising English
outside class and that had given them a greater measure of confidence
and independence. She was also convinced that the intervention tasks
that were part of the research had modelled behaviours and strategies
that the students could continue to use. A further significant aspect was
that she had learned to be less teacher-centred and to include her
students more comprehensively in explorations of learning processes
and opportunities.

Janette was at a stage in the action research spiral where she could
continue to pursue broader questions and she extended her interests by
looking at what facilitates and motivates longer-term use of English
outside the classroom. To supplement her findings, she interviewed

students in other teachers' classes and followed up others who had left the centre. This has given Janette an even broader picture of the range of informal learning strategies that learners use, which informs her own teaching and enables her to disseminate her findings and insights in professional discussions with other interested teachers in her teaching centre.

8.4 The Teams/Competencies Project

The staff of Wilkins Intensive English Centre

Whole-school action research aims to engender school improvement in a number of directions simultaneously (Calhoun 1994). One way is bringing staff members together to solve problems, thereby strengthening their collegiality and capacity to work together to identify and address areas for change. Because initiatives involve all faculty or staff members, a second goal is that all students benefit, rather than those taught by the few teachers who are engaged in action research. Third, there should be a breadth and volume of enquiry that permeates areas that potentially concern all teachers. A further potential is that school-wide growth may extend to involve other participants, such as local administrators, school aides, students, parents or other community members.

It would be naive to see action research as a panacea for school-wide curriculum innovation. Not all teachers will be equally enthused and, in any event, change presupposes a complex and long-term process. Nevertheless, much of the literature on educational reform (e.g. Fullan and Pomfret 1977; Fullan 1991; Markee 1997) teaches us that curriculum innovation is most effective when teachers experience and implement it first-hand. Developing critical changes in practice from the basis of teachers' collective research on school problems would therefore seem to be a fruitful direction in which to go. This section examines an example of collaborative action research within the context of one school's curriculum change initiatives.

Wilkins Intensive English Centre is an inner-city school that offers three terms of English language preparation for entry into high school to recently arrived immigrant students. For some time, teachers at the school had expressed dissatisfaction at their staff meetings about the literacy competence of students exiting the school, in the key learning areas of the high school curriculum. Unhappy that their students may not be adequately prepared linguistically, the school proposed several key innovations, for which they received special state government funding for schools designated as 'disadvantaged'. The changes proposed represented a multi-layered series of curriculum, pedagogical and workplace restructuring reforms within which action research became a component for implementation and monitoring.

As a first major decision, the staff decided to focus primarily on preparing the students for the linguistic demands and text types embedded in high school subject areas, rather than on curriculum content. Mathematics teaching, for example, would highlight the language of mathematics as well as mathematical operations, while visual arts teaching would develop the language needed to write descriptive and evaluative texts as well as skills in artistic production. A further development was to reconstitute the students' achievement of language skills in competency terms, a move that required the staff to agree on criteria for making reliable judgements about students' language acquisition at different class levels. A third change was a radical shift from individual class teaching at beginner and intermediate levels to a cross-team approach. Groups of three or four teachers would be expected to collaborate on the planning and teaching of various areas of the curriculum to the same groups of students.

One advantage in the move towards these reforms was that, despite movements in staffing, the majority of staff had been active in the preliminary planning and trialing of the changes. This provided a 'critical mass' of key players who had already reflected on the need for changes and had initiated them because they were seeking ways of improving their students' learning. Also, because of the changes already discussed, the concept of teaching in this school was inevitably moving from individualistic to collaborative practice. Action research was envisaged as a way of dovetailing some of these processes of change. The project report (Wilkins Intensive English Centre 1996: 2) explains:

> The project involves two cycles of supported professional
> development of staff. The first, covering semester one, focuses on
> developing teachers' theoretical awareness of competency-based
> programming and assessment and supporting them in their
> practice. The second, covering semester two, focuses on teachers
> reflecting on change by undertaking action research. The support
> provided by the project involves the use of a consultant. Both
> cycles follow a pattern of professional development early in the
> semester through a full staff development day with the consultant.
> This is followed by two half days with the consultant in teams and
> a full day for each teacher without consultant support.

A school-based evaluation of the first semester's initiatives, conducted through an 'Awareness Survey', indicated that most teachers felt positive about the changes that had been made. Many felt that they had gained support for their teaching from a team structure, although sometimes team dynamics were still being negotiated, especially where it was felt that there was insufficient cross-team sharing. Other comments suggested that curriculum processes were now more focused as teachers were working to a common understanding of required outcomes, which in turn led to improved achievement by students. However, some stated that the new approach had increased their workload and that the specified outcomes were not possible for all students to achieve. The report summarises (pages 6–7):

> There appears to be strong approval for the team/competencies approach with the need to address team dynamics, to assist teachers to help students to achieve competencies and to facilitate sharing of ideas and resources across teams. In addition, attitudes to the team/competencies approach were further canvassed during a session at the second staff development day, indicating a far greater number of 'positives' than 'problems'.

> Two strategies were used to determine the extent of collaboration by teachers in planning, implementation and evaluation of programs. The first was the Teacher Practice Survey administered in July, which addressed the question about how teachers write programs. The second was the Teams Survey, also administered in July which asked how teams used their meeting time. The majority of responses to the Teacher Practice Survey indicated a high degree of collaboration. On average, however, only about a sixth of team meeting time is devoted to program development, although over a quarter of time is devoted on average to student progress and nearly a quarter to program allocation. Teachers mentioned often in the Awareness Survey, that knowing what other teachers are teaching in their class was a positive outcome and remarked that this represents a difference to the situation which prevailed before.

Having achieved the major change areas during the first half year, the staff were now prepared for a period of reflection on teaching practices which would enhance the changes. They were in a sound position to determine areas for action research activity. These evolved as four team-based concerns (page 22):

> *Constructive oral interaction* – will the inclusion in every lesson of strategies to elicit oral response improve the constructive oral interaction of students?
> *Feedback to students to help them attain competencies* – how is feedback given and what do students do with it?
> *Learning styles* – are there strategies such as drama and games which will enable more 'withdrawn' students to become more participative?
> *Listening* – are there incidental and indirect instructional practices and cultural and external factors which interact to inhibit or interfere with students' listening?

Although staff changes and other unforeseen circumstances inter-
vened in the operation of some teams, team-based action research
meetings continued with and without the external consultant
throughout the second half-year. The meetings acted as forums where
teachers collectively planned and trialed teaching strategies directed at
their research areas. Perceived learning problems and needs were
constantly analysed and observed and data were collected through a
variety of techniques that included lesson plans, journal and 'day book'
entries, video and audio recordings, interviews and surveys, collections
of teaching materials and samples of student work. Data were displayed
at meetings and teachers exchanged interpretations and reflections on
their students' learning. Similarly, classroom materials and teaching
strategies were shared and evaluated.

A major, and perhaps unanticipated, outcome was that team
members learned from each other about teaching. They shared knowledge and personal theories and values and grew to recognise and
appreciate each other as professional resources with many talents and
strengths. At the end of the project, all the teachers believed they could
attribute specific learning gains to the research for most students. Where
they felt students were not achieving, they were able to pinpoint reasons
for this more systematically and to develop appropriate new teaching
strategies. Notwithstanding some of the frustrations of carrying out the
research, including technical and logistical impediments to data collection, time constraints, timetabling changes, changes in team composition and the need to finalise the project at the busy end of the academic
year, the majority of the staff indicated that their experiences of action
research had been very valuable.

> Both the staff and the consultant were most enthusiastic about this
> experience of carrying out action research. Plans to provide further
> opportunities for more in-depth research have been incorporated
> into the 1997 plan.
>
> (unpublished report)

Perhaps, a final comment should be left to a teacher. Throughout the
project, he frequently observed how professionally challenging and
revealing he had found the research:

> Benefits were gained from discussing how I teach, what I teach,
> how successful it is and from seeing me in action in class on video
> (wish I'd seen that 20 years ago – could have done more about it!).
> There will be long-term benefits!
>
> (teacher evaluation form)

8.5 Strategies for 'non-language' outcomes

Lenn de Leon, New South Wales

Lenn de Leon's research was collaborative in a threefold way. She volunteered to be a member of an action research group in her state, where teachers were jointly exploring different teaching strategies for diverse learner groups. She researched in combination with her colleague, Linda Ross, who taught a very similar class at the same small teaching centre (see Chapter 1). And she made a deliberate decision to invite her students to become co-investigators. These three collaborative dimensions interacted to provide her with a rich network of data sources and reflections.

Lenn realised as soon as she met them that her new class at Campbelltown Adult Migrant English Centre in New South Wales would inevitably take her in a completely new direction as a teacher. Not only was she faced with a group composed mainly of English speakers, but the purpose of the class was adult literacy and numeracy, the latter an area which was new to Lenn. Moreover, the students were involuntary and reluctant participants, as Lenn explains:

> All the students were of English speaking background, except for Steve who had been in Australia for 25 years. The students' ages ranged from 19–54 and their education ranged from 4–9 years. [They] were products of the school system where they had failed (or did the school system fail them?). They came to our courses with traumatic experiences as kids in school and carried baggage with them as adults.
>
> The majority of students were in class because the Commonwealth Employment Service had determined that they required literacy/ numeracy training as a pre-requisite to vocational training. Although all of them had signed a CES contract, that did not necessarily reflect their willingness to be in class and this feeling was strong at the start of the course.

(de Leon 1997: 108)

Originally Lenn conceptualised her teaching goals in terms of her students achieving the competency-based language outcomes stipulated in the curriculum framework for her programme. However, as her research proceeded, she became acutely aware of the personal and affective factors that were having an impact on the classroom situation.

> Learners have different personal and emotional problems that affect their participation in class and their commitment to the course. One morning Barnes was in a foul mood. It turned out that he had had 'a fight with me old man'. On another occasion, he turned up in need of emergency accommodation after being kicked

out of his father's house. At 19, his concern for his young family of
four took priority over his training and he eventually left the class.

Another feature of this group was their lack of self-confidence.
Their long-term unemployment, failure in school, and the
awareness that they were lacking in skills all contributed to their
low self-esteem. One day I called Barnes in class and at the
mention of his name, his instant response was, 'Now what'd I do?'
All I wanted to say was that he had done a good job. Apparently
the only time his name was called in class at school was when he
was reprimanded.

(page 109)

The learners' antagonism to being in class permeated much of the
classroom interaction in the first weeks of the course. Another major
concern for Lenn was how she could respond to the very diverse needs
of her learners and the demands of the group as a whole. Wondering
about her students' attitudes to their participation in a class where
individuals exhibited such different learning needs, Lenn decided to
explore their perceptions through regular discussions, which she documented through notes and short recounts. She also asked her learners to
write about how they felt. These data soon led her to reconceptualise
the focus of the research.

It is interesting that as teachers we recognise difficulties in teaching
disparate learner groups. But, as I discovered, disparateness does
not seem to be considered a problem by the learners ... Robert
summed up the general perceptions of the other learners in class
when he said, 'Don't worry me. I just work at my own pace'. Is my
concern about disparate learner groups overrated?

(page 109)

As the class settled into an established working pattern and became
more actively involved and enthusiastic, Lenn realised that although her
learners were making progress, she could see very little evidence that
they would achieve the required competencies in the time allocated to
the course. Analysing the discussion data she had collected with the
students so far, she discovered that she needed to reorient her concerns
towards 'non-language' outcomes, that is towards questions to do with
greater self-esteem, more positive attitudes towards learning and increased autonomy.

The issue of non-language gains became the focus of my research
and a number of questions emerged. Was it possible for learners
with limited literacy and numeracy to develop the skills to be
independent learners? Could contract learning be an effective
learning strategy? Would giving homework to students be an
effective strategy in developing independent learning? How did the

learners feel about being in class? Would this perception change at the end of the course? Could the learners take on a teacher role? Could I share the teacher role?

(page 110)

Experimenting with homework tasks and contract learning strategies and discussing them actively with her learners, Lenn began to gain a greater appreciation of what would lead towards increasing her learners' responsibility for learning.

> When I introduced this idea [of homework], practically the whole class protested. I realised that the word 'homework' elicited this negative response because it brought back unpleasant memories of school experiences. I introduced the word 'task' and we renegotiated the term 'homework' to mean any task not done in the classroom. An 'out-of-class task' was a more acceptable term to the learners. Out-of-class tasks became an integral part of the students' learning. They found their way into learning contracts and the majority of students invested considerable time at home completing tasks ...

> Each learner was given a learning contract and this was where learning started to be individualised. Students made decisions about what they wanted to focus on by using the range of available resources in class. They also identified what they needed to learn and this was different for each one. For example, Rob needed to work on his reading, so he might select a text from our reading book, while Bruce worked on his maths book ...

> One incident gave me an insight into the extent to which contract learning had helped students on their way towards becoming more independent. One day I had to be away from class but no relief teacher could be organised. In the absence of a teacher, the learners took control and each one worked on his or her learning contract.

(page 111)

A major turning point in teacher–student roles and relations came when Lenn was persuaded by one of the students, Bruce, to go to the local club where he was a member, for a game of darts. Initially very reluctant, Lenn changed her mind when she began to realise that she could turn the occasion into a language learning opportunity. Lenn prepared the class for the outing by getting them to study the points on a darts board and doing some mathematical problem-solving exercises. What she was not prepared for was the appropriation of the actual event by the students.

> The excursion activity was initiated by one of the students who played at a local darts competition. As he was well in control of the topic, he began to take on the role of the teacher. It took me some

time to act on his suggestion because firstly, I was not sure about taking the class to the club; secondly, I had never played darts before and thirdly, I had to feel comfortable with the student taking control of the task.

As it turned out I did not have to worry because the students took me to the club, they taught me to play darts and I learned that it was OK for students to take control of a task ... The game of darts added a new dimension: it was no longer just a social event – it had become a numeracy event as well. The students' feedback was that it was excellent.

Bruce assumed the teacher role seriously. He made sure that each one calculated his own score by multiplying, adding, and then subtracting from the target score ... There was a lot to learn from the reversal of roles. As I was not contributing much to my team, Bruce and Robert started to coach me by showing me some strategies. As teachers they were very supportive and encouraging – I even won the game! Afterwards in one of our collaborative discussions, I asked Bruce his thoughts on the teacher role that he had played and he said:

Bruce: I thought I was very good
Sam: He was, actually
Lenn: Yeah, I thought you were
Bruce: Never got agro [aggressive]. When they got stuck I helped out
Sam: He was placid about it
Lenn: You were very encouraging as a teacher should be, right, and you were very supportive
Bruce: Yeah, I should try it at home!

(page 112)

A significant aspect of this example is the way that Lenn's involvement of her students in her research expanded her vision of how she could best help them to learn. This involvement led to genuine collaboration so that Lenn was able to find ways to address factors inhibiting learning and enable her students to perceive themselves as learners. Because of the level of trust and honesty that built up between herself and her students, Lenn gained the confidence to reshape her concept of her role as a teacher. She expresses it as follows:

As I reflected on the task, I realised that the teaching-learning cycle involves a constant reversal of roles. It is a matter of being open and recognising students as teachers and allowing them to take control and feel successful about it ...

My students' willingness to be seen with their teacher in their own territory, where they knew practically everyone, is significant considering their negative feelings about being in class at the start of the course. To me, it was a statement that they had come to

terms with their role as students and that, as their teacher, I had
been accepted.

(page 113)

Lenn saw the various collaborative processes inherent in her research
as a significant catalyst for change. She had taken the risk of making
her, initially hostile, students her co-researchers, which led her into the
previously uncharted territory of explicitly teaching independent
learning strategies. Her students' roles as co-researchers had also
inspired changes in themselves and their attitudes to learning. Her
collaboration with Linda Ross resulted in shared reflections and solutions throughout the project, as well as decisions to continue exploring
the area of teacher–learner roles together. In collaboration with their
students, they went on to use video techniques to capture classroom
discussions about learning perceptions and to present their findings at a
literacy and numeracy teachers' state conference. Lenn found the
participatory dialogues with other researchers meaningful, as they
compelled her to examine the relevance of her data in a systematic way.
She also found listening to other teachers' research issues a rich source
of insights and the experience of joining them in collaborative research
'the most powerful and meaningful form of staff development I have
participated in this year'.

8.6 Concluding remarks

One of the most striking aspects of an overview of teacher accounts
such as those presented in this chapter is that there is no 'one size fits all'
pattern in collaborative action research. Teachers research a wide range
of issues using a wide range of methods and adopt approaches to
reporting their research that often differ from the more established
genres of formalised academic research studies. The examples presented
in this chapter illustrate the kinds of professional concerns that may
motivate collaborative enquiries and ways of reporting them. An
important point to be made is that the enquiries all emerge from felt
needs on the part of the researchers to improve or change their practice
or to tackle problems in their teaching context that they believe will
benefit from the professional support of others. What is also noticeable
is that the research is exponential, usually raising new areas or questions
that take the researchers deeper into their investigations. Thus, the
initial research often becomes a springboard for further cycles.

These studies also capture the variety and flexibility of action
research techniques. Notably, they illustrate the power of collaborative
discussions between co-researchers, students, team teachers, interested

colleagues, administrators and research consultants. Formalising the discussions by documenting key insights or recording what has been said takes the procedures one step further than routine activities that are commonly part of teaching–learning interactions. Surveys and questionnaires, again common classroom activities, are harnessed for the purposes of data collection, as are collections of students' work and classroom materials. Information is exchanged on teaching strategies and materials and their strengths and weaknesses are analysed for further trialing. Audio and video taping to focus discussion of both teaching and learning are productively utilised and lead to further insights and strategic actions.

Above all, experimenting with collaborative action research builds a professional learning community with other teachers. In a profession generally characterised by practitioner isolation, the research process empowers teachers by reaffirming their professional judgement and enabling them to take steps to make reflection on practice a regular part of everyday teaching.

In this book I have been an advocate for language practitioner action research. My advocacy stems from the overwhelmingly positive responses of the many teachers whose work has been personalised throughout these chapters and who have been my partners in research endeavours. At the same time, I hope I have painted a realistic picture of the highs and lows for teachers contemplating a research perspective on their practice. To this end, I give the final word to a teacher, Meg Quinn (1997a), whose honest appraisal will encapsulate for many teachers the prevailing complexities and dilemmas of the current 'teacher as researcher' movement. If this movement is to become a reality, it is teachers who must ultimately define its possibilities.

> I learnt much from the close observation of the students and recording the comments they made both in the classroom and in the interview. I also learnt much from being able to share my reflections with other teachers. In particular, I was fortunate to have another teacher from my centre in the research project, who was also teaching at the same level. As we became more involved in the research we used each other to reflect on what was happening and to develop ideas. This shared reflection became part of the project and contributed to the decisions I made and the conclusions I came to.

> However, there is a conflict between the dual roles of classroom teacher and researcher. Often the demands of one seem to get in the way of the demands of the other. It is often hard to maintain the role of both observer and participant in the classroom situation and the time required to write observations and keep a journal, so essential to an ethnographic study, can be difficult to fit into a

teaching day. Another factor that I found personally frustrating was the time constraint on the project. I felt that just as I knew what I was doing and starting to see some results, the project was finished. This is also partly due to the fact that it was a ten-week class. Students usually change classes after those ten weeks so it would be difficult to follow a longer study through. However, longer study is required to properly investigate this subject.

My involvement in the project has provided an opportunity for reflection on both practice and the theory of practice. Even though I feel that the results may be of limited value for a wider audience, the personal and professional benefits have been great and will hopefully have an ongoing impact on my teaching.

Further reading

Books and articles

There is now a large number of publications which provide discussions and guidance on action research in the general educational literature. These provide extensive information for the more 'advanced' action researcher as well as for those new to this approach to research.

There are several well-known, even 'classical', accounts of early large-scale action research projects. Many of the earlier readings are British in origin, reflecting substantial initiatives in action research, such as the Humanities Curriculum Project and the Ford Teaching Project, which emerged in the 1960s and 1970s. Amongst these accounts are:

Ebbutt, D. 1983. Educational action research: some general concerns and specific quibbles. Mimeo. Cambridge Institute of Education.

Elliott, J. 1978. What is action research in schools? *Journal of Curriculum Studies*, 10, 4: 355–7.

Elliott, J. 1977. Developing hypotheses about classrooms from teachers' practical constructs: an account of the Ford Teaching Project. *Interchange*, 7, 2: 2–20.

Elliott, J. and C. Adelman. 1973. Reflecting where the action is: the design of the Ford Teaching Project. *Education for Teaching*, 92: 8–20.

Stenhouse, L. 1971. The Humanities Curriculum Project: the rationale. *Theory into Practice*, X, 3: 154–62.

Stenhouse, L. 1975. *An Introduction to Curriculum Research and Development*. London: Heinemann.

Readings developed from work in Australia and Britain which reflect the more recent development of a critical dimension to action research are:

Carr, W. and S. Kemmis. 1986. *Becoming Critical: Education, Knowledge and Action Research*. London: Falmer Press.

Lomax, P. and J. Whitehead. 1987. Action research and the politics of educational knowledge. *British Educational Research Journal*, 13, 2: 175–90.

Nixon, J. 1981. *A Teacher's Guide to Action Research: Evaluation Enquiry and Development*. London: Grant MacIntyre.

Rudduck, J. and D. Hopkins (eds). 1985. *Research as a Basis for Teaching*. London: Heinemann.

Winter, R. 1989. *Learning from Experience: Principles and Practice in Action Research*. London: The Falmer Press.

There are a number of major publications which reflect the resurgence of an interest in action research in the North American context:

Argyris, C., R. Putnam and D. Smith. 1985. *Action Science: Concepts, Methods and Skills for Research and Intervention*. San Francisco: Jossey-Bass.

Bissex, G. and R. Bullock. 1987. *Seeing for Ourselves: Case Study Research by Teachers of Writing*. Portsmouth, NH: Heinemann.

Cochran-Smith, M. and S. Lytle. 1990. Research on teaching and teacher research: the issues that divide. *Educational Researcher*, 19, 2: 2–11.

Connelly, F. M. and J. D. Clandinin. 1988. *Teachers as Curriculum Planners: Narratives of Experience*. New York: Teachers College Press.

Gore, J. and K. Zeichner. 1991. Action research and reflective teaching in preservice teacher education: a case study from the United States. *Teaching and Teacher Education*, 7, 2: 119–36.

Goswami, D. and P. R. Stillman (eds.). 1987. *Reclaiming the Classroom: Teacher Research as an Agency for Change*. Upper Montclair, VT: Boynton/Cook.

Lytle, S. and M. Cochran-Smith. 1990. Learning from Teacher Research. A Working Typology. *Teacher College Record*, 92, 1: 83–102.

Mohr, M. and M. McLean. 1987. *Working Together: A Guide for Teacher Researchers*. Urbana, IL: National Council of Teachers of English.

Myers, M. 1985. *The Teacher-Researcher: How to Study Writing in the Classroom*. Urbana, IL: National Council of Teachers of English.

Oja, N. and L. Smulyan. 1989. *Collaborative Action Research: A Developmental Process*. Philadelphia: Falmer Press.

Sorotnik, K. A. and J. I. Goodlad (eds.). 1988. *School–University Partnerships in Action*. New York: Teachers College Press.

Strickland, D. 1988. The teacher as researcher: Towards the extended professional. *Language Arts*, 65, 8: 754–64.

Books which are useful in providing extensive practical guidance for conducting action research include:

Altrichter, H., P. Posch and B. Somekh. 1993. *Teachers Investigate their Work*. London: Routledge.

Hitchcock, G. and D. Hughes. 1995. *Research and the Teacher*. Second edition. London: Routledge.

Hopkins, D. 1993. *A Teacher's Guide to Classroom Research*. Second edition. Buckingham: Open University Press.

Hustler, D., A. Cassidy and E. C. Cuff (eds.). 1986. *Action Research in Classrooms and Schools*. London: Allen and Unwin.

Kemmis S. and R. McTaggart (eds.). 1988. *The Action Research Planner*. Third edition. Geelong, Victoria: Deakin University Press.

McKernan, J. 1996. *Curriculum Action Research. A Handbook of Methods and Resources for the Reflective Practitioner*. Second edition. London: Kogan Page.

McNiff, J. 1988. *Action Research. Principles and Practice*. London: Routledge.

Walker, R. 1985. *Doing Research. A Handbook for Teachers*. London: Routledge.

Resources which provide practical information on conducting action research in the second language field are still relatively few in number. They include:

Bailey, K. and D. Allwright. 1991. *Focus on the Language Classroom: An Introduction to Classroom Research for Language Teachers*. Cambridge: Cambridge University Press.

Freeman, D. 1998. *Doing Teacher Research: From Enquiry to Understanding*. Boston: Heinle and Heinle.

McDonough, J. and S. McDonough. 1997. *Research Methods for English Language Teachers*. London: Arnold.

Nunan, D. 1989. *Understanding Language Classrooms. A Guide for Teacher-Initiated Actions*. Englewood Cliffs, NJ: Prentice-Hall.

Nunan, D. 1990. Action research in the language classroom. In J. C. Richards and D. Nunan (eds.). *Second Language Teacher Education*. New York: Cambridge University Press.

Wallace, M.J. 1998. *Action Research for Language Teachers*. Cambridge: Cambridge University Press.

Two key articles that discuss action research in second language education are:

Crookes, G. 1993. Action research for second language teachers: going beyond action research. *Applied Linguistics*, 14, 2: 130–42.

van Lier, L. 1994. Action research. *Sintagma*, 6: 31–7.

There are other recent second language publications which may be useful in identifying focus areas or issues for action research, although they do not provide direct accounts of how to do action research. They include:

Edge, J. and K. Richards (eds.). 1993. *Teachers Develop Teachers Research. Papers on Classroom Research and Teacher Development.* Oxford: Heinemann.

Nunan, D. and C. Lamb. 1996. *The Self-Directed Teacher.* Cambridge: Cambridge University Press.

Parrott, M. 1993. *Tasks for Language Teachers.* Cambridge: Cambridge University Press.

Reay-Dickins, P. and. K. Germaine. 1992. *Evaluation.* Oxford: Oxford University Press.

Richards, J. and C. Lockhart. 1993. *Reflective Teaching in Second Language Classrooms.* Cambridge: Cambridge University Press.

van Lier, L. 1996. *Interaction in the Language Curriculum: Awareness, Autonomy and Authenticity.* London: Longman.

Wajnryb, R. 1992. *Classroom Observation Tasks.* Cambridge: Cambridge University Press.

There is a growing number of accounts by second and foreign language teachers who have conducted action research in their own classrooms or schools. Amongst them are:

Burns, A. and S. Hood (eds.). 1995. *Teachers' Voices: Exploring Course Design in a Changing Curriculum.* Sydney: National Centre for English Language Teaching and Research.

Burns, A. and S. Hood (eds.). 1997. *Teachers' Voices 2: Teaching Disparate Learner Groups.* Sydney: National Centre for English Language Teaching and Research.

Burns, A. and S. Hood (eds.). 1998. *Teachers' Voices 3: Teaching Critical Literacy.* Sydney: National Centre for English Language Teaching and Research.

Kebir, C. 1994. An action research look at the communicative strategies of adult learners. *TESOL Journal,* 4, 1: 28–31.

Snow, M. A., J. Hyland, L. Kamhi-Stein and J. H Yu. 1996. US language minority students: voices from the junior high classroom. In K. Bailey and D. Nunan (eds.), *Voices from the Language Classroom: Qualitative Research in Language Education.* Cambridge: Cambridge University Press.

Szostek, C. 1994. Assessing the effects of cooperative learning in an Honours foreign language classroom. *Foreign Language Annals,* 27: 252–61.

Tsui, A. 1996. Reticence and anxiety in second language learning. In K. Bailey and D. Nunan (eds.), *Voices from the Language Classroom: Qualitative Research in Language Education.* Cambridge: Cambridge University Press.

Journals

Specialist journals on action research are few in number. There are no journals to date which focus exclusively on action research in second language education, but three recent journals in the general educational field are listed below.

Educational Action Research: An International Journal
This is a journal of the Collaborative Action Research Network (CARN) based in the United Kingdom, which began in 1993. Information obtainable from:
Triangle Journals Ltd, PO Box 65, Wallingford, Oxfordshire, OX10 0YG, UK
Email: journals@triangle.co.uk
http://www.triangle.co.uk

Teacher Research: The Journal of Classroom Inquiry
This journal has been published by the University of Maine in the USA since 1993. Information obtainable from:
Johnson Press, 49 Sheridan Avenue, Albany, NY 12210, USA

Networks: An Online Journal of Teacher Research
This is a journal which was set up on the world-wide web in 1998. Its aim is to encourage teachers internationally who are undertaking action research in their classrooms to publish through the internet. Information obtainable from:
http://www.oise.utoronto.ca/~ctd/networks

ELT journals which are directed at a teacher readership include:

Asian Journal of English Language Teaching
English Language Teaching Unit, The Chinese University of Hong Kong, Shatin, New Territories, Hong Kong
Email: ggong@cuhk.edu.hk or georgebraine@cuhk.edu.hk

Canadian Modern Language Review
University of Toronto Press, Journals Division 5201, Dufferin Street, North York, Ontario, M3H 5T8, Canada
Email: cmir@gpu.utcc.utoronto.ca

ELICOS Association Journal
PO Box 30, Pyrmont, NSW 2009, Australia

ELT Journal
Oxford University Press, Walton Street, Oxford, OX2 6DP, UK
Email: 10064133@compuserve.com

English Teaching Forum
Room 304, 301 4th Street, SW Washington DC, 20547, USA
Email: etforum@usia.gov

English Teaching Profession
The Swan Business Centre, Foshers Lane, Chiswick, London,W4 1RX, UK
Email: 101723.563@compuserve.com

ESP Malaysia
Department of Modern Languages, Faculty of Management and Human Resource Development, Universiti Teknologi Malaysia, Karung NBerkunci 791, 80990 Johor Bahru, Johor Darul Takzim, Malaysia

Guidelines
SEAMEO Regional Language Centre, 30 Orange Grove Road, Singapore, 258352, Republic of Singapore

JALT Journal
Osaka Jogakuin Junior College, 2–26–54 Tamatsukari, Chuo-ku, Osaka, 540 Japan

Language Issues
NATECLA National Centre, South Birmingham College, 520–524 Stratford Road, Birmingham, B11 4AJ, UK

Language Learning
Ontario Institute for Studies in Education, Modern Language Centre, Room 10–237, Bloor St West, Toronto, Ontario, Canada M5S 1V6
Email: acumming@oise.on.ca

Language Teacher
Osaka Jogakuin Junior College, 2–26–54 Tamatsukari, Chuo-ku, Osaka, 540 Japan

Language Teaching
2–91 Shinchon-dong, Suhdaemoon-ka, Seoul 120–140, Korea
Email: dstrawn@bubble.yonsei.ac.kr

Language Teaching Research
Arnold, 338 Euston Road, London, NW1 3BH, UK

Modern English Teacher
PO Box 5141, London, W4 2WQ, UK

ORTESOL Journal
c/o Department of Applied Linguistics, Portland State University, PO Box 751, Portland, OR 97207, USA
Email: dbkh@odin.cc.pds.edu

Further reading

Practical English Teacher
Pilgrims Language Courses, 8 Vernon Place, Canterbury, Kent, CT1 3NG, UK

Prospect
National Centre for English Language Teaching and Research, Macquarie University, Sydney, NSW 2109, Australia
Email: nceltr@mq.edu.au

RELC Journal
SEAMEO Regional Language Centre, 30 Orange Grove Road, Singapore, 258352, Republic of Singapore

TESL Canada Journal
6th Floor, Education North Department of Educational Psychology, University of Alberta, Edmonton, Alberta, T6G 2G5, Canada

TESOL in Context
The Journal of the Australian council of TESOL Associations, 81 Swanbourne Street, Fremantle, Western Australia, 6160, Australia

TESOL Journal
Cameron Street, Suite 300, Alexandria, VA 22314–2751, USA

Thai TESOL Bulletin
Center for Language and Educational Technology, Asian Institute of Technology, PO Box 4, Pathumthani 12120, Thailand
Email: nick@ait.ac.th

Mailing lists

ARLIST is an electronic mailing list which aims to provide a forum for people interested in discussing issues about the theory and practice of action research. To subscribe, email the message **subscribe arlist** to: arlist-request@psy.uq.oz.au.
   Information obtainable from: Bob Dick, bd@psy.uq.oz.au.

Action research networks

The best-known teacher network focusing on action research is:
Classroom Action Research Network (CARN)
School of Education, University of East Anglia, Norwich, NR4 7TJ, UK

References

Agar, M. 1980. *The Professional Stranger: An Informal Introduction to Ethnography*. New York: Academic Press.

Allan, L. 1994. *Reflections and Teaching: Cooperative Workshops To Explore Your Experience*. Sydney: Adult Literacy Information Office.

Allwright, D. 1988. *Observation in the Language Classroom*. London: Longman.

Allwright, D. 1991. Exploratory language teaching: a mini-course for XI ENPULI. *Working Paper*, 9. Centre for Research in Language Education, Lancaster: Lancaster University.

Allwright, D. 1993. Integrating 'research' and 'pedagogy': appropriate criteria and practical possibilities. In Edge and Richards (1993).

Allwright, D. and K. M. Bailey. 1991. *Focus on the Language Classroom*. Cambridge: Cambridge University Press.

Allwright, D., M. I. Cunha, R. Lenzuen, T. Mazillo, and I. Miller. 1997. Achieving sustainability in teacher research: problems and possibilities. Colloquium presented at the 31st Annual TESOL Convention, Orlando, Florida, March 1997.

Anderson, G. L., K. Herr and A. S. Nihlen. 1994. *Studying Your Own School: An Educator's Guide to Qualitative Practitioner Research*. Thousand Oaks, CA: Corwin Press.

Apple, M. 1982. *Education and Power*. Boston: Routledge and Kegan Paul.

Argyris, C. and D. Schön. 1991. Participatory action research and action science compared: a commentary. In W. F. Whyte (ed.), *Participatory Action Research*. Newbury Park, CA: Sage.

Bailey, K. M. 1983. Competitiveness and anxiety in adult second language acquisition: looking at and through the diary studies. In H. W. Seliger, and M. H. Long (eds.), *Classroom Oriented Research in Second Language Acquisition*. Rowley, MA: Newbury House.

Bailey, K. M. 1990. The use of diary studies in teacher education programmes. In Richards and Nunan (1992).

Bailey, K. M. 1998. Approaches to empirical research in instructional settings. In H. Byrnes, (ed.), *Perspectives in Research and Scholarship in Second Language Learning*. New York: The Modern Language Association of America.

Bailey, K. M. and R. Ochsner. 1983. A methodological review of the diary studies: windmill tilting or social science? In K. M. Bailey, M. H. Long and S. Peck (eds.), *Studies in Second Language Acquisition: Series on Issues in Second Language Research*. Rowley, MA: Newbury House.

References

Bartlett, L. 1992. Teacher development through reflective teaching. In J. Richards and Nunan (1992).

Bassey, M. 1986. Does action research require sophisticated research methods? In D. Hustler *et al.* (1986).

Beales, A. 1995. The special considerations in selecting and sequencing course content in workplace courses. In Burns and Hood (1995).

Beasley, R. and L. Riordan. 1981. The classroom teacher as researcher. *English in Australia*, 55:36–41.

Belenky, M. G., B. M. Clichy, N. R. Goldberger and J. M. Tarule, 1986. *Women's Ways of Knowing: The Development of Self, Voice, and Mind.* New York: Basic Books.

Bell, J. 1993. *Doing Your Research Project.* Second edition. Buckingham: Open University Press.

Bello, T. 1994. Respecting and serving the needs of ESL senior citizens. *TESOL Journal*, 4, 1:36–9.

Benson, M. 1994. Writing an academic article. An editor writes ... *Forum*, 32, 2 6–9.

Berwick, R. 1989. Needs assessment in language programming: from theory to practice. In R. K. Johnson (ed.), *The Second Language Curriculum.* Cambridge: Cambridge University Press.

Block, D. 1992. Metaphors we teach and learn by. *Prospect*, 7, 3:42–55.

Bogdan R. and S. K. Biklen. 1982. *Qualitative Research for Education: An Introduction to Theory and Methods.* First edition. Boston: Allyn and Bacon.

Bogdan R. and S. K. Biklen. 1998. *Qualitative Research for Education: An Introduction to Theory and Methods.* Third edition. Boston: Allyn and Bacon.

Bottomley, Y., J. Dalton and C. Corbel. 1994. *From Proficiency to Competencies – A Collaborative Approach to Curriculum Innovation.* Sydney: National Centre for English Language Teaching and Research.

Bradley, P. 1995. Open letters to reflect on. In Riddell (1995).

Brindley, G. 1990. Towards a research agenda for TESOL. *Prospect*, 6, 1:7–26.

Brindley, G. 1991. Becoming a researcher: teacher conducted research and professional growth. In E. Sadtono (ed.). *Issues in Language Teacher Education.* Singapore: SEAMEO Regional Language Centre.

Brindley, G. 1992. Towards a collaborative research agenda for TESOL. Paper presented at the 26th Annual TESOL Convention, Vancouver, March 1992.

Brophy, M. 1995. Helena's perspective. In Riddell (1995).

Brown, C. 1995. A question of action. In Riddell (1995).

Brown, G. and G. Yule. 1983. *Teaching the Spoken Language: An Approach Based on the Analysis of Conversational English.* Cambridge: Cambridge University Press.

Brown, J. D. 1988. *Understanding Research in Second Language Learning: A Teacher's Guide to Statistics and Research Design.* New York: Cambridge University Press.

Brown, J. D. 1991. Statistics as a foreign language – Part 1: what to look for in reading statistical studies. *TESOL Quarterly*, 25, 4:549–86.

Brown, J. D. 1992. Statistics as a foreign language – Part 2: more things to consider in reading statistical language studies. *TESOL Quarterly*, 25, 4:629–664.

Brumfit, C. and R. Mitchell. 1989. The language classroom as a focus for research. In C. Brumfit and R. Mitchell (eds.), *Research in the Language Classroom*. ELT Documents 133. London: Modern Language Publications.

Burgess, R. (ed.). 1993. *Educational Research for Policy and Practice*. London: Falmer Press.

Burns, A. 1991. Action research: reflecting on practice in the classroom. Paper presented at the 4th Congress of the Latin-American British Council Institutes. Santiago, Chile, July.

Burns, A. 1995. Teacher researchers: perspectives on teacher action research and curriculum renewal. In Burns and Hood (1995).

Burns, A. 1996. Starting all over again: from teaching adults to teaching beginners. In Freeman and Richards (1996).

Burns, A. 1997. Action research, curriculum change and professional growth. In Field *et al.* (1997).

Burns, A. and S. Hood (eds.). 1995. *Teachers' Voices: Exploring Course Design in a Changing Curriculum*. Sydney: National Centre for English Language Teaching and Research.

Burns, A. and S. Hood (eds.). 1997. *Teachers' Voices 2: Teaching Disparate Learner Groups*. Sydney: National Centre for English Language Teaching and Research.

Burns, A. and S. Hood (eds.). 1998. *Teachers' Voices 3: Teaching Critical Literacy*. Sydney: National Centre for English Language Teaching and Research.

Burns, A., S. Hood, A. Lukin and P. McPherson. 1996. Expanding the professionalism of TESOL practitioners through action research. Paper prepared for the Research Symposium, 30th Annual TESOL Convention, Chicago, March 1996.

Burns, A., H. Joyce and S. Gollin. 1996. *'I see what you mean'. Using Spoken Discourse in the Classroom: A Handbook for Teachers*. Sydney: National Center for English Language Teaching and Research.

Burns, R. B. 1994. *Introduction to Research Methods*. Melbourne: Longman.

Burton, J. and P. Mickan. 1993. Teachers' classroom research: rhetoric and reality. In Edge and Richards (1993).

Butler-Wall, B. 1979. Diary studies. In E. Arafa, C. Brown, B. Butler-Wall and M. Early (eds.), *Classroom observation and analysis*. Unpublished manuscript, Applied Linguistics Ph.D. Program, University of California, Los Angeles.

Calhoun, E. F. 1994. *How to Use Action Research in the Self-renewing School*. Alexandria, VA: Association for Supervision and Curriculum Development.

Campbell, V. 1995. Competency-based vocational language learning: exploring learners' views. In Burns and Hood (1995).

Candlin, C. N. 1995. Networking and professional development. *News from the Forum*, 2, 4:2–3.

References

Candlin, C. N. 1996. Resourcing the resourceful. *Outreach*, 5, 3:1.

Cane, B. and C. Schroeder. 1970. *The Teacher and Research*. London: National Foundation for Educational Research in England and Wales.

Carew, M. 1995. The effects of educational background in the program of beginning learners: a case study. In Burns and Hood (1995).

Carr, W. and S. Kemmis. 1986. *Becoming Critical: Knowing through Action Research*. Geelong, Victoria: Deakin University.

Carroll, M. 1994. Journal writing as a learning and research tool in the adult classroom. *TESOL Journal*, 4, 1:19–22.

Carroll, M. 1995. Developing integrated approaches towards assessment. In Burns and Hood (1995).

Chaudron, C. 1988. *Second Language Classrooms: Research on Teaching and Learning*. Cambridge: Cambridge University Press.

Cochran-Smith M. and S. Lytle. 1990. Research on teaching and teacher research: the issues that divide. *Educational Researcher*, 19, 2:2–11.

Cohen, L. and L. Manion. 1985. *Research Methods in Education*. Second edition. London: Croom Helm.

Cohen, L. and L. Manion. 1994. *Research Methods in Education*. Fourth edition. London: Croom Helm.

Congdon, P. 1978. Basic principles of sociometry. *Association of Education Psychologists Journal*, 4, 8:5–9.

Connelly, F. M. and J. D. Clandinin. 1988. *Teachers as Curriculum Planners: Narratives of Experience*. New York: Teachers College Press.

Connelly, F. M. and J. D. Clandinin. 1990. Stories of experience and narrative inquiry. *Educational Researcher*, 19, 5:2–14.

Corbel, C. 1992. The AMES Victoria approach to professional development for teachers. Presentation at the Train the Trainer Workshop, National Centre for English Language Teaching and Research, Macquarie University, Sydney, March 1992.

Corey, S. M. 1953. *Action Research to Improve School Practices*. Columbia, New York: Teachers' College.

Cronbach, L. J., S. R. Ambron, S. M. Dornbusch, R. D. Hess, R. C. Hornik, D. C. Philips, D. F. Walker and S. F. Weiner. 1980. *Towards Reform of Program Evaluation*. San Francisco: Jossey-Bass.

Crookes, G. 1989. Grassroots action to improve ESL programs. *University of Hawai'i Working Papers in ESL*, 8, 2:45–61.

Crookes, G. 1993. Action research for second language teachers: going beyond teacher research. *Applied Linguistics*, 14, 2:130–44.

Dalton, J. and Y. Bottomley. 1994. From proficiency to competencies. *Prospect*, 9, 2:70–5.

Davis, K. 1995. Qualitative theory and methods in applied linguistic research. *TESOL Quarterly*, 29, 3:427–454.

Day, R. R. 1990. Teacher observation in second language education. In J. C. Richards and D. Nunan (eds.), *Second Language Teacher Education*. Cambridge: Cambridge University Press.

Day, A. 1996. *How to Get Research Published in Journals*. Aldershot: Gower.

de Leon, L. 1997. Strategies for non-language outcomes. In Burns and Hood (1997).

Denzin, N. K. (ed.). 1978. *Sociological Methods: A Source Book*. Chicago: Aldine.

Dewey, J. 1929. *The Sources of a Science of Education*. New York: Liveright.

Dillon, J. 1983. Problem solving and findings. *Journal of Creative Behaviour*, 16, 2:97–111.

Dingle, N. 1995. Collaboration in action research: the role of the research coordinator. In Burns and Hood (1995).

Dominice, P. F. 1990. Composing educational biographies: group reflection through life histories. In J. Mezirow (ed.), *Fostering Critical Reflection in Adulthood*. San Francisco: Jossey-Bass.

Ebbutt, D. 1985. Educational action research: some general concerns and specific quibbles. In R. Burgess, (ed.), *Issues in Educational Research*. Lewes: Falmer Press.

Edge, J. and K. Richards (eds.). 1993. *Teachers Develop Teachers Research. Papers on Classroom Research and Teacher Development*. Oxford: Heinemann.

Elliott, J. 1991. *Action Research for Educational Change*. Milton Keynes: Open University Press.

Elliott, J. and C. Adelman. 1973. Reflecting where the action is: the design of the Ford Teaching Project. *Education for Teaching*, 92:8–20.

Elliott, J. and C. Adelman. 1976. *Innovation at the Classroom Level: A Case Study of the Ford Teaching Project. Course CE203*. Milton Keynes: Open University.

Erickson, F. 1986. Qualitative methods in research on teaching. In M. C. Wittrock (ed.), *Handbook of Research on Teaching*. New York: Collier-Macmillan.

Erickson F. and J. Wilson. 1982. *Sights and Sounds of Life in Schools*. Research Series No. 125. Ann Arbor, MI: Institute for Research in Teaching, College of Education, University of Michigan.

Field, J., A. Graham, E. Griffiths and K. Head. 1997. *Teachers Develop Teachers Research 2*. Whitstable: International Association of Teachers of English as a Foreign Language.

Firestone, W. A. 1987. Meaning in method: the rhetoric of quantitative and qualitative research. *Educational Researcher*, 16, 7:16 21.

Fowler, A. 1997. Developing independent learning. In Burns and Hood (1997).

Freeman, D. 1991. Learning teaching: 'Inter-teaching' and other views of the development of teachers' knowledge. Plenary paper presented at the Annual Washington Area TESOL Conference, Washington, DC, October 1991.

Freeman, D. 1998. *Doing Teacher Research: From Inquiry to Understanding*. Boston: Heinle and Heinle.

Freeman, D. and J. Richards (eds.). 1996. *Teacher Learning in Language Teaching*. New York: Cambridge University Press.

Fullan, M. (with S. Stiegelbauer). 1991. *The New Meaning of Educational Change*. New York: Teachers' College Press.

Fullan, M. and A. Pomfret. 1977. Research on curriculum and instruction implementation. *Review of Educational Research*, 47, 2:335–93.

Fulwiler, T. (ed.). 1987. *The Journal Book*. Portsmouth, NH: Boynton/Cook.

Glaser B. G. and A. L. Strauss. 1967. *The Discovery of Grounded Theory: Strategies for Qualitative Research*. New York: Aldine de Gruyter.

Glickman, C. 1993. *Renewing America's Schools: A Guide for School-Based Action*. San Francisco: Josey-Bass.

Goetz, J. L. and M. D. LeCompte. 1984. *Ethnography and Qualitative Design in Educational Research*. New York: Academic Press.

Golombek, P. 1994. Putting teachers back into teachers' knowledge. *TESOL Quarterly*, 28, 2:404–7.

Goodman, J. 1997. At home in the workplace. In Burns and Hood (1997).

Goswami, D. and J. Stillman. 1987. *Reclaiming the Classroom: Teacher Research as an Agency for Change*. Upper Montclair, NJ: Boynton/Cook.

Grayson, K. 1997. Incorporating students' views into the planning process. In Burns and Hood (1997).

Griffiths, M. 1990. Grassroots practice or management tool? In P. Lomax (ed.), *Managing Staff Development in Schools: An Action Research Approach*. Bera Dialogues, No. 3. Clevedon: Multilingual Matters.

Hadfield, J. 1992. *Classroom Dynamics*. Oxford: Oxford University Press.

Halliday, M. A. K. 1985. *An Introduction to Functional Grammar*. London: Edward Arnold.

Halliday, M. A. K. and G. Plum. 1985. On casual conversation. In R. Hasan (ed.), *Discourse on Discourse*. Occasional Paper No. 7. Applied Linguistics Association of Australia.

Halsey, A. H. (ed.). 1972. *Educational Priority: Volume 1: E.P.A. Problems and Policies*. London: HMSO.

Hambling, V. 1997. Customising worksheets and activities. In Burns and Hood (1997).

Hamilton, J. 1997. Action research as professional development. In Burns and Hood (1997).

Hammond, J., A. Burns, H. Joyce, L. Gerot and D. Brosnan. 1992. *English for Social Purposes*. Sydney: National Centre for English Language Teaching and Research.

Harmey M., P. Sansey and D. Sinclair. 1996. Generating a positive learning environment. Unpublished action research report.

Hatcher-Friel, L. 1997. Collegiate reflections on methodology. In Burns and Hood (1997).

Heritage, J. 1984. *Garfinkel and Ethnomethodology*. Cambridge: Polity Press.

Hill, J. E. and A. Kerber. 1967. *Models, Methods and Analytical Procedures in Educational Research*. Detroit: Wayne State University Press.

Hitchcock, G. and D. Hughes. 1995. *Research and the Teacher*. Second edition. London: Routledge.

Hodgkinson, H. L. 1957. Action research – a critique. *Journal of Educational Sociology*, 31, 137–53.

Holly, M. 1984. *Keeping a Personal-Professional Journal*. Geelong, Australia: Deakin University Press.

Holly M. and J. Smyth, 1989. The journal as a way of theorising teaching. *The Australian Administrator*, 1:1–8.

Hopkins, D. 1993. *A Teacher's Guide to Classroom Research*. Second edition. Buckingham: Open University Press.

Hudelson, S. J. and J. W. Lindfors (eds.). 1993. *Delicate Balances: Collaborative Research in Language Education*. Urbana, IL: National Council of Teachers of English.

Humphries, S. 1984. *The Handbook of Oral History: Recording Life Stories*. London: Inter-Action Trust Limited.

Hustler, D., A. Cassidy and E. C. Cuff (eds.). 1986. *Action Research in Classrooms and Schools*. London: Allen and Unwin.

Jarvis, G. 1980. Action research vs. needed research for the 1980s. In ACTFL: Proceedings of the National Conference on Professional Priorities. Hastings-on-Hudson: American Council for Teaching of Foreign Languages.

Jarvis, G. 1991. Research on teaching methodology: its evolutions and prospects. In B. F. Freed (ed.), *Foreign Language Acquisition Research and the Classroom*. Lexington, MA: D. C. Heath.

Johnson, D. M. 1992. *Approaches to Research in Second Language Learning*. New York: Longman.

Johnson, K. and K. Morrow. 1981. *Communication in the Classroom*. London: Longman.

Kebir, C. 1994. An action research look at the communication strategies of adult learners. *TESOL Journal*, 4, 1:28–31.

Kellehear, A. 1993. *The Unobtrusive Researcher: A Guide to Methods*. Sydney: Allen and Unwin.

Kemmis, S. and R. McTaggart (eds.). 1982. *The Action Research Planner*. First edition. Geelong, Victoria: Deakin University Press.

Kemmis, S. and R. McTaggart (eds.) 1988. *The Action Research Planner*. Third edition. Geelong, Victoria: Deakin University Press.

Kerlinger, F. N. 1970. *Foundations of Behavioural Research*. New York: Holt, Rinehart and Winston.

Koenig, J. and J. Zuengler. 1994. Teacher/researcher collaboration: studying student and teacher goals in oral classroom activities. *TESOL Journal*, 4, 1:40–3.

Kohn, J. 1997. Using English outside the classroom. In Burns and Hood (1997).

Koster, P. 1996. In the mood. In *Investigating the Teaching of Grammar. Reports from a Collaborative Action Research Project Conducted by NSW AMES*. NSW AMES Occasional Papers Volume 1. Sydney: Program Support and Development Services.

Kumarivadivelu, B. 1994. The postmethod condition: (e)merging strategies for second/foreign language teaching. *TESOL Quarterly*, 28, 1:27–48.

LeCompte, M. and J. Preissle. 1993. *Ethnography and Qualitative Design in Educational Research*. Second edition. New York: Academic Press.

Lewin, K. 1946. Action research and minority problems. *Journal of Social Issues*, 2:34–46.

Lincoln Y. S. and E. G. Guba. 1985. *Naturalistic Inquiry*. Beverley Hills, CA: Sage.

Llewelyn, S. 1995. Topics, text types and grammar: making the links. In Burns and Hood (1995).

Lomax, P. 1990. An action research approach to developing staff in schools. In P. Lomax (ed.), *Managing Staff Development in Schools: An Action Research Approach*. Bera Dialogues, No. 3. Clevedon: Multilingual Matters.

Long, M. 1980. Inside the 'black box': methodological issues in classroom research on language learning. *Language Learning*, 30, 1:1–42.

Low, G. 1989. Appropriate design: the internal organisation of course units. In R. K. Johnson (ed.), *The Second Language Curriculum*. Cambridge: Cambridge University Press.

Lukin, A. 1995. Functional grammar in the classroom. In Burns and Hood (1995).

Malamah-Thomas, A. 1987. *Classroom Interaction*. Oxford: Oxford University Press.

Markee, N. 1997. *Managing Curricular Innovation*. Cambridge: Cambridge University Press.

Marrow, A. J. 1969. *The Practical Theorist: The Life and Works of Kurt Lewin*. New York: Basic Books.

Maykut, P. and R. Morehouse. 1994. *Beginning Qualitative Research. A Philosophical and Practical Guide*. London: Falmer Press.

Mazillo, T. 1994. On becoming a researcher. *TESOL Journal*, 4, 1:45–6.

McCormick R. and M. James. 1983. *Curriculum Evaluation in Schools*. London: Croom Helm.

McDonald, R., G. Hayton, A. Gonczi and P. Hager. 1993. *No Small Change: Proposals for a Research and Development Strategy for Vocational Education and Training in Australia*. Sydney: Research Centre for Vocational Education and Training, University of Technology, Sydney.

McDonough, J. and S. McDonough. 1990. What's the use of research? *ELT Journal*, 44, 2:102–9.

McDonough, J. and S. McDonough. 1997. *Research Methods for English Language Teachers*. London: Arnold.

McKay, S. L. 1997. Writing for publication. *The Language Teacher*, 21, 6:15–18.

McKernan, J. 1993. Varieties of curriculum action research: constraints and typologies in American, British and Irish projects. *Journal of Curriculum Studies*, 25, 5:445–58.

McKernan, J. 1996. *Curriculum Action Research. A Handbook of Methods and Resources for the Reflective Practitioner*. Second edition. London: Kogan Page.

McNiff, J. 1988. *Action Research: Principles and Practice*. London: Routledge.

McPhail, A. 1995. Investigating with learners their perceptions of competency-based language. In Burns and Hood (1995).

McPherson, P. 1995. Classroom research. Presentation at The Context of English Language and Literacy in the 90s, NSW AMES Regional Conference, Burwood, Sydney. October 1995.

McPherson, P. 1997a. Action research: exploring learner diversity. *Prospect*, 12, 1:50–62.

McPherson, P. 1997b. Social and cultural differences in the classroom. In Burns and Hood (1997).

McPherson, P. 1997c. *Investigating Learner Outcomes for Clients with Special Needs in the Adult Migrant English Program*. Research Report Series No. 9. Sydney: National Centre for English Language Teaching and Research.

McTaggart, R. 1991. *Action Research: A Short Modern History*. Geelong, Victoria: Deakin University Press.

Merriam, S. B. 1988. *Case Study Research in Education: A Qualitative Approach*. San Francisco: Jossey-Bass.

Miles, M. and M. Huberman. 1984. *Qualitative Data Analysis: A Sourcebook of New Methods*. First edition. Beverley Hills, CA: Sage.

Miles, M. and M. Huberman. 1994. *Qualitative Data Analysis: A Sourcebook of New Methods*. Second edition. Beverley Hills, CA: Sage.

Miller, J. 1990. *Creating Spaces and Finding Voices: Teachers Collaborating for Empowerment*. Albany: State University of New York Press.

Muldoon, M. 1997. A profile of group diversity. In Burns and Hood (1997).

Mulvaney, H. 1997. Making the most of support resources. In Burns and Hood (1997).

Munn, P. and E. Drever. 1990. *Using Questionnaires in Small-Scale Research*. Edinburgh: Scottish Council for Research in Education.

Murphy, D. 1996. The evaluator's apprentice: learning to do evaluation. *The International Journal of Theory, Research and Practice*, 2, 3:321–38.

Myers, M. 1985. *The Teacher-Researcher: How to Study Writing in the Classroom*. Urbana, IL.: ERIC Clearing House on Reading and Communication Skills and the National Council of Teachers of English.

Naidu, B., K. Neeraja, E. Ramani, J. Shivakumar, and V. Viswanatha, 1992. Researching heterogeneity: an account of teacher-initiated research into large classes. *ELT Journal*, 46, 3:252–63.

Nunan, D. 1987. *The Teacher as Curriculum Developer*. Sydney: National Centre for English Language Teaching and Research.

Nunan, D. 1988. *The Learner-Centred Curriculum*. Cambridge: Cambridge University Press.

Nunan, D. 1989. *Understanding Language Classrooms. A Guide for Teacher-Initiated Action*. Hemel Hempstead: Prentice Hall.

Nunan, D. 1992. *Research Methods in Language Learning*. Cambridge: Cambridge University Press.

Nunan, D. 1993. Action research in language education. In Edge and Richards (1993).

Ochs, E. 1979. Transcription as theory. In E. Ochs and B. Schieffelin (eds.). *Developmental Pragmatics*. New York: Academic Press.

Oja, S. N. and L. Smulyan 1989. *Collaborative Action Research: A Developmental Approach*. London: Falmer Press.

Patton, M. Q. 1980. *Qualitative Evaluation Methods*. Beverley Hills, CA: Sage.

Perkins, J. 1997. Unpublished report from the NCELTR Teaching Critical Literacy Action Research Project.

Perkins, J. 1998. Developing critical literacy with post-beginner learners. In Burns and Hood (1998).

Phillips, J. 1996. Stress for success. Unpublished Masters of Applied Linguistics dissertation, Macquarie University, Sydney.

Pierson, C. 1997. Finding common goals. In Burns and Hood (1997).

Popham, W. J. and D. Carlson. 1977. Deep, dark deficits of adversary evaluation. *Educational Researcher*, 6:3–6.

References

Prabhu, N. S. 1990. There is no best method – why? *TESOL Quarterly*, 24, 2:161–76.

Quinn, M. 1997a. 'Ah ... writing ... it's OK now': perceptions of literacy learning. In Burns and Hood (1997).

Quinn, M. 1997b. The experience of action research: a teacher's perspective. *Outreach*, 6, 3:4.

Rapoport, R. N. 1970. The three dilemmas in action research. *Human Relations*, 23, 6:499.

Reichardt, C. S. and D. Cook (eds.). 1979. *Qualitative and Quantitative Methods in Evaluation Research*. Beverley Hills, CA: Sage Publications.

Reynolds, M. J. 1982. The choice of frame and focus in a data-driven case study: a description of a research process. In S. Dingwall and S. Mann (eds.), *Methods and Problems in Doing Applied Linguistic Research*. University of Lancaster: Department of Linguistics and Modern English Language, September 1982.

Richards, J. C. (ed.). 1998 *Teaching in Action: Case Studies from Second Language Classrooms*. Alexandria, VA: TESOL.

Richards, J. C. and D. Nunan (eds.). 1992. *Second Language Teacher Education*. New York: Cambridge University Press.

Richards J. C and D. Freeman. 1992. Conceptions of teaching and the education of second language teachers. *TESOL Quarterly*, 27, 2:193–216.

Riddell, C. (ed.). 1995. *Journeys of Reflection: ESL Action Research in TAFE*. Melbourne: Office of Training and Further Education and Western Metropolitan College of TAFE.

Roberts, J. 1998. *Language Teacher Education*. London: Arnold.

Ross, L. 1997. Changes in practice: steps in action research. In Burns and Hood (1997).

Rudduck, J. 1981. *Making the Most of the Short Inservice Course*. London: Methuen.

Samway, K. D. 1994. But it's hard to keep fieldnotes while also teaching. *TESOL Journal*, 4, 1:47–8.

Schön, D. A. 1983. *The Reflective Practitioner: How Professionals Think in Action*. New York: Basic Books.

Schwab, J. J. 1969. *College Curricula and Student Protest*. Chicago: University of Chicago Press.

Schwab, J. J. 1970. *The Practical: A Language for Curriculum*. National Education Association, Washington. DC.

Seliger, H.W. and E. Shohamy. 1989. *Second Language Research Methods*. Oxford: Oxford University Press.

Shaw, S. 1997. Taking a whole group approach. In Burns and Hood (1997).

Silverman, D. 1993. *Interpreting Qualitative Data. Methods for Analysing Talk, Text and Interaction*. London: Sage.

Smith, J. K. and L. Heshusius. 1986. Closing down the conversation: the end of the quantitative-qualitative debate among educational inquirers. *Educational Researcher*, 15:4–12.

Somekh, B. 1993. Quality in educational research – the contribution of classroom teachers. In Edge and Richards (1993).

Somekh, B. 1994. Inhabiting each other's castles: towards knowledge and mutual growth through collaboration. *Educational Action Research*, 2, 3:357–81.

Somekh, B. 1996. Beyond common sense: action research and the learning organisation. *ELT Management*, 22:3–7.

Spada N. and M. Fröhlich. 1995. *COLT Observation Scheme. Coding Conventions and Applications*. Sydney: National Centre for English Language Teaching and Research.

Spradley, J. 1979. *The Ethnographic Interview*. New York: Holt, Rinehart and Winston.

Spradley, J. 1980. *Participant Observation*. New York: Holt, Rinehart and Winston.

Stake R. E. and C. Gjerde. 1974. An evaluation of TCITY, the Twin City Institute for Talented Youth 1971. In R. Kraft *et al.* (eds.). *Four Evaluation Examples: Anthropological, Economic, Narrative and Portrayal*. AERA Monograph Series on Curriculum Evaluation. Chicago: Rand McNally.

Stenhouse, L. 1975. *An Introduction to Curriculum Research and Development*. London: Heinemann.

Stenhouse, L. 1981. What counts as research? *British Journal of Educational Studies*, XXIX, 2:113.

Strickland, D. 1988. The teacher as researcher: towards the extended professional. *Language Arts*, 65, 8:74–64.

Taba, H. and E. Noel. 1957. Steps in the action research process. In *Action Research: A Case Study*. Washington, DC: Association for Supervision and Curriculum Development.

Tobin, K. 1990. Metaphors and images in teaching. In *What Research Says to the Science and Mathematics Teacher*. Monograph Series Paper No. 5. Curtin University: The Key Centre for School Sciences and Mathematics.

Troupiotis, D. 1994. The teaching of grammar. Unpublished action research report.

Troupiotis, D. 1995. What about grammar? In Burns and Hood (1995).

Tudor, I. 1996. *Learner-Centredness as Language Education*. Cambridge: Cambridge University Press.

Valeri, L. 1997. What do students think about group work? In Burns and Hood (1997).

van Lier, L. 1988. *The Classroom and the Language Learner*. London: Longman.

van Lier, L. 1994. Some features of a theory of practice. *TESOL Journal*, 4, 1:6–10.

van Lier, L. 1996. *Interaction in the Language Classroom: Awareness, Autonomy and Authenticity*. London: Longman.

van Manen, M. 1991. *The Tact of Teaching: The Meaning of Pedagogical Thoughtfulness*. Albany: State University of New York Press.

Walker, R. 1985. *Doing Research: A Handbook for Teachers*. London: Routledge.

Walker, R. 1991. Finding a silent voice for the researcher: using photographs in evaluation and research. In M. Schratz (ed.), *Qualitative Voices in Educational Research*. London: Falmer Press.

References

Walker R. and C. Adelman. 1972. *Towards a Sociography of Classrooms*. Final Report, Social Science Research Council Grant HR-996–1: The long-term observation of classroom events using stop-frame cinematography.

Wallace. M. J. 1998. *Action Research for Language Teachers*. Cambridge: Cambridge University Press.

Watson-Gegeo, K. A. 1988. Ethnography in ESL: defining the essentials. *TESOL Quarterly*, 22:575–92.

Whitehead J. and J. Barratt 1985. Supporting teachers in their classroom research. Collection of papers produced by Values in Education. School of Education, University of Bath.

Whitford, B. L., P. C. Schlechty and L. G. Shelor. 1987. Sustaining action research through collaboration. Inquiries for invention. *Peabody Journal of Educational Research*, 64, 3:151–69.

Whitham, S. 1997. How do you feel about this class? In Burns and Hood (1997).

Widdowson, H. 1990. *Aspects of Language Teaching*. Oxford: Oxford University Press.

Wiersma, W. 1986. *Research Methods in Education: An Introduction*. Boston: Allyn and Bacon.

Wilkins Intensive English Centre. 1996. Disadvantaged Schools' Component Project Evaluation Report. Unpublished report.

Winter, R. 1982. 'Dilemma analysis': a contribution to methodology for action research. *Cambridge Journal of Education*, 12, 3:11–74.

Winter, R. 1989. *Learning from Experience. Principles and Practice in Action Research*. London: Falmer Press.

Wolcott, H. 1992. Posturing in qualitative research. In M. LeCompte, W. Millroy and J. Preissle (eds.). *The Handbook of Qualitative Research in Education*. New York: Academic Press.

Wolf, R. L. 1975. Trial by jury: a new evaluation method. 1. The process. *Phi Delta Kappa*, 185–7.

Woods, D. 1996. *Teacher Cognition in Language Teaching*. Cambridge: Cambridge University Press.

Yow, V. R. 1994. *Recording Oral History*. Thousand Oaks, CA: Sage.

Index

action research
  analysis of data in, 152–179
  as professional development, 15,
    215–22
  benefits of for teachers, 14–18,
    48–49
  circumventing obstacles towards,
    49–53
  cyclical nature of, 32
  constraints and impediments on,
    45–, 48
  critical dimension in, 30–31
  criticism and defence of as valid
    form of research, 24–26, 27–28
  data collection and analysis in *see*
    data collection, data analysis
  definitions of, 29–34
  dissemination of results, 181–200
  flexibility of, 32
  finding a focus for, 37, 53–56
  features and nature of, 30–34
  in school renewal, 209–212,
    225–228
  in social context, 22, 32–34,
  motivation for carrying out,
    14–17
  origins of, 26–29
  phases of, 35, 36–43
  processes of, 35–43
  rationale for, 48
  validity of findings in, 160–166
Adelman, C., 28
Adult Migrant English Program, 1, 2,
  3–5, 7, 34, 59, 73, 215, 218
Agar, M., 153
alienation, 49
Allan, L., 138–139, 147–149
Allwright, D., 46, 52, 80, 206

Allwright, D. and K. M. Bailey, 52,
  99, 181
AMEP *see* Adult Migrant English
  Program
Anderson, G. L. *et al.*, 107, 150, 161,
  162, 208
Apple, M., 48
Argyris, C. and D. Schön, 152,

Bailey, K. M., 24, 90, 167
Bailey, K. M. and R. Ochsner, 90
Bassey, M., 191
Beales, A., 92
Beasley, R. and L. Riordan., 14
Belenky, M. G., 13
Bell, J., 192
Bello, T., 101
benefits of action research, Ch. 1
Benson, M., 190
bias, 166
Block, D., 147
Bogdan, R. and S. K. Biklen, 30, 168
Bottomley, Y. and J. Dalton, 204
Bradley, P., 145–146
Brindley, G., 24, 46, 53, 54, 78, 207
Brophy, M., 133
Brown, C., 8, 95–96, 97
Brown, G. and G. Yule, 99
Brown, J. D., 20
Brumfit, C. and R. Mitchell, 24
Burgess, R., 182
Burns, A., 97
Burns, A. and S. Hood, 59, 65, 205,
  206
Burns, A., H. Joyce and S. Gollin, 99
Burns, A., S. Hood, A. Lukin and P.
  McPherson, 79
Burns, R. B., 23, 30, 31, 87, 163

Burton, J. and P. Mickan, 46, 206
Butler-Wall, B., 167

Calhoun, E. F., 209–211, 225,
Camm, E., 197–198
Campbell, V., 73, 74, 135, 171
Candlin, C., 204–205
Cane, B. and C. Schroeder, 184
Carew, M., 91–93, 123–126
Carr, W. and S. Kemmis, 30, 153, 154
Carroll, M., 74, 89, 90, 127, 168
*Certificates in Spoken and Written
    English*, 4, 90–91, 187, 188, 203
Chaudron, C., 20, 80
Cochran-Smith, S. and M. Lytle, 53
codes (in data analysis)
    activity, 171
    definition of the situation, 169
    event, 172
    perspectives of subjects, 169–170
    process, 171
    relationship and social structure,
        172–173
    setting/context, 168–169
    strategy
    situation, 169
    ways of thinking, 170
coding
    categories, 166–168
    data, 157–158
Cohen, L. and L. Manion, 20, 29, 30,
    31,34, 59, 152, 163
collaborative research, 7, 11–12,
    13–14, 15, 31, 34, 59–68, 174,
    181, 203–204, 207–212,
    214–215;, 215–229
COLT, 80
Congdon, P., 110, 111
Connelly, F. M. and J. D. Clandinin,
    136
Corbel, C., 203
Corey, S., 27–28
Cronbach, L. J. *et al.*, 24
Crookes, G., 31, 49–50, 53, 182, 184
CSWE *see Certificates in Spoken and
    Written English.*
curriculum, 4, 14, 28–29, 56,
    201–202, 209

cycles in action research, 32, 156

Dalton, J. and J. Bottomley, 204
data analysis, 38–39
    assembly, 157
    classroom talk analysis, 173–179
    coding conventions, 99
    content analysis, 166–167
    data assembly, 157
    data comparison, 158–159
    definitions of, 153–154
    interpreting data, 159–169
    processes for, 156–160
    techniques for, 166–179
    validity of, 162–166
data collection, 25, 38, 71, 222
    formal observation schemes for,
        79–80
    non-observational techniques for,
        117–150; *see also* non-
        observational techniques
    observational techniques for,
        78–115; *see also* observational
        techniques
    triangulated *see* triangulation
Davis, K., 68, 153, 161
Day, R. R., 190
de Leon, L., 121–122, 170, 229–233
Denzin, N. K., 164
Dewey, J., 26
Dillon, J., 68
Dingle, N., 120
dissemination of research, 181–200
    through networks, 181–182;
        through presentations, 192–197;
        group, 193–195; individual,
        192–193; interactive, 195–197
    through visual displays, 197–201
    through written formats, 183–192
documents in data collection
    letters, 143–146
    student texts, 140–143
Dominice, P. F., 138

Ebbutt, D., 32, 183
Edge, J. and K. Richards, 214
educational biographies, 138–140
Elliott, J., 28, 32, 185

Erickson, F., 153, 161
Erickson, F. and J. Wilson, 101, 198–199
ethical considerations, 70–75
exploratory teaching, 52

Field, J., 214
Firestone, W. A., 24
Fowler, A., 130–132
Freeman, D., 13, 53, 214–215
Freeman, D. and J. Richards., 214
Fullan, M., 225
Fullan, M. and A. Pomfret., 225
Fulwiler, T., 90

Glaser, B. G. and A. L. Strauss, 25
Glickman, C., 209
Goetz, J. L. and M. D. LeCompte, 153
Golombek, P., 13
Goodman, J., 88, 173
Goswami, D. and P. R. Stillman, 10, 16, 90
Grayson, K., 169
grassroots action, 49–51
Griffiths, M., 208
'grounded' theory, 25

Hadfield, J., 144
Halliday, M. A. K., 141
Halsey, A. H., 30
Hambling, V., 82–84, 215, 216, 217, 219
Hamilton, J., 204, 215–221
Hammond, J., 65
Hannon, C., 181
Harmey, M. *et al.*, 36, 177–179
Hatcher-Friel, L., 82–84, 172, 215, 216, 217
Henry, C., 5
Heritage, J., 100–101
Hill, J. E., and A. Kerber, 31
Hitchcock, G., and D. Hughes, 21, 71, 87, 89, 102, 106, 107, 136–137, 165
Hodgkinson, H. L., 28, 29
Holly, M., 90
Holly, M. J. and J. Smyth, 90

Hopkins, D., 14, 32, 49, 63, 69, 101, 110, 136, 154, 166, 186, 202
Hudelson, S. J. and J. W. Lindfors, 206
Humphries, S., 136
Hustler, D. *et al.*, 183

IEC, 36, 225
Intensive English Centres *see* IEC
intervening, 39–40
interviews for data collection
    structured, 119–120
    semi/unstructured, 120–126
Introduction to Curriculum Research and Development, 28

Jarvis, G., 24, 46,
Johnson, D. M. and K. Morrow., 20, 98
journals, 189–192

Kebir, C., 73, 98, 176–177
Kellehear, A., 101
Kemmis, S. and R. McTaggart, 5, 12, 16, 32, 35, 38, 51, 54, 55, 110, 111
Koenig, J. and J. Zuengler, 182
Köhn, J., 214, 221–225
Koster, P., 141–143

LeCompte, M. and J. Preissle, 166
Lewin, K., 26–27, 32
Lincoln, Y. S. and E. G. Guba, 165, 166
Llewelyn, S., 188
Lomax, P., 202
Long, M., 80
Lukin, A., 81, 187

Malamah-Thomas, A., 80
Markee, N., 225
Maykut, P. and R. Morehouse, 153
Mazillo, T., 200–201
McCormick, R. and M. James, 165
McKay, S. L., 190
McKernan, J., 24, 26, 46, 47, 89, 94, 136, 156, 202, 206–207
McDonald, R. *et al.*, 182

McDonough, J. and M. McDonough, 5, 14
McNiff, J., 35, 51, 54, 158
McPhail, A., 132
McPherson, P., 79, 85–86, 89, 107, 111–114, 159–160, 192
McTaggart, R., 27, 28
member checks, 165
Merriam, S.B., 166
metaphor development, 147–150
Miles, M. and H. Huberman., 153, 180
Miller, J., 90, 208
Muldoon, M., 117, 137–138, 170
Mulvaney, H., 164, 169
Munn, P. and E. Drever, 130
Murphy, D., 206
Myers, M., 46

Naidu, B., K. Neeraja, E. Ramani, J. Shivakumar, and V. Viswanatha, 191
National Centre for English Language Teaching and Research, 2
NCELTR *see* National Centre for English Language Teaching and Research
non-language outcomes, 122, 229–233
non-observational techniques for data collection
    classroom discussions, 127–129
    documents *see* documents in data collection
    life and career histories, 136–140
    metaphor development, 147–150
    semi-structured and unstructured interviews, 120–126
    structured interviews, 118–120
    student diaries and journals, 133–136
    surveys and questionnaires, 129–133
    unstructured interviews, 118–120
Nunan, D., 5, 12, 20, 24, 25, 46, 78, 80, 97, 206,

Observation, 22, 40–41, 80–84

participant, 82–85
non-participant, 82–85
observational techniques for data collection
    audio and video recording, 94–98
    notes, 85–89
    proformas, 90–94
    social organisation, 105–115; layouts and maps, 106–110; sociometry, 110–115
    teacher diaries, 85–87, 89–90
    teacher journals *see* teachers diaries
    teacher notes, 87–89
Ochs, E., 99
Oja, S. N. and L. Smulyan., 206
operationalisation of terms, 21
outcomes reporting, 160

Patton, M. Q., 166
Pearson, C., 149–150
peer examinations, 165
Perkins, J., 66–68
Phillips, J., 69–70, 172
photographs
    in data collection, 101–105
    in displays, 199–200
Pierson, C., 149–150, 169
planning, 37–38
portrayals, 186–189
presentations, 42–43
    group, 193–195
    individual, 192–193
    interactive, 195–197
    photographic, 199–200
    poster displays, 200
    video displays, 197–199
professional development, 202–203, 215–233
Pupil Autonomy in Learning with Microcomputers, 72

qualitative research approach, 20, 22–23, 24, 25, 78, 161, 162
quantitative research approach, 20, 21–22, 23, 24, 78
Quinn, M., 155, 156–158, 181, 191, 234

Rapoport, R. N., 29
Reflective Practitioner, 26
reflexivity, 12, 154–155
reliability of results
    internal reliability, 21
    external reliability, 21–22
reports, 41, 183–186
research partnerships, 206–209
research questions, 36–37, 60–70
Reynolds, M. J., 22
Richards, J. C., 214
Richards, J. C. and D. Freeman, 12
rival explanations, 165
Roberts, J., 5, 214
Ross, L., 7–11, 62–63, 108–109, 229
Rudduck, J., 202

Samway, K. D., 86
Schwab, J. J., 28
scientific approach to research, 21
Seliger, H. W. and E. Sohamy, 20
Shaw, S., 144–145, 192
Silverman, D., 163
Smith, J. K. and L. Heshusius, 23
Somekh, B., 32–34, 72, 102, 154,
Spada, N. and M. Frohlich, 80
spiral process, 27, 28, 32, 156
Spradley, J., 121
Staff development *see* professional
    development
Stake, R. E. and C. Gjerde, 186, 187,
    195
Stenhouse, L., 17, 28, 29, 44, 183,
    201
steps in action research
    six-step procedure, 28
    four steps, 32
Strickland, D., 53
student participation, 95, 224,
    229–232

Taba, H. and E. Noel, 28

teacher networks, 204–205
Tobin, K., 147
transcription of recorded material,
    98–101, 176–177
triangulation, 25, 163–165
    investigator, 164
    space, 164
    theoretical, 164
    time, 164
Troupiotis, D., 92–94
Tudor, I., 5

Valeri, L., 114–115, 214
validity criteria, 161–162
    catalytic validity, 162
    democratic validity, 162
    dialogic validity, 162
    process validity, 162
    outcome validity, 162
validity of findings, 160–162
    external validity, 160
    internal validity, 160
van Lier, L., 20, 46, 49
van Mannen, M., 202
video displays, 197–199

Walker, R., 101, 105, 181, 182, 186,
    192, 195, 197
Walker, R. and C. Adelman, 101
Wallace, M. J., 30, 80
Watson-Gegeo, K. A., 22
Whitehead J. and J. Barratt, 54
Whitford, B. L. *et al.*, 206
Whitham, S., 127–129
Wiersma, W., 20
Wilkins Intensive English Centre *see*
    Harmey *et al.*
Winter, R., 71, 152, 186
Woods, D., 214
written updates, 190–192

Yow, V. R., 136